WOMEN'S RIGHTS

Social Issues in American History Series

Immigration

Women's Rights

African Americans and Civil Rights:
From 1619 to 1995

WOMEN'S RIGHTS

by
Christine A. Lunardini

Foreword by Betty Friedan

Social Issues in American History Series

Oryx Press
1996

The rare Arabian Oryx is believed to have inspired the myth of the unicorn. This desert antelope became virtually extinct in the early 1960s. At that time several groups of international conservationists arranged to have 9 animals sent to the Phoenix Zoo to be the nucleus of a captive breeding herd. Today the Oryx population is over 1000 and over 500 have been returned to the Middle East.

© 1996 by Christine A. Lunardini
Published by The Oryx Press
4041 North Central at Indian School Road
Phoenix, Arizona 85012-3397

Cover photograph: A parade in New York City promoting woman suffrage, May 6, 1912. Courtesy of the Library of Congress.

Illustrations on pages 4, 11, 17, 19, 27, 40, 43, 77, 124, 143, and 156 courtesy of the Library of Congress; photographs on pages 64, 91, and 104 courtesy of The Schlesinger Library, Radcliffe College; photographs on pages 67 and 174 courtesy of the Photographs and Prints Division, Schomburg Center for Research in Black Culture, The New York Public Library, Astor, Lenox and Tilden Foundations; photograph on page 126, copyright unknown; photograph on page 145 courtesy of The Hearst Newspaper Collection, Department of Special Collections, University of Southern California Library; photograph on page 175 courtesy of the Archives of Labor and Urban Affairs, Wayne State University; photograph on page 177 courtesy of the Cherokee Nation; photo on page 180 courtesy of NASA.

Published simultaneously in Canada
Printed and bound in the United States of America

∞ The paper used in this publication meets the minimum requirements of American National Standard for Information Science—Permanence of Paper for Printed Library Materials, ANSI Z39.48, 1984.

Library of Congress Cataloging-in-Publication Data

Lunardini, Christine A., 1941–
    Women's rights / by Christine A. Lunardini.
        p.   cm. — (Social Issues in American history series)
    Includes bibliographical references (p.   ) and index.
    ISBN 0-89774-872-7 (cloth)
        1. Women's rights—United States—History. 2. Women—United States—History. I. Title. II. Series: Social Issues in American history.
HQ1236.5.U6L85   1995
305.42'0973—dc20   95-21712
                                                                          CIP

CONTENTS

• • • • • • • • •

FOREWORD

• • • • • • • •

by
Betty Friedan

I n 1963, my book, *The Feminine Mystique*, was published with a 2,000 copy
printing. Not even the publisher, W.W. Norton, expected the explosive
response to the ideas presented in the book—that many women in America
were dissatisfied with their proscribed roles as wives, mothers, and homemakers. In it I described the vague feelings that many of them had that their lives
were not as fulfilling as they were told—by social scientists, the media, and
many others—that they should be. Thinking they were the only ones who felt
unhappy, most women kept these feelings to themselves and tried instead to
conform. Indeed, the book must have touched a cord, for it sold 3 million
copies during the next ten years. I am proud that *The Feminine Mystique*
helped women to realize that they had alternatives in their lives and that they
could fight to live for their own dreams and ambitions.

Many consider *The Feminine Mystique* one of the works that launched the
women's movement in America. However, as Christine A. Lunardini describes in *Women's Rights*, the women's fight for equality in America began
with this country's very first settlers. Since then women have faced years of
one-step-forward, two-steps-back movement towards their goals of equality
and choice in all areas of their lives. Thousands of women have played a role
in this fight for women's rights in America, as have thousands of works and
speeches and protests and activities.

What is most important for the student of women's history to understand
is that this is a struggle with ebb and flow, one that the participants themselves, women in America, reevaluate and redirect on a regular basis. Like
any fight, it is also affected by surrounding circumstances—legislation, popular opinion, the media, etc.—things not completely within women's control.

However, we keep pursuing our goals, and little by little we make headway. Today, women have a more equal position in business, education, the professions, than ever before. We have many more choices than our mothers and our mothers' mothers. And we have more control over our lives. However, our fight continues, for we are still paid less than our male counterparts, and we still carry the majority of the burden of birth control, child care, and management of the household. We are grossly underrepresented in the upper echelons of the corporate world and politics, and we still face serious threats to our equality in many facets of our lives.

There are myriad inspiring stories in this book of women who pushed on in the face of adversity, of how they rallied to tackle the next problem oppressing women. Take from this history the motivation needed to press on with the fight and face challenges—new and old—with the enthusiasm and inspiration of millions of women from the centuries and decades before this one.

PREFACE

· · · · · · · · ·

Women's Rights, part of the Social Issues in American History Series, was undertaken to provide a concise overview of the issues and ideas that have influenced women's history from the earliest European settlements at Jamestown, Virginia, and Plymouth, Massachusetts, to the most recent events that continue to affect the lives of women today. The women's movement in America is not a new phenomenon peculiar to the 1970s and 1980s, contrary to what many younger Americans believe. Women have always been active participants in American life and culture and will continue to remain so. However, though a fully self-conscious women's movement has existed since the first women's rights convention in Seneca Falls, New York, in 1848, both historians and the public have pushed the movement into the background of American consciousness from time to time. Thus, every reincarnation of the women's movement, every new effort to deal with the variety of issues that affects women's lives, is treated as a novel idea—a movement without a past.

Relying on the wealth of histories that deal with various aspects of women's past, this book is intended to provide a fuller explanation of that past to both high school and college students, as well as anyone else interested in how women have influenced American history, culture, and politics. The book is arranged chronologically, though time periods overlap as the women's movement has evolved from one priority to the next. Although the major themes and points of women's history are included in the text, the book was never intended to be a complete history of women in America, including every historical event in which women were involved or that affected them directly. Decisions to leave out some material were made only with an eye to keeping the project both as comprehensible and as manageable as possible. The book includes a chronology of important dates that highlights some people or events not specifically discussed in the text; entries in the bibliography guide the reader to further exploration. Like other books in the series, *Women's Rights* features biographical profiles of women who made a significant contribution to the fight for equal rights. Unlike the other books, these profiles appear after each chapter instead of in a separate section at the end of the book. This organization was used because the lives of the women profiled illustrate so well the particular themes discussed in each chapter. Many of the women profiled are less famous than others, though every bit as fascinating. The individuals profiled were selected because they pushed the boundaries that defined women's roles during the eras in which they lived. In some cases, their contributions to American life and culture and to women's rights constituted only a brief public moment in otherwise private lives. In other cases, the women profiled lived very public lives. All of them paid a price for their activities and, unfortunately, many of them never lived long enough to see the consequences of their refusal to accept the status quo. It is hoped that the material covered in the text and the biographical profiles will inspire readers to explore further the richness that is women's history. A selective bibliography for further reading and study is provided, as well as a glossary of important terms and legislation.

As with any project of this nature, thanks are due to many people for their assistance. I would like to thank the staffs of the New York Public Library and the Pace University Library for their assistance; Anne Thompson and Karla Olson, editors at Oryx Press, for their patience and help; and Elizabeth Knappman for making this opportunity possible. On a personal note, I would also like to thank those people who continue to be so supportive and encouraging—not to mention tolerant: Maureen Callahan, Catherine Clinton, Steve Victore, Noah Callahan-Bever, Edward Bever, Chloe Callahan-Flintoft, Sheila Callahan-Victore, Sheila and Kit Thompson, Maureen Tsuchiya, Pat and Kevin Donahue, Jerome Dumain, Rosemary Lunardini, and Donna Lunardini.

INTRODUCTION

· · · · · · · · ·

T hat women have played a key role in the development of American culture and society is indisputable. As well as being crucial to the success of the first colonies, women in America have fought in every war, including the Revolution and the Civil War; they have labored for industrial growth; and they have been instrumental in social and political reforms, from abolition and temperance to the New Deal and civil rights.

What is truly remarkable, however, is that women have influenced the course of American history so profoundly despite limitations to their personal freedom. In fact, it is the indefatigable struggle to overcome these limitations that is the history of women's rights.

At times the struggles that women have faced have focused on broadening their rights. For example, Emma Willard, among others, exhibited extreme dedication in her fight for a woman's right to an education equal to that of a man. Susan B. Anthony and Elizabeth Cady Stanton devoted their lives to pursuing political and legal rights for women. For more than half a century, both women worked tirelessly for suffrage and equal rights. Along the way they attracted thousands of other women to the fight.

Just as often, however, women's struggles have focused on issues not directly related to women's rights. Women in the Revolutionary era, for example, were responsible, in large measure, for keeping the economy intact. They planted and harvested the crops necessary to sustain the Continental army, took care of the wounded, buried the dead, and traveled with the troops, serving as everything from cooks to laundresses. As the evils of slavery became more and more apparent, greater and greater emphasis was placed on banning it altogether. Lucretia Mott, Fanny Kemble, and the Grimké sisters were just a few of the women among the prime supporters of the movement. They willingly risked even their personal safety to see slavery abolished. Their involvement in these causes provided women with the experience, skills, and confidence necessary to pursue women's rights issues.

Other themes that emerge time and again in American history include the willingness of women to put their own interests aside to pursue specific goals for other groups. When the Civil War erupted, for instance, participants of the still-fledgling women's movement volunteered to suspend their reform activities to support the Union fully. From the first settlements to the present, the symbiotic relationship between women's private lives and experiences and their public activities has also been a consistent theme. Women, to a far greater extent than men, have responded to domestic conditions by trying to change public policy and/or law. Determined to protect and provide for their children, women have been in the forefront of the birth control and family planning movement and efforts to enact protective legislation prohibiting child labor. Concerned over the effects of excessive alcohol consumption on the family, women mobilized not only to make alcohol a moral issue, but to ban it altogether.

Depending on the time and the circumstances, the struggle for women's rights has been sporadically more public and more acceptable than at other times. Yet, the issues that have motivated women throughout history have a certain similarity. Concerns about family, marriage, children, control over one's life and destiny on issues dealing with birth control and abortion are but one set of concerns. Educational opportunities, occupational choices, even the right to work outside of the home are another set of concerns. And civil rights and equality constitute yet another set of issues with which women have had to deal throughout the country's history. Although each of these issues, or often a combination of issues, has been at the forefront of public awareness, it is also true that the public has been as quick to overlook or ignore gains made at great cost. The result, for anyone who has studied women's rights, is the realization that issues that seem so contemporary today are in fact ages old and, though they should have been resolved, are the stumbling blocks that continue to prevent women from realizing their full potential as equal members in society. They also continue to motivate women to work to secure equality.

CHAPTER 1

Women in Colonial America

B ecause every historical situation has a context in which it must be understood, this recounting of women's rights in America begins with a brief overview of the conditions in 16th and 17th century England that influenced the first European settlements in the New World.

ENGLAND'S CENTURY OF TURMOIL

Fundamental and profound changes that transformed England in the 16th century were an important catalyst that motivated settlers to venture to America. England had been a Catholic nation until Henry VIII ascended to the throne. In his zeal to produce a male heir, Henry broke with the Roman Catholic Church and established the Church of England, conveniently installing himself as its head. In so doing, Henry could give himself permission to shed wives who failed to provide the son he wanted. Supporters of the Protestant Reformation, whose previous efforts to establish a stronghold had been only sporadically successful, now found a new opportunity, particularly after Henry seized property and land from the Catholic religious orders throughout the country.

Not only did Henry change the contours of English religious life, but his actions affected England's role internationally as well. When Henry divorced his Spanish wife, Catherine, he created a rift between Spain and England that grew in intensity and culminated with the defeat of the Spanish Armada. With their navy in disarray, Spain was no longer able control the Atlantic, making ocean travel, previously an impediment to English colonization of the New World, suddenly much less risky.

In the meantime other events caused equally significant changes in English—particularly agrarian—society. Spurred by a dramatic increase in population and economic dislocation as a result of rising inflation and the sale of church lands, England suddenly found itself with a highly mobile population, in both class and geographical terms. As in any period of economic turmoil, fortunes were made and lost. Families that had worked on particular lands for generations were forced to seek other means of sustenance when their landlords, either nobles or gentry, suddenly went bankrupt. At the same time, merchants, who had benefited greatly from rising prices, began to look for ways to capitalize on the economic changes in an organized fashion. They financed trading companies to find new markets for the increased production of goods made possible by a larger pool of cheap labor. By 1600 there were 200 English joint-stock trading companies operating in Europe and Asia.

Though Henry VIII started this massive social, political, demographic, and economic change, he was not terribly interested in exploring the New World. Undoubtedly, Henry's almost unceasing religious and political conflicts, not to mention his search for the perfect wife, left him little time for more visionary exploits. Given his legendary difficulties in siring a male successor to the throne, it is ironic that his only son, Edward VI, was a sickly child who died at the age of 13, less than six months after becoming king. Though Henry did manage to bring an end to the War of the Roses, which had kept the royal houses of England locked in a deadly feud for generations, it was his second daughter, Elizabeth I, who calmed the political and economic turbulence that had prevented any long-term national endeavors. It was Elizabeth who oversaw the defeat of the Spanish Armada and Elizabeth who favored and encouraged New World exploration and settlement.

COLONIES IN THE NEW WORLD

Even with the encouragement of the Crown, the success of permanent colonies in the New World was not guaranteed. Two early English attempts met with failure. Sir Humphrey Gilbert, armed with a charter granted by Elizabeth in 1578, set forth in 1583, hoping to found a new colony. Shortly after claiming Newfoundland for England, Gilbert disappeared at sea. His half-brother Sir Walter Raleigh was also granted a charter to establish a colony. Raleigh tried twice. First, in 1585 a company of 100 men settled on Roanoke island off the coast of North Carolina. The settlement failed, primarily because the men turned to the pursuits of gold and finding a passage to the Indies. Two years later Raleigh sent another company to Roanoke, this time including women and children. To survive the first winter, the colonists had to depend on supplies from England. However long they waited, it was in vain, for when the supply party reached Roanoke, the settlers had disappeared without a trace. It was more than two decades before another attempt at colonization was made.

THE IMMIGRATION IMPULSE

The stories of the first permanent settlements at Jamestown, Virginia, in 1607 and at Plymouth and Massachusetts Bay a short time later compose a well-known chapter in American history. Three characteristics distinguished these colonies from the earlier settlements: 1) rather than seeking to turn a quick profit from settlements that few considered a permanent home, the new colonists intended to build lasting communities, 2) the new colonists had ongoing support from their sponsors in England, and 3) perhaps most importantly, women were considered a crucial component to success, particularly in the Puritan colonies of New England. In the Puritans' view, order and discipline were essential to survive the harshness of the first years, and an orderly society required family-based settlement. Even in the southern colonies, though, where the social and political structure was less rigid, the necessity for women in the colonies was recognized early on. George Calvert, the founder of Maryland, who was appointed the first Lord Baltimore by James I, noted that the survival of his colony depended on the ability to import white women from Europe. Without them the chance of establishing a stable environment was rather remote. Throughout the colonies, it was perceived that women brought with them domestic cohesion and often a sense of tranquillity. But more important, without women settlers, population increases would have been possible only through constant immigration. Failure to build a stable base population with a healthy birthrate would have eventually undermined the stability of the community itself.

Even so, almost the same mistakes were made at the Virginia colony that had caused earlier colonies to fail so miserably. The first company of 600 settlers were all men. Moreover, most of the colonists, many former soldiers, were really more interested in making money than in establishing a settlement. Except for the leadership of John Smith, a member of the first governing council of Virginia, the internal conflicts, particularly disagreements over individual duties and responsibilities and lines of authority, and an antagonistic relationship with the powerful Powhattan Indians could have sounded the death knell for the colony. Smith helped to reduce tensions, by acting as a mediator to settle disagreements and by exercising his authority unequivocally, and held the colony together through the first terrible winter. Still, within 18 months, the original 600 colonists had dwindled to less than 200.

During that first year, Smith discovered that it was inordinately difficult to persuade a company of bachelors to do some of the work necessary to make the settlement a success. Homemaking tasks, such as doing laundry; making

Rendering of an 18th-century colonial family. Notice the numerous activities the family members are engaged in.

candles, brooms, and other household utensils and tools; making clothing; fetching firewood and water; baking; cooking; preserving meats; gardening; and raising small livestock were extremely labor intensive and, along with childrearing, dominated the daily lives of women back home. On their own men tended to ignore all but the most rudimentary and necessary household chores. Such inattention to homemaking had predictable results and threatened the entire colonial enterprise.

The first two women to settle in Jamestown—Anne Forrest, the wife of a colonist, and her 13-year-old servant, Anne Buras—arrived the following year in 1608. They were outnumbered by almost 200 to one, and the colony's managers recruited other women as quickly as possible. In 1609 over 100 women arrived in Jamestown. This first group, however, joined an ill-planned colony that was little equipped to ward off the multitude of problems inherent in settling a new land. The winter of 1609–1610 became known as the "starving time," when lack of supplies, the harshness of the winter, and the inability to fend off disease combined to kill about 90 percent of the settlers. However, the high mortality rate did not deter others from immigrating. Women who became known as "tobacco wives" arrived with the expectation that, much like slaves, they would be bid for by settlers who had the equivalent to approximately 80 dollars in tobacco.

Women had as many different reasons for immigrating to the New World as men did. Their reasons covered a broad spectrum, including the desire to start a new life, the opportunity to own their own home and land in a fertile new environment, high probability that they would marry and have a family, or the need to escape from the burdens of a life encumbered by poverty and debt and circumscribed by political and religious stagnation. Of course, many women came as part of a family unit already, following the lead of a husband who made the decision to go. However, for single women as well as those who were married, despite the profound difficulties of the first years in the colonies, the possibility of success outweighed the probability of failure.

Still, during the 17th century and for much of the 18th century, the shortage of women remained acute. It is not surprising, then, that a concentrated effort was made to entice women to immigrate. The Jamestown colony, for example, offered women free land, attractive to individuals who could otherwise never expect to own land. The practice was discontinued fairly soon after it was started, however, for the colony managers discovered that women who received the free land often preferred to live alone rather than to marry. Colony sponsors soon resorted to other enticements, including prenuptial agreements that would allow women to retain control of their property after marriage. It was clear that there were women willing to accept the risks if the potential opportunity was significant, and that following husbands or looking for husbands was not necessarily the only reason they immigrated.

The Pursuit of Religious Freedom

Just as many women as men emigrated for religious reasons. After a century of Henry's manipulations, both the Pilgrims and the Puritans believed that the Church of England had become corrupt. The Pilgrims, or Separatists, who advocated complete independence of their congregation, settled in Plymouth, Massachusetts. The Puritans, by far the more influential group in terms of the development of the New World, sought to purify the church rather than to leave it altogether. The Puritans found out fairly quickly that trying to reform the church from within and to disassociate themselves from the church's corrupt policies was more than they could handle. In 1628, under John Winthrop's leadership, they set sail for what was to be a "city upon a hill" for all the world to see and emulate—a nucleus dedicated to God, corruption free, and with every resident in deed and word striving to attain sainthood. If the Puritans sought the freedom to establish a religious colony in the Massachusetts Bay Colony, they did not extend that same freedom to other groups, particularly those that tried to make inroads into Puritan communities.

Another religious group, smaller than the Puritans but who, in many ways, had as significant an effect in the New World, was the Quakers. The Quakers settled primarily in William Penn's colony of Pennsylvania and in New Jersey. They were much less structured than were the Puritans and did not maintain a professional ministry, so the church was not dominated by male clerics as was Puritanism. Moreover, the Quakers allowed women to pursue roles other than that of wife and mother, as was generally proscribed by the English male hierarchy. Quaker doctrine allowed all persons who professed to have found their "inner light" to speak out in public, to become lay ministers, and to proselytize on behalf of Quakerism. Not everyone welcomed Quakers, or women with as broad a role as the Quakers allowed, into their communities, of course. For example, when Mary Dyer traveled to Boston to preach Quakerism, she was expelled. Three times she returned, and three times she was asked to leave. Finally, the Puritans chose to exercise the ultimate form of expulsion—they executed Dyer in the late 1650s.

Though the Puritans were uncomfortable with dissenters, they rejected women dissenters completely. Puritan life was based on a clearly defined and rigid hierarchy. When anyone stepped outside the bounds of that structure, they were quickly discouraged. Women dissenters represented a double threat because they questioned not only the theological hierarchy but the social hierarchy as well. To be confronted time and again with a Mary Dyer was simply too much to bear.

It is, of course, true that there were few women dissenters in the colonies. Perhaps the best known woman dissenter to settle in Massachusetts was Anne Hutchinson (see profile, page 13). Hutchinson and her family left England in the vain attempt to find a place where they could practice their own brand of religion, free from the constraints imposed by authorities. Ultimately, Hutchinson was tried as a heretic, and she and her family were expelled from Massachusetts.

While the Puritans were not particularly open to tolerating other religions within their communities, the New World was, nevertheless, a fairly liberal environment in which to establish a religious community. Other religious communities in the colonies included New York State's Shaker community; the Moravians, who could be found in colonies throughout the settled areas; Catholic communities, again located throughout the settled colonial area and especially in the South; and a Jewish synagogue, founded in Rhode Island. With very few exceptions, these religious groups relegated women to a position of second-class citizenship.

Women as Indentured Servants

Though many women came to the New World willingly, most women who immigrated in the 17th century did not come of their own free will or they came as indentured servants. Some indentured servants did not come of their own free will either, but were indentured as payment for crimes of which they had been convicted. Others signed on to serve for several years, after which they gained their independence. Once they had paid off their debts to their sponsors, these women usually married rather quickly, given the scarcity of eligible women in the community. Though in England these servants would have likely remained servants for life, in America their status usually changed from servant to wife and mother, which often usually meant having a home and sometimes even their own indentured servant.

The promise of change did not soften the harshness with which indentured servants could expect to be treated, however. They faced several years of extremely hard work with significant personal restrictions. They were obliged to perform any task their sponsors required of them. Generally, the servants were supervised by the wife, who may have been an indentured servant herself. In spite of this—or perhaps because of it—former indentured servants were not inclined to treat their servants any less harshly than they had been treated. If servants ran afoul of their masters or the law, it was often for engaging in premarital sex or for pregnancy. Regardless of who her partner was, the woman generally bore the brunt of the blame, a common societal attitude even today. The punishment for such indiscretion frequently included an extended period of servitude.

The Forced Immigration of African Women

Unlike indentured servants, who knew they would eventually be free to improve their social status, African women, who were almost without exception kidnapped from their homes by unscrupulous slave traders and sold as slaves, saw no such hope of ultimate redemption. Slaves, who were introduced into the colonies very soon after colonization began in earnest, would be slaves for life. By 1648 they accounted for about 2 percent of the total population of about 15,000. Twenty years later the percentage of slaves in the population had more than doubled, to 5 percent. While the percentage of slaves in the population never exceeded 10 percent, their concentration in the southern colonies was significant, especially after the plantation system began to flourish and expand. On the eve of the Revolutionary War, half the population of Virginia was slaves, and in South Carolina two out of every three residents were Africans. Female slaves were especially valuable during their childbearing years, and their importance to the system continued to grow, particularly after the slave trade was abolished in the early 19th century. Even so, they were subjected to all of the abuses of indentured servants without the promise of eventual freedom. Moreover, their children, born into slavery and likely at some point to be sold and taken away from them, would also remain slaves for life.

NATIVE AMERICAN WOMEN IN THE NEW WORLD

In addition to free white women, indentured servants, and slaves, a third group of women were influenced by the settlements in the New World. Though Native American women did not really live in the colonies, their lives were changed by the presence of the colonists, most significantly by the religious missionaries, mostly Catholics, who considered it their duty to convert the Native Americans to Christianity. To that end women were important because the missionaries believed that if the women could be converted, they in turn would convert the men. Their relatively low success rate, either to convert the Native Americans or find Native Americans willing to work to convert their comrades, did not deter the missionaries from making a sustained effort.

A more significant consequence of New World settlements for Native American women was their gradual loss of status within their communities. Though it is true that women in agricultural tribes had more power than those in the hunting tribes of the Great Plains, in general they all had tribal powers ranging from moderate to significant. The Iroquois, for example, were organized along matrilineal lines. Women owned the longhouses, mothers arranged marriages, sons-in-law lived with the wife's family, and women generally managed the farming activity. Among the Senecas women were allowed to vote for male chiefs and to participate in other political activities as well.

When Europeans began to make significant inroads in North America, they began to encourage Native Americans to alter their culture to fit a European ideal. Notions of land ownership, a concept not unlike ownership of the sun or the air to the Native Americans, also changed their concept of materialism. Gradually, the power base enjoyed by Iroquois and Cherokee women began to erode. Women in both those tribes traditionally enjoyed generous representation in tribal councils and, in some instances, even dominated. Women in other tribes enjoyed less influence, but eventually all were affected by European culture. Missionaries and religious schools that were established to educate the Native American imposed European culture on the grounds that it was superior. Young girls were taught homemaking skills as though they were going to inhabit societies identical to the European settlements. They were chided or even ridiculed for wearing customary clothing and for speaking in their native tongue. Finally, most Native American tribes were moved further and further west as whites advanced further into the interior. Time after time, whites designated certain areas as Native lands, then only a short time later ignored that designation, particularly if the lands were found to have additional value, such as mineral resources.

Before Europeans arrived in North America, Cherokee women were able to exercise a good deal of power, though not as chiefs. They played a crucial role in agriculture, they had the right to speak in village councils, and some

Cherokee women accompanied their men when the tribe went to war. The erosion of Native American culture began almost as soon as white feet set down on American soil. One consequence of white settlements was the removal of Indians, time after time and despite valid treaties, to lands farther and farther west. The confinement of Indians to reservations began in the late 18th century and have characterized Indian-white relations up to the present. For example, a series of treaties initiated between the Cherokees and the United States government in 1791 designated parts of Georgia as an independent Indian nation. When gold was discovered, the Indians protested white trespassers, initiating a Supreme Court case, *Cherokee Nation v. Georgia*. The court, with John Marshall acting as chief justice, held for the Indians. But President Andrew Jackson, who had little regard for Indians, refused to uphold the law. "John Marshall has made his decision," he is said to have remarked. "Now let him enforce it." The Cherokees were forced to leave Georgia, again with government assurances for new lands, and eventually they settled in Oklahoma.

THE VALUE OF WOMEN IN SOCIETY

Within the colonies women played important roles, both domestically and economically, inside and outside of the home. In the Puritan communities, they were recognized as a stabilizing influence. Winthrop and his ministers believed that the family unit was the foundation of a well-ordered society. The Puritans, as well, felt society was well ordered with a clearly defined hierarchy that was both understood and accepted and believed that family structure mirrored society.

The foundation of Puritan society was the covenant—a required mode of behavior recognized by all participants. Marriage was the appropriate living arrangement for adults, and widows and widowers were urged to remarry as quickly as possible. Husbands were, unequivocally, the authority figure in the family; wives and children were duty bound to obey their husbands and fathers. Men were also responsible for enforcing the proper religious behavior within the home. In return, women could expect that their husbands would support and protect them. Parents were expected to protect their children and to provide them with the proper religious education. Children obeyed their parents and were prohibited from showing any disrespect. Although there is no evidence to suggest it was ever enforced, even minors could be mortally punished if they demonstrated extreme disrespect for their parents.

The covenants by which the Puritans lived were undoubtedly more closely observed in some relationships than in others. Regardless, members of Puritan communities and others throughout the colonies believed that women maintained cultural ties and encouraged domestic tranquillity. In fact the Southern colonies, which did not emphasize the value of women as did the

Puritans, did not stabilize nearly as quickly as the New England colonies, and not at all until a permanent family and community orientation was present.

Life in the colonies was never easy, and it was always harder and riskier for women because of the high rate of childbirth mortality. The cause of one-fifth of the deaths of adult women, it was so commonplace that an advice pamphlet in 1663 cautioned expectant mothers to prepare for both the birth of their child and their own possible demise as they approached their delivery time. (Woloch, *Women and the American Experience*, pp. 23-24.)

Yet, women did enjoy some liberties that they would not have had back home. For example, they were so necessary to the success of the colonies that they were allowed to participate in jobs that were ordinarily prohibited. Though it was not common, neither was it unique to find women merchants, printers, artisans, and even business managers. Generally speaking, colonial women—excluding slaves—had a greater chance to rise up the economic ladder than they would have had in Europe.

The Puritan determination to avoid as much divisive conflict as possible within the community led to a series of laws that favored women. Husbands, for example, could not abandon their wives, but were obligated to support them under penalty of law. Nor could they strike their wives or inflict any bodily harm on them. Incorrigible husbands could be divorced by their wives when the marriage was in such disarray that it became a threat to the well-being of the community. Widows were able to gain some autonomy over their lives and property. Still, these apparently liberal privileges were not extended because of a desire to grant women greater freedom. The goal was simply to maintain as much colonial stabilization as possible, and if the threat of retribution to unruly males enhanced the lot of women, that was merely a necessary accident.

In some communities the consequences of greater freedoms for women sometimes became too much for the communities to endure. For example, female ownership of property proved to be a threat that legislators were unwilling to tolerate. In 1634 Maryland passed a law requiring women who inherited property to marry within seven years or lose it. And, if women in the community could not be controlled by any other means, unofficial community sanctions could be imposed. Until almost the 18th century, women in New England who were outspoken, critical, or in some other fashion considered a community nuisance left themselves vulnerable to accusations of practicing witchcraft.

The Salem Witch Trials

In the second half of the 17th century, these accusations increased. The first recorded execution of a so-called witch was that of Margaret Jones in 1648, condemned for, among other things, her intemperate behavior. A few years

Depiction of the Salem Witch Trials, in which a "possessed" defendant has caused the collapse of one of her interrogators. Note that most of the witnesses are women.

later in 1658, Anne Hibbens was executed for having a suspiciously crabby nature.

However, nothing compared to the Salem Witch Trials in 1692. Before the trials ended, a total of 141 persons were accused of witchcraft, almost all of whom were women, many of them middle-aged housewives. Over 100 of the accused were convicted, and eventually, 20 "witches" were executed. Almost all of the accusations were made by a group of teenage girls and were often based on no more than a "look" that the accuser claimed caused abnormal behavior. Explanations for what happened in Salem have been the focus of historical interest ever since. The age of the accusers persuaded more than one historian that jealousy and spitefulness played a prominent role in the whole episode. At bottom, it was one way to eliminate people whose behavior did not conform to the norm. The Salem frenzy seemed to jolt people back to reality, however, because witch hunts dwindled rapidly after that.

A SLOWING BIRTH RATE AND CHANGES IN THE CHURCH

The more removed the colonies became from Europe in both time and distance, the more significant became the changes that affected not only women but all of the colonists. In the years leading up to the American Revolution, two changes took place that greatly affected women and were a

Revolution, two changes took place that greatly affected women and were a foundation for even greater changes in the 19th century. They were the slowing of the birth rate in the colonies and changes in religious institutions.

Most early colonial families were large, especially by modern standards. Cotton Mather, the minister who Anne Hutchinson followed to America, fathered 16 children and did not think that an unusually great number. In his diaries, Mather talks about families of 20 and 25 children, which were considered unusually large. The average "completed fertility" for colonial women was from six to eight children, with as many as three or four miscarriages interspersed. But the birth rate began to drop by the late 18th century and continued to do so throughout the 19th century. Quality of life was almost certainly a factor in the declining birthrate. Fewer children meant that families were not as stretched economically. Moreover, because childbirth continued to be a risky health proposition for women, the fewer pregnancies, the less risk a woman faced. Though the reasons for the declining birth rates are not entirely clear, smaller families, especially as the 19th century unfolded, allowed women greater opportunity to move beyond the circle of the home and to become more involved in issues outside of the home.

Religion also affected women. The first religious revival in America, the Great Awakening in 1740, refocused attention away from Puritan theology in favor of a much more personal theology centered on conversion experience. The "New Light" preachers openly challenged patriarchal and hierarchical church authority. Not surprisingly, this message appealed to many women, who made up a significant proportion of evangelical congregations. In fact, evangelical ministers particularly praised women for their ability to teach children religious values and to spread religion throughout the community. Women's increased status within religious organizations helped to create the "feminization of religion," which in turn became the foundation for the 19th century charitable and voluntary activities that provided women with the skills necessary to pursue their own rights.

Colonial women benefited from an unusual set of frontier circumstances that improved their options, at least in comparison to their counterparts in Europe. Although there was nothing even close to a self-conscious women's rights awareness, the approaching Revolutionary War and the events surrounding the creation of a nation caused more women to think about their own status in society and encouraged them to question male authority.

• • • • •

Anne Hutchinson, Religious Dissenter
1591–1643

The theological underpinnings of Puritanism are, at best, difficult to understand. A fundamental tenet, however, was the belief that the way to salvation lay in entering into a Covenant of Works and progressing to a Covenant of Grace. Embracing the Covenant of Works meant viewing one's life as infinitely improvable and accepting that the road to improvement lay in performing good works or deeds on a daily basis. It was believed that if a Puritan faithfully kept the Covenant of Works, he or she would become one of the elect, chosen by God to achieve ultimate salvation. Standing in the community and wealth were two of the outward signs that an individual was among the elect. The Covenant of Grace was the enlightened step forward that Anglican Minister Cotton Mather took to relieve some of the anxiety and oppression that arose from never being certain of ultimate salvation. Therefore, Mather preached that if one reached a point where one felt an intuitive knowledge of salvation, that person had achieved salvation.

Mather's relative liberalism brought down the wrath of traditional Anglicanism, and in 1633 he was forced to leave England and flee to Boston, in the Massachusetts Bay Colony. Some of Mather's flock followed him, including Anne Hutchinson, who had found in Mather's preaching and perspective some hope for coming to terms with her own imperfections and for the souls of her two young daughters, who had died within a month of each other. Unlike most of her peers, however, Hutchinson had taken Mather's interpretation of Puritanism to its logical conclusion: an individual's internal acceptance of the state of grace and, therefore salvation, in the simplest terms put that person in direct contact with God. It also rendered some things unnecessary, including the concept of the Covenant of Works. All in all, it was a very dangerous personal theology because it flew in the face of traditional and even liberal Protestantism.

Hutchinson (of whom a portrait is unavailable), her husband William, and their family arrived in Boston in September 1634. William Hutchinson's successful entry into the cloth trade brought the family prestige and enough wealth to purchase land tracts and invest in other businesses. His elevation to Boston selectman and deputy to the Massachusetts General Court indicated that the family had reached the highest level of colonial society. Anne, in the meantime, with her outgoing personality and nursing skills, became a welcome presence in the community, particularly among the women. Distressed to discover that most women were still bogged down in the Covenant of Works, Hutchinson began sharing her interpretation of Mather's theology. She soon had a large following that included the wealthiest merchants and craftsmen and even the governor, Henry Vane.

Despite the "publicness" of her preaching, events might have transpired unnoticed had Hutchinson not invoked the anger of Mather's fellow minister, John Wilson. Hutchinson did not like Wilson's conservatism and made that clear to all who cared to listen, contrasting his beliefs with that of Cotton Mather. In the controversy that arose, the entire city of Boston took sides, and before long other communities did as well. When John Winthrop, one of the founders of the Bay Colony, was elected governor, he reasserted control over the General Court by removing Hutchinson's sympathizers. When a church committee condemned Hutchinson for numerous errors in her theological interpretations, Cotton Mather sided with the committee. Later, apparently regretting his actions, he came to Hutchinson's assistance during her trial, but by then the damage had been done. The General Court tried Hutchinson in 1637, found her guilty of preaching heresy, and banished her from the Bay Colony. In 1638 Anne Hutchinson and her family left Massachusetts, going first to Rhode Island, where, she mistakenly believed, she could find peace of mind among the more liberal colonists led by Roger Williams. Finally, the Hutchinsons moved to New York. In 1643 Hutchinson, her family, and her neighbors were the victims of a Native American attack in what is now Pelham Bay Park in the Bronx.

In the eyes of the ruling elite, the danger posed by Anne Hutchinson lay not only in her interpretation of theology, but in the fact that she was a woman. Her eloquent self-defense before the General Court proved that she was the theological equal of her accusers. But, as Cotton Mather noted at her trial, "she is only a woman and many unsound and dangerous principles are held by her." The most dangerous principal she held was the notion of independent thinking, for that threatened the entire structure of colonial society. Violating the Puritan standards of acceptable female behavior, Hutchinson threatened to bring down not only the theological covenental relationships, but the covenental relationships that governed behavior within the family as well. If she exercised independence in determining which Puritan beliefs she would accept, others could do the same thing. If people questioned Puritan beliefs, they would surely begin to question civil authority and family structure as well.

CHAPTER 2

Revolutionary Spirits

With the dawn of the 17th century, the garrison mentality of many colonists in the New World, wherein they felt besieged by forces over which they had little or no control, began to fade. As conditions improved, the constant struggle for mere survival became less and less consuming. Of course, this was primarily true for those living in the more settled areas. The closer one was to the frontier, the more one had to be concerned about the trials of an unforgiving environment. In the older, settled areas and the emerging cities, survival was rapidly giving way to competition and the drive for commercial profit. Moreover, the unbalanced sex ratios that had characterized the early settlements had already begun to disappear along the East Coast.

All these factors affected women's lives to a certain degree. Marriage options in a society with balanced sex ratios were far different from those in a society where men outnumbered women by as many as 200 to one. And changes in the economy, especially the economy of the cities, affected women's domestic roles as more and more goods and services became available. However, for most of the 18th century, women were bound by the same constraints that had defined their lives in the 17th century. Almost 90 percent of women lived on farms, and the changes that affected city women took much longer to reach the rural areas

Very few women in the 18th century had the opportunity to exercise their independence even if they wanted to. Indeed, married women were regarded as *feme coverts*. Under that definition, a woman's right to her property, possessions, inheritance, and wages reverted to her husband when she married. The husband alone determined the disposition of the family wealth and property, with the exception that a wife could veto the sale of family property. She also retained the right to dower, which is designating or setting aside possessions and/or money for her daughter or daughters to bring to their own marriages. For the most part, married women had and would continue to have fewer rights than did either single women or widows, both of whom were exempted from the laws of coverture and therefore were free to own property, enter into contracts, and act as guardians and administrators of estates.

While there were a few unusual women of the era who exercised some control over their own lives and destinies, for most that was not an option. Most were homebound, tied to the daily routine of chores and child rearing. Unlike their husbands, fathers, and brothers, who could gather both formally and informally, women had little contacts beyond family and church. Eventually, the church took on greater and greater importance in the lives of women—and conversely, women became more important in the church—though that transformation did not occur until the 19th century. Even though the success of colonies depended on women's participation, in the opening decades of the 18th century they remained largely marginal in the public life of the colonies.

POLITICS AND PATRIOTISM

Despite their subordinate status throughout the colonies, women responded with enthusiasm in the politically divisive years leading up to the American Revolution and during the war itself. Very few women questioned or saw anything wrong with the social hierarchy as it existed, so their status was no impediment to developing the same patriotic sensibilities as the male colonists. Indeed, women made crucial contributions to the quest for independence, contributions that were recognized by countrymen and foe alike. One American editor praised the "industry and frugality of the American ladies," and went on to point out how "greatly they are contributing to bring about the political salvation of a whole Continent." On the other side, a British officer reported to Lord Cornwallis, the commanding general of the British forces, that "We may destroy all the men in America, and we shall still have all we can do to defeat the women."

During the early years of the 18th century, the British government, preoccupied with momentous events on the Continent, was content to leave the colonies to their own devices. But by the 1760s, faced with debt and heavy taxes at home, and the necessity of maintaining an army in America, George Grenville, the Chancellor of the Exchequer, imposed the first of a series of taxes over which the colonists and the Crown locked horns. The Sugar Act of 1764 was the first law passed by Parliament for the express purpose of raising money in the colonies for the use by the Crown. As new

Husband and wife prepare for his departure for the Continental Army. While men were off at war, women had to maintain home and family, often under great duress.

taxes were imposed on a variety of goods, the colonists denounced what most considered an oppressive burden on the colonies. For the first time, the cry of "taxation without representation" was raised. The reaction from the colonies was enough to bring down Lord Grenville in 1766. His replacement, Lord Townshend, considered colonial objections to English taxes as "so much nonsense" and immediately set about imposing new taxes on imported goods.

Daughters of Liberty

In the colonies, angry merchants agreed to impose another economic boycott against English goods, as they had done a short time earlier when Parliament passed the Stamp Act in 1765. Colonial women responded by organizing informally and calling themselves the Daughters of Liberty. In an effort to lessen the hardships imposed by a shortage of goods due to the boycott, they instituted substitutes for unavailable goods. They experimented with tea substitutes, raised sheep and wove their own cloth from the wool, and relied on homemade goods rather than imported ones. More importantly, the Daughters of Liberty acted as both teachers and enforcers of the patriotic message, making sure that other women observed the ban on imports. Joining with the Sons of Liberty in meetings and marches, the Daughters of Liberty were not adverse to engaging in physical confrontation, especially with Loyalists who disagreed with them.

On the Home Front

By the time the Revolutionary War started in 1776, many women were as versed in the politics and rhetoric of independence as any male colonist. Moreover, their patriotism was no less fervent. The manner in which women contributed to the war effort varied markedly, however. Many women were left to manage the family farm while their husbands were off fighting. Few women, however, had Eliza Pinckney's experience at running the family business.

In 1740, at the age of 17, Eliza Lucas Pinckney began managing her father's plantations in the Carolinas. A resourceful and innovative young woman, Eliza had received most of her education in England and brought back with her to the Carolinas a fairly sophisticated perspective. George Lucas had enormous confidence in Eliza, and he advised his daughter to try experimenting with the crops, a suggestion she lost no time in pursuing. Once in control, she succeeded in finding the right seed that, when cultivated in the Carolina soil, produced a grade of indigo, a seed used in making blue dye, far superior to anything currently available in the Americas or Europe. Until then about the only product exported from the Carolinas was rice, which was vulnerable to both natural forces that harmed the crops and unfavorable fluctuations in the price of the crop abroad. Indigo seeds became the Carolinas' second most important export.

Pinckney's powerful influence in family and community was notable, for she had served as both custodian and transmitter of family property and the republican values of the Revolution. Even after her marriage in 1744, Pinckney endeavored to keep abreast of intellectual trends and political developments in the colonies. She instilled values in each of her four children, including moderation and self-control, which became characteristics of the colonists and helped to shape their politics. Similar values helped those women who did not have Pinckney's background, but who found themselves in her situation.

Most women's lives were not as publicized as Pinckney's, but they nevertheless helped to impart the same kinds of values to their children as Pinckney did. In this fashion the generations directly succeeding the Revolution generation came to hold a common set of values and beliefs.

Abigail Adams, the wife of John Adams and resident of the Massachusetts colony, also found herself running the family business when John began spending months away from home as a member of the Continental Congress. To Abigail fell the task of raising four children and maintaining two homes. She did so willingly, first because the couple loved each other wholly and

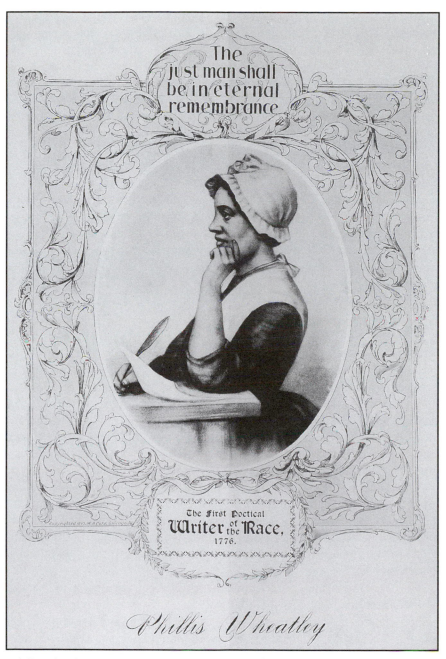

The just man shall be in eternal remembrance

The First Poetical
Writer of the Race,
1776.

Phillis Wheatley

Phillis Wheatley, a Boston slave, became the first African American woman to have her poetry published, in a 1773 volume.

completely from courtship to death, and second because Abigail possessed the strength of character, intelligence, and resourcefulness that made her equal to the task. John Adams grew to depend on her expertise and was proud of her managerial skills. Abigail gained a well-deserved reputation as a shrewd caretaker of her family's resources, buying farm stock, hiring help, buying pieces of land, paying bills, raising the children, and living as economically and prudently as possible. On top of all this, she was a voluminous letter-writer, preserving for posterity testimony to Adams's values and political acumen.

Although most women did not leave the kind of documentation that Eliza Pinckney or Abigail Adams did, they performed the same duties and held the same responsibilities for their husbands and children. Despite their protestations that family management was beyond the scope of their skills, women became quite adept at running family farms or businesses during the long separation from their husbands. And, like Adams and Pinckney, thousands of mothers instilled in their children the same values and ideals that had helped to produce a generation of patriots. When the opportunity presented itself, these children were ready to stand and fight.

Ladies' Associations

The Daughters of Liberty, who had been so supportive of the independence movement ten years earlier, remained active supporters once the fighting started. Women such as Sarah Franklin Bache, the daughter of Benjamin Franklin, and Esther DeBerdt Reed stepped to the forefront, and in 1780 reorganized the formerly loose coalition of activists into the Ladies Association of Philadelphia. Informally known as "George Washington's sewing circle," the Ladies Association engaged in relief work, donating clothing and medical supplies to the colonial patriots as an "offering of the Ladies." In Philadelphia alone the Ladies Association collected about $300,000 in Continental money. At Washington's request the money was used to purchase linen shirts for his army, each one embroidered with the name of the woman who made it. In gratitude, Washington awarded the members of the association "an equal place with any who have preceded them in the walk of female patriotism."

The ladies association idea quickly spread and became a nationwide voluntary effort. Members included the wives of prominent political and military figures, such as Martha Jefferson, the daughter of Thomas Jefferson. During the Revolution, men who probably would have frowned upon their wives and daughters engaging in such activity in less critical times, encouraged their involvement. The associations were mostly sewing circles, consisting of as many as 60 or 70 women who would spin, weave cloth, and make clothing for the troops. They also passed resolutions supporting the rebel cause and pledged not to do business with merchants who did not honor the non-importation agreements or in some other way did not support the independence movement. On one occasion 500 Boston women held a protest against a merchant found to be hoarding coffee. One North Carolina association declared, "We cannot be indifferent on any occasion that appears to affect the peace and happiness of our country." The Daughters of Liberty and the Ladies Association of Philadelphia preceded by many years the voluntary associations that women organized in the early 19th century. Still, the organizations mirrored in remarkable ways how women would later join together to work for specific changes.

URBAN AND RURAL RESPONSES

Most Americans' lives were disrupted in one way or another by the war, the men's with fighting, the women's with changes on the home front. In major cities, such as Boston, New York, and Philadelphia, long occupations by the British army forced many women to pack up and leave with their children in tow. Those who had nowhere to go or remained behind for other reasons had to endure long periods of siege. Many of those who stayed did so because they owned small businesses in the community. These women, whether they were minding the business for an absent husband or owned the business themselves, found themselves in dire straits because of the disruption in goods and the economic chaos that was a constant during the war.

Rural farm women were equally affected by the war, though in a different way. Their common experience was most often isolation. Left alone to cope with farm and family, these women often had no one to turn to for help or advice. As time went on, however, these rural women turned to each other. In South Carolina, Mary Gill Mills organized a band of 11 women who traveled from farm to farm during the harvest season helping each other bring in the crops.

The war helped to generate a widespread sense of outrage and anger among women, first directed at a political system that repressed the colonies as a whole and, as time went on, at a system that continued to repress women specifically. During the Revolution they assuaged their anger somewhat by taking matters into their own hands.

For some women farmers, such as the wife of one American general, Catherine Van Rensselaer, a scorched earth policy seemed the wisest course of action when faced with an approaching enemy force. The alternative, seeing all their hard work go to support the enemy, was too painful to watch. Other women did not have enough time to destroy their crops before the British confiscasted them. Anne Kennedy of South Carolina tried to harvest her crops before the British arrived. She almost succeeded, but had to fight with the troops who destroyed all her hard work. Although she was injured in the scuffle, Kennedy managed to throw a soldier down a staircase and save her home from being burned to the ground. In another instance, a South Carolina woman actually burned her home to the ground to drive out the British troops quartered there. In the process she drove them straight into a force of advancing American rebels.

The young officer who advised Lord Cornwallis of the difficulties that American women presented for British success, undoubtedly had in mind women like Mary Lindley Murray, Emily Geiger, and Nancy Morgan Hart. Murray invited a British general and his staff to enjoy a leisurely breakfast at her New York home. The soldiers, though perhaps a little surprised at the gracious invitation, nevertheless accepted. They never dreamed that as they sat about enjoying the meal, American patriots were escaping. When young Geiger agreed to carry a message from General Nathanial Greene to General Thomas Sumter, she had to ride on horseback for two days across the South Carolina wilderness. Stopped by British troops, Geiger was taken into custody, but she managed to talk her way out of it and safely deliver the crucial information. Hart, a Georgia resident, succumbed to the demands of a group of Tories to prepare a meal for them. When the interlopers, fearing little from their female captive, began to eat the meal she had prepared for them, Hart drew a gun and held them all captive until local forces came and relieved her. The demanding Tories were all hung.

These incidents of protest on the part of colonial women were played out in varying degrees throughout the war and throughout the colonies. While it is true that most women were never placed in a position of physical risk, opportunities were taken to engage in rebellion against the British on a variety of levels. For most women it was simply the willingness to maintain the home and take care of the family while the men were fighting. For others, the rebellion was more immediate and held greater risks.

WOMEN AT RISK

Several groups of women were particularly vulnerable during the war. Slave women, loyalists, and the wives of either political or military leaders were all faced with a unique set of circumstances. For slave women the war had mixed consequences. As they had done in other situations in the past, the British encouraged slaves to join them in the fight against the colonists, promising them freedom in exchange for siding with the Crown. As many as 3,000 slave women left the plantations, many of them taking their children and little else. For some this was indeed a route to freedom, but for many slaves the defeat of the British meant a return to the whites who claimed to own them. One can imagine the reception with which the returned slaves were greeted. Very few slaveholders recognized the parallels between their own desire to break free of England and the slaves' desire to be free from bondage.

Loyalist women were in a much more precarious situation, for their political loyalties—or their husbands'—made them easy targets for patriots. Like their patriot counterparts, the loyalists often found themselves left alone to mange homes and businesses. For most loyalists, however, the most prudent course of action was to head for a safer climate, frequently Canada. If they stayed, they were often harassed by neighboring patriots. The harassment could be fearsome depending on how active the loyalists were. One New York woman accused of actively supporting the British was stripped naked by a mob of angry patriots. Ultimately, loyalists suffered more than other vulnerable groups, because the outcome went against them. Those who could, left the country after the British surrendered.

One of the more colorful loyalists was Mary Brant. Brant was the daughter of a Mohawk religious leader and the sister of Mohawk warrior Joseph Brant. Brant married the Superintendent of Indian Affairs, Sir William Johnson, and was influential in persuading the Iroquois to side with the British during the Revolution. Brant eventually went to Canada and was awarded a pension from the British government for her services to the Crown.

Several patriot women whose husbands were influential in the Revolution also faced grave danger and sometimes even death. Their homes were burned and their possessions looted, and some women went into hiding because they were afraid that the British would capture them. The wife of a physician who ministered to patriot troops was forced to watch British soldiers shoot her husband to death. In an act of bravery that placed her in mortal danger, Annis Stockton of Princeton, New Jersey, hid the papers of Princeton rebels from approaching British soldiers. Had the British secured the papers, which were considered rebellious, it would have meant death for all involved.

On the Battlefield

While such acts of bravery were carried out throughout the colonies, some women went even further to support of the Revolution. Margaret Corbin, of Pennsylvania, headed east with her husband John when the fighting broke out. When her husband, an artillery gunner, was shot during the battle of Fort Washington on November 16, 1776, Corbin immediately took his place and kept up the cannon fire, even after she was wounded. Permanently disabled by her wounds, Corbin was awarded a pension by the Continental Congress three years later, in honor of her "distinguished bravery." Betsy Hagar of Massachusetts, orphaned at age nine and an ardent revolutionist by the time she was 21, was particularly adept at mechanical things. She worked for a prorevolution Boston blacksmith and, when the war broke out, refitted hundreds of muskets to be issued to patriot soldiers. A volunteer nurse at the Battle of Concord, Hagar recognized the value of six damaged cannons left behind by the British. She hid them, rebuilt them, and then saw them turned against the British. Politically outspoken, Hagar spent the war making ammunition and offering her opinion on events of the day.

Another Pennsylvanian, Mary Ludwig Hays McCauley, known far and wide as Moll of the Pitcher or simply Molly Pitcher, also joined her husband on the battlefield. Her courage in braving the battlefield to carry water to the wounded and those still fighting became legendary. After the war Pitcher received the explicit thanks of George Washington, who recommended that Congress commission her as a sergeant and that she receive half-pay for the remainder of her life.

Other women were equally willing to place their lives on the line for liberty, including Lydia Darrah, a Pennsylvania Quaker who, by eavesdropping on British troops quartered in her home, was able to warn Washington of an impending attack. Deborah Sampson (see profile page 27) disguised herself as a man to fight with a Massachusetts unit. Sarah Bradley Fulton engaged in guerrilla warfare, making the lot of British soldiers in her area more difficultit might have been.

A number of women who became involved in battle situations did so because they were present when the battles erupted. Because many married women had no other means of support, they often accompanied their husbands when they left to do battle, especially when the couple owned no property and had no children. Furthermore, because the finances of the Continental Army were shaky much of the time, soldiers frequently went for months without any pay at all. As camp followers, women could earn money to support themselves and their husbands by doing laundry and cooking. So routine were the camp followers, in fact, that the Continental Army specifically excluded them from rum and whiskey rations, lest anyone assume that the camp followers were in fact legitimate members of the army and due all the benefits thereof.

THE NEW NATION

Historians have frequently made the observation that neither the Declaration of Independence nor the Constitution of the United States were seminal documents as far as women were concerned. It is true that the Revolution brought only minor legal changes where women were concerned. Despite their outpouring of support for the Revolution, their obvious patriotism, and their new-found political awareness, women were not transformed into full citizens with the ratification of the Constitution. Abigail Adams was extremely critical of the legal and social status ascribed to women, as she made clear in a number of her letters to friends. She also admonished her husband to "Remember the Ladies, and be more generous and favorable to them than your ancestors. Do not put such unlimited power into the hands of the Husbands. Remember," she added, "all men would be tyrants if they could"

(James, et al., eds., *Notable American Women*). Adams was not pleading with her husband to include women in public life, but rather to redistribute power within the family, encouraging the arrangement she enjoyed within her marriage. "Emancipating all nations, you insist upon retaining absolute power over Wives," she went on to say. "If particular care and attention is not paid to the Ladies, we are determined to foment a Rebellion, and will not hold ourselves bound by any Laws in which we have no voice, or Representation."

Adams may have thought it humorous to use the same rhetoric that the Americans used when complaining to the English government. However, her concerns about the rights of women within the family reflected those of many women in the revolutionary era. It was, of course, expected that women would revert to their former roles, as most women did and would do after all the wars in history. Nevertheless, some women wanted recognition for the invaluable service they had rendered, and many were fairly outspoken about their expectations. Mary Willing Byrd of Virginia expressed the discontent of many women when she noted that despite all she had done, despite the fact that she was a model citizen, despite her patriotism, she "paid [her] taxes and have not been Personally or Virtually represented. My property is taken from me and I have no redress."

Despite such concerns, the Constitution did not address the rights of women because for most Americans—male and female—it was not an issue. Indeed, women were not even mentioned in the document, though both Native Americans and slaves, who had few if any rights, were included. Native Americans were given special status, and slaves were determined to be "three-fifths" of a person when determining a state's population and proportional representation in the legislature. Women, however, neither received new legal codes nor were relieved of dependence on coverture, whereby all their rights reverted to their husbands in marriage. Women were given no values in representation. Nor were they given suffrage—voting privileges—because the right to vote was extended to those who owned property. Unmarried women were also excluded.

Only in New Jersey were women allowed to vote. A statute enacted in 1783 extended voting rights to "all inhabitants of this state, of full age, who are worth fifty pounds proclamation money, clear in the same." The election law of 1790 clearly referred to voters as "he or she." For over two decades, women in New Jersey voted in local elections. In some instances they voted as a block to support a candidate who represented the ideals they valued or oppose a candidate who did not. Female support for candidates who held particular views that women agreed with became more pronounced as time went on. For example, women supported protemperance and prosuffrage candidates as the century wore on. Indeed, many politicians feared that after suffrage was won, women would consistently vote as a bloc in support of issues that most directly affected them. This was the case in an Essex County election in 1797, when large numbers of women turned out to vote for the Federalist candidate. How widespread this trend was, or how much fuel it provided for those who opposed women voters, is unclear. What is clear is that the controversy over women voters—and incidentally, African Americans voters, because they, too, were eligible under the statute—never abated. Finally, in 1807 a new statute was written into law and women and African Americans were written out. It is clear from reading the preamble to the new law that all troublesome factions were lumped together in an effort to do away with any controversy whatsoever: "Whereas doubts have been raised and great diversities in practice obtained throughout the state in regard to the admission of aliens, females, and persons of color, or Negroes to vote in elections . . . it is highly necessary to the safety, quiet, good order, and dignity of the state, to clear up said doubts." New Jersey cleared them up by limiting voting rights to adult white male property owners.

Revolutionary Aftermath

For all intents and purposes, after the Revolution home and family remained woman's domain. But if legal and political equality still eluded women, there were positive, though much more subtle changes as a result of the Revolution. The war had brought women of business and politics and provided them with a greater sense of the value of their own contributions. For women, the ideal of Republican motherhood was very positive, for it vested in women especially the power to instill in their children and future generations the values and ideals to which they subscribed. Republicanism included the themes of freedom and independence for which the colonists had fought, as well as the belief in democracy as the foundation for nationhood and the informed participation of all citizens in pursuing a democratic society.

One of the ideals to which more and more women subscribed was education, not only for their sons, but for their daughters as well. Women had long been denied access to education, but their new responsibility—to pass on the virtues of Republicanism—prompted many women to demand the education they felt they needed to meet this responsibility.

As early as 1790, Judith Sargent Murray was arguing for equal education for women. Even as a child, Murray demonstrated an intellectual bent. As an adult, she wrote essays to while away the time while her seagoing husband was away. Initially, she wrote under a pseudonym, "Constantia," but eventually her essays were published under her own name. An essay in *Massachusetts Magazine* posed the question that has fueled the women's movement ever since—that of nurture versus nature. Did the role of women in society depend entirely on biological determinants? "Suffer me to ask," she wrote, "in what the minds of females are so notoriously deficient?" She went on to ponder whether "the judgment of a male of two years old is more sage than that of a female's of the same age?" She also made the observation that, from age two on, the partiality shown males was totally out of proportion with circumstances. "How is the one exalted and the other depressed. . . . The one is taught to aspire and the other is early confined and limited." Murray's pleas for equal education for both girls and boys, though not immediately heeded, signaled the beginning of a long campaign that would eventually lead to the establishment of regular education for women.

The new sensibility of many women throughout the new United States accelerated the rate of change in the 19th century. The Revolutionary generation fulfilled their new-found responsibility and indeed gave birth to a new generation much more determined to pursue their rights and explore their own talents, despite the limitations they suffered because of their gender.

• • • • •

Deborah Sampson, Revolutionary Soldier
1760–1827

Deborah Sampson, the oldest of three daughters and three sons of Jonathan Sampson and Deborah Bradford, was born in 1760, on the eve of the Revolutionary War. On her mother's side, Sampson was a descendent of Massachusetts Governor William Bradford. On her father's side, her ancestors included Miles Standish and John and Priscilla Alden. Despite her lineage Sampson was indentured at the age of 10 because her father was incapable of supporting his family. The family she served treated her quite well, and she even acquired enough education to go into teaching when her servitude ended in 1779. In November 1780 Sampson became a member of the First Baptist Church of Middleborough. Shortly thereafter, she set out on foot for Boston. She was intent on serving her country in its fight for liberty, and on May 20, 1782, she enlisted in the Continental Army under the name of Robert Shurtleff. Taller than the average woman, she was able to carry off her disguise as a young man and marched off with the Fourth Massachusetts Regiment under the command of Captain George Webb. By this time her church back in Middleborough had learned of her ruse and excommunicated her for "dressing in men's clothes and enlisting as a Soldier in the Army." Fortunately for Sampson, her regiment had already left Boston, and her secret remained intact as far as her superiors were concerned.

Even before her enlistment, the war had pretty much concluded, but peace negotiations dragged on for more than a year, making it necessary to keep troops on the alert in areas that were particularly vulnerable. The Fourth Massachusetts was sent to West Point, New York, and actually engaged in several skirmishes with British troops. In one battle near Tarrytown, New York, Sampson was wounded. However, her true identity was not discovered until her regiment moved to Philadelphia. There she fell ill with a severe fever and was hospitalized. Though her physician discovered her secret, he refused to disclose his information to army officials, apparently out of admiration for the young woman's dedication to her country. Back at West Point, Sampson was discharged from the Continental Army on October 25, 1783 by General Henry Knox, who later became the first Secretary of War.

Sampson married and raised three children. In later years she went on speaking tours, talking about her experiences as a soldier. She had been awarded a pension shortly after her discharge, and after her death in 1827, admirers petitioned the government to extend the pension to her children.

Deborah Sampson's war experience was not one that most women had, but she did represent a sensibility among most women that they, too, were true patriots in the cause of freedom. Some, like Sampson, wanted to and did go a step further in demonstrating their patriotic fervor. Those who did appear in retrospect to be harbingers of women's growing willingness to step outside the bounds of acceptable behavior to pursue their beliefs and goals.

CHAPTER

The Revolution in Education

Almost a decade before the American publication of Mary Wollstonecraft's seminal book, *Vindication of the Rights of Women* (1792), American essayist Judith Sargent Murray published essays expressing almost identical ideas. In 1784 Murray's essay, "Desultory Thoughts Upon the Utility of Encouraging a Degree of Self-Complacency, Especially in Female Bosoms," appeared in *Gentlemen and Ladies Town and Country Magazine*. Murray argued that instilling in young women a healthy self-respect and a recognition of their innate value as human beings would prevent them from succumbing to the pressures of social mores and rushing into marriage simply to avoid spinsterhood and gain the status usually accorded to wives and mothers. Murray firmly believed that women could aspire to be more in life than just someone's wife.

Murray's essays on education, politics, religion, and the social issues of the day began appearing in the *Massachusetts Magazine* in 1792 as a series written under the pseudonym "Constantia." The series enjoyed a popular following, but the theme that Murray returned to again and again was the raising of young girls. By this time Wollstonecraft's book had appeared, and Murray found within its pages some support for the ideas that she had been espousing for years. Murray had problems endorsing Wollstonecraft because the Englishwoman led a lifestyle, which included a divorce, that was an anathema to most American women. And Murray did not agree with everything that Wollstonecraft said, especially concerning her views on politics. Wollstonecraft was a staunch supporter of the French Revolution, which many Americans, including Murray, believed had been carried to an unacceptable extreme. However, both Murray and Wollstonecraft believed in equal education for women and that women would be more productive if they were offered more opportunities in life.

Judith Sargent Murray's ideas may not have overtly influenced the ideas of early Americans. However, they surely resonated with people who read and discussed them, and may have formed a backdrop for the emerging role and status of women in the early republic. The entire nation was experiencing unprecedented change. A constantly expanding frontier and economy both worked to open new avenues for all Americans. To a large extent, social status was no longer dependent entirely on lineage, but on initiative, ambition, and achievement, all of which helped to produce a growing middle class whose boundaries continued to shift as fortunes rose and fell. Few constants identified the middle class, but one was the new sense of family structure, dominated as never before by women.

By the late 1820s, the transformation in domestic life was well under way, particularly in the commercialized urban Northeast. Before the Revolution most people lived on farms, where the family unit was also the work unit. Because it was a self-contained unit, there was little differentiation between work done outside the home and work done inside. Everyone, including the children, had assigned tasks that had to be done for the family to prosper. With the development of a market economy, however, men began to leave the home to find work that was not necessarily connected to anything his family did, except that he was paid wages that helped support the family. The home stopped being the center of production and became instead a place of retreat, insulated from the commercial world.

A consequence of this transformation was that the home became truly the woman's domain, no longer under the constant domination of the male head of the family. Women had primary responsibility for raising children, maintaining the home, and imparting the moral and religious virtues to other family members. Moreover, because the home was no longer a self-sustaining operation, women had more autonomy to venture out into the world, purchasing supplies for the home.

None of this would have been possible without an informal agreement between both parties that man's domain had shifted from the home to the world, encompassing business, politics, and money, while women were expected to give themselves over entirely to the household. The value systems of in both worlds were not necessarily the same, nor even compatible. But the values reserved for home were of paramount importance as far as society in general was concerned. And, unlike homes in the pre-Revolutionary period, women possessed much more autonomy.

The shift in the division of labor and the separation of workplace from home was accompanied by a change in attitude about the significance of home and home-oriented tasks. With the emergence of a market economy driven by goods, services, and capital, the workplace became the profit-center and the home a cost-center. Housework became more and more devalued because it did not produce an obvious profit. But in the wake of the Revolution to which they had contributed so much, women were not about to let their role be devalued. Instead, from the end of the Revolution, statesmen, politicians, and ministers had all extolled the virtues of virtue. The highest calling to which women could aspire had become the raising of republican sons and daughters. Women had become the crucial dispensers of values, morals, and character. As one magazine of the day observed, "Her character is felt throughout the intricate workings of society."

This economic and social shift created for women a paradox that continued to delay and promote women's status in society for the next century and beyond. On the one hand, that a woman's primary role did not produce a material benefit in a market economy worked to belittle her value to society in general. Women had very little cash with which to bargain for more rights and privileges. On the other hand, a woman, as mother and caretaker of the next generation, was placed on a pedestal to be looked up to and admired. It is important to keep in mind that the women placed on pedestals were primarily middle-class women, but the imagery that went along with that elevation became very much accepted by most Americans, including women, as the ideal. Eventually, such an image became little more than a sentimentalized ideal to which everyone could aspire but no one could really attain. By then middle-class women in particular had begun to use their idealized status to help them achieve more rights.

THE ARGUMENT FOR EQUAL EDUCATION

With so much responsibility placed on the shoulders of women, pleas for educated women, such as those made by Abigail Adams and Judith Sargent Murray, were given much more consideration than before. Murray argued strenuously for "sensible and informed" women, who, she said, would at the very least make better companions for men. Encouraged by the establishment of female academies, Murray looked upon her children's generation of young girls as the forerunners in "a new era in female history."

Arguments in favor of female education dated all the way back to the late 17th century when, for example, Cotton Mather believed that education would both make a woman a better wife and prevent her from straying into what he defined as the wickedness that was woman's more natural state. Education for both sexes was most often carried out in the home and tended to be occupation oriented. For boys there was some variety depending on the desires of their fathers and on their own abilities and inclinations. For girls, however, there was only one occupation in their futures: homemaking.

Consequently, their education centered on homemaking skills rather than intellectual development. Girls in the colonial period learned cooking, weaving, sewing, child care, cleaning, candle making, baking, and whatever other skills their mothers believed they should know. In the cities and in the plantation South, daughters of the merchant and planter classes sometimes had tutors, or they might attend one of the local finishing schools. There they were taught by women whose formal education was no better than their own and learned additional skills appropriate for their class, including French, dancing, needlepoint, drawing, and music. Relatively few girls learned more advanced skills, such as reading and writing. Protestantism encouraged these skills, however, using the spiritual rationale that girls who learned to read would have greater familiarity with the Bible and would be better able to instruct their own children. To prepare thoroughly for conversion and thereby help to secure ultimate salvation, women had to be able to study the Scriptures. Nevertheless, the literacy rates for boys and girls resembled the sex ratios of males to females in the earliest colonial days.

Over the next century, the education available to girls was at best very rudimentary and, even then, accessible only to the wealthiest of families. To be sure, most families could not afford to educate their children—boys or girls—but when the means existed for some education, it went to the boys of the family. By the end of the 18th century, the secondary education available for the sons of families able to afford it was quite advanced.

THE RISE OF FEMALE ACADEMIES

The Revolution, however, intensified concerns over the preparedness of girls to take on the new responsibilities required of them in the new republic. Mothers required an entirely new set of skills to properly raise good citizens with the ideals and values of the republic. Just as statesmen and military leaders had praised women's performances during the war, many leaders made themselves heard on the issue of female education. Philadelphian physician and statesman Benjamin Rush, who had been a member of the Second Continental Congress and a signer of the Constitution, offered his "Thoughts on Female Education" at the opening of the Philadelphia Young Ladies Academy in 1787. Women in the new republic, Rush argued, needed to be prepared for every eventuality, including widowhood at a young age. As a wife, the educated woman would be better able to relieve her husband of the tasks associated with home management, thus allowing him to achieve in the outside world. Not only should she be intellectually capable helping her husband, she also needed to be prepared to teach her children the virtues of republicanism and patriotism. A young widow might find herself raising several young children on her own, making it even more imperative that she be able to carry on alone if the worst happened. Educated women, Rush went on, make better wives, better mothers, better managers, and better citizens.

Rush argued that American women needed to be educated as broadly as possible, and he advocated instruction in English language arts, mathematics, bookkeeping, geography and travel, history and biography, and enough instruction in natural and physical sciences to enhance domestic skills. He also believed that dancing would provide a good form of exercise and that vocal lessons would provide cultural entertainment. Rush was also careful to point out that advances in women's education depended in large part upon the manner in which women deported themselves, for society would not support education if it masculinized the female population. The arguments that Rush put forth supported the advocates of equal education and helped to legitimize the concept.

Taking another tack, Thomas Jefferson—ever the pragmatist—conceded that there was no guarantee that a woman would marry someone with the intellectual capability of educating children if that woman herself had no education. Speaking of his own daughter, Jefferson noted, "The chance that in marriage she will draw a blockhead I calculate at about 14 to one." In that event, "the education of her family will probably rest on her own ideas and direction without assistance." These arguments began to carry greater and greater weight as time went on. Thus, the whole ideology upon which republican motherhood rested carried within it the logical conclusion that female education would enhance the performance of both woman's domestic role and her patriotic responsibility.

Republican rhetoric eventually gave rise to the establishment of female academies, which were intended to be the equivalent of secondary education available for boys. At the best of the female academies, the education indeed was on a par with male educational institutions. But most female academies offered a curriculum that was supposed to provide a basic education while still weighing heavily on the side of developing domestic skills. One of the first, if not the first, female academies was established in Philadelphia by a consortium of wealthy patrons, including Benjamin Rush, in 1787. The Philadelphia Young Ladies Academy offered a curriculum that paralleled the college preparatory curriculum at male schools. The Young Ladies Academy also served as the prototype for future institutions, with the greatest number of female secondary schools established after 1820. Sometimes referred to as the "age of the academy," the years between 1820 and 1860 witnessed a proliferation of secondary schools for both boys and girls. For women the turning point came in 1818, in the person of Emma Willard.

Emma Willard and the Troy Seminary

Like many notable American women, Emma Willard, the founder of the Troy Female Seminary in Troy, New York, became an influential public figure because economic necessity forced her to supplement her family's income. When her husband John was confronted with severe economic problems, Willard quit her job as a teacher at a small local school and opened her own school, the Middlebury (Connecticut) Female Seminary. Though she originally planned to realize more income, Willard quickly became convinced that she could make an important difference in the lives of young women, as well as an important change in education, "by the introduction of a grade of schools for women higher than any heretofore known."

Never one to let convention determine her life, Willard had always believed that women were far more capable than society gave them credit for. When she was 17, she taught herself geometry—a subject that male educators believed to be beyond a woman's capability. (Even the advocates of female education as a means to strengthen the republic believed that women were capable of learning only the most rudimentary of mathematical skills.)

The major advantage enjoyed by schools for young men, in Willard's view, was their funding. Taking a bold approach that no one previously had considered, Willard decided that she would go directly to the source—the state legislature—to get funding for her school. Connecticut, however, was not receptive to the idea. Several of her students suggested that Willard might reach more sympathetic ears in New York State. Committed now to her strategy, the Willards moved the school to Waterford, New York, and submitted to the governor and the legislature *An Address to the Public: Particularly to the Members of the Legislature of New York, Proposing a Plan for Improving Female Education.* Willard's *Address*, delivered in 1818, asked that taxes be allocated for the education of young women.

This pamphlet was followed in 1819 by a written proposal, in which Willard once again argued for taxpayer support in funding female education. In her *Plan for Improving Female Education,* Willard also suggested a course of study that included anatomy, philosophy, and higher mathematics. The Willards then lobbied the legislature. While some members of the legislature were indeed receptive to the idea, most were intolerant, believing that Willard's proposals were contrary to God's will for women. How the legislators arrived at this conclusion is unclear, but they were shocked that anyone, much less a woman, could propose teaching anatomy to women. Needless to say, the necessary funding failed to materialize. Publication of her proposal, however, brought far-reaching support, including that of former president Thomas Jefferson, who, undoubtedly, was still concerned about potential blockheads in the marriageable population. Luckily, not everyone in New

York State agreed with the majority of legislators. In 1821 Willard agreed to move to Troy, New York, when the Common Council of that town offered to provide $4,000 to fund a school.

The Troy Female Seminary, which opened in September 1821, offered a full curriculum comparable to those found in the best men's schools. Classes in mathematics and science were quickly added as well, something that no other women's schools offered. The school quickly became successful and self-supporting, and Willard, anxious to return to Connecticut to continue spreading her message, turned it over to her son and daughter-in-law in 1838.

The female academies were a significant development for women because their establishment signaled at least some recognition that women were capable of learning on a level beyond pure application. There was no dearth of students to fill up available spaces at the new schools. Girls and young women had been eager for many years to have the same opportunities to learn that their brothers had always enjoyed. At places like the Troy Seminary, young women were taught to appreciate their own intellectual abilities, though even Willard believed that the vast majority of her students would continue to find the focus of their lives as wives and mothers. Nevertheless, the academies provided women with an alternative to immediate marriage, an interim period between being a daughter and a wife.

The academies also provided women with an opportunity to contribute to the family income, even after marriage. It was not unusual for a young woman with one or two years of academy behind her to open her own school and begin teaching. Nor was it unusual for a married woman with little or no formal schooling to open a school to supplement the family income. Teaching, in the 19th century, became an acceptable occupation for middle-class women.

For those who were interested in education beyond simply attending a school, the opportunity was also there to embark on a career as an educator and to help bring about reforms in the current system of education. Emma Willard believed in public service and an educated population that would act responsibly as citizens. To do that, women needed to be educated as fully as men. Many of those who Willard had educated at the Troy school were already helping to promote Willard's educational philosophy. Having trained a new generation of teachers, Willard's students were her best advocates.

EDUCATIONAL REFORMERS

Even those who had not been taught directly by Willard knew what she had accomplished and followed her example in their own efforts to improve female education. Catherine Beecher grew up in Litchfield, Connecticut, one of 12 children of minister Lyman Beecher. Her brother Henry Ward Beecher became an influential minister, and her sister, Harriet Beecher Stowe, wrote *Uncle Tom's Cabin*. Another sister, Isabella Beecher Hooker, became a women's rights activist. Catherine followed her own star, becoming one of the most influential educational reformers of the era. In 1823 Beecher founded the Hartford Female Seminary, which her father encouraged her not to allow to become "only a commonplace, middling sort of school." Beecher published several articles on education, including "Female Education," which appeared in the *American Journal of Education*, and a fund-raising pamphlet entitled *Suggestions Respecting Improvements in Education* (1829). After several years in Hartford, she was restless, so accompanied her father to his new post as president of Lane Theological Seminary in Ohio. She opened another school, the Western Female Institute, co-authored an elementary reader with William McGuffey—*McGuffey's Eclectic Fourth Reader*—and continued to develop her ideas on educational reform. The *McGuffey Readers* became the first universally used reading texts in public schools in the United States.

After several more years, Beecher concluded that the major challenge facing the nation was the enormous number of children who were growing up beyond the reach of schools. In an 1845 article, *The Duty of American Women to Their Country*, Beecher argued that ignoring the nearly two million children who were growing up uneducated posed a grave danger to the nation, a danger that could lead to anarchy and bloodshed. The following year, women in the Mount Vernon Church of Boston formed a society for the purpose of sending female teachers to the West. In 1847 the former governor of Vermont, William Slade, founded the Board of National Popular Education in Cleveland. Beecher was in charge of selecting, training, and placing teachers in areas where there were no schools. The board placed over 500 schoolteachers throughout the West, where they in turn trained and educated other young women to teach.

Increasingly interested in setting up facilities in the West rather than importing teachers from the East, Beecher left the board in 1848 to establish the American Women's Educational Association. Largely through her efforts, schools were opened in Milwaukee, Wisconsin; Dubuque, Iowa; and Quincy, Illinois. In general, Catherine Beecher helped to professionalize teaching and was probably more responsible than any other single individual for the enormous increase in the numbers of women who became teachers in the 19th century.

After Zilpah Grant had been teaching for a dozen years in East Norfolk, Massachusetts, she enrolled in Emerson's school in Saugus, Massachusetts to continue her own studies. There she met Mary Lyon, another educational reformer. With Lyon's encouragement Grant took on the administration of a succession of private academies, until, in 1828, she went to the Ipswich Female Seminary in Massachusetts. The following year, Catherine Beecher tried to enlist her as principle religious teacher and director of religious studies at the Hartford Seminary, but Grant had other ideas that she wished to pursue. At Ipswich Grant advanced the idea of a boarding school for females. It was a notion too radical to bring up publicly at the time, though there was at least one local school already set up to accept boarders. (The Canterbury [Connecticut] Female Boarding School, run by Prudence Crandall, was established under unusual circumstances. [See profile, page 40.]) Zilpah Grant's idea was to house both students and faculty in one building, with each member of the faculty responsible for the health, welfare, and intellectual and moral development of the students assigned to her. Because the idea was so radical, it did not receive enough financial support to get it started. Still, Grant continued on as head of the Ipswich Female Academy for another five years, until she retired in 1839. While she was at Ipswich, Grant developed a rigorous academic curriculum that prompted one observer to write, in 1833, "The primary objective of the school seems to be to provide faithful and enlightened teachers, but the course of instruction is such as to prepare the pupil for any destination in life."

When Mary Lyon, the founder of Mount Holyoke College, wanted to establish a school in Massachusetts, she had already had years of experience working with her friend and colleague, Zilpah Grant. She sought Willard's advice as well. Lyon was determined to maintain the high academic standards that people like Willard, Grant, and Beecher supported for women. But she was also ready to proceed further with Grant's idea for a boarding school situation. While still at Ipswich Academy, Lyon began raising money for her own school. Her goal was to prepare young women for the larger social roles that would be demanded of them. "Our future statesmen and rulers, ministers and missionaries must come inevitably under the moulding hand of the female," Lyon believed. After she looked for several months for a location, three towns expressed an interest in having her school in their communities, including South Deerfield, Sunderland, and South Hadley, Massachusetts. Ultimately, Mount Holyoke College was established in South Hadley because the town, like Troy, New York, was willing to make an investment in women's education. The town pledged $8,000 in support of Lyon's school. By 1836, with the South Hadley commitment and money raised from Ipswich housewives, Lyon obtained a charter and selected a committee of advisors. A four-story, red brick Georgian building, serving as both academic building and dormitory, was ready the following year when the first class of 80 students arrived on campus at the new Mount Holyoke Seminary.

Mount Holyoke has the distinction of being the first women's college in the United States, though it did not officially become a full-fledged college until 1888. From the start it offered courses ranging from Greek and Latin to human anatomy. Mary Lyon had the highest hopes for her students and encouraged them to go out into the world prepared to make changes. The 1839 catalog noted that a Mount Holyoke graduate was expected to be an efficient auxiliary in the great task of renovating the world." Like Willard, Beecher, and Grant, Lyon saw hundreds of young women leave Mount Holyoke to become missionaries and teachers.

THE SOUTH LAGS BEHIND

The move towards more educational opportunities for both sexes, but especially for females, was not uniform throughout the country. As with many other experiences, education reform began in the East and gradually spread to the Midwest and the West. The one area that lagged far behind was the South. To be sure, the South's unique economic, cultural, and geographic circumstances impeded the kind of progress witnessed in other areas. For one thing, plantation life was isolated in a way that life in few other regions was, with the exception of the frontier. The main form of recreation for southern women was visiting, but even that required planning, because it required transportation. Plantation owners might have hired tutors for their sons and perhaps their daughters, but even that was not a constant. The educational opportunities that did exist for southern females tended to focus exclusively on domestic skills, preparing southern daughters to become southern matrons. Common school systems existed only in two of the southern states, Kentucky and North Carolina; consequently, the daughters and sons of those who did not belong to the plantation class generally had no schooling at all. And, of course, slave children, male and female, were not allowed to learn to read or write. Finally, at the time when the rest of the country was experiencing the greatest surge of educational reform, the South was limiting outside influences because of the increased agitation over slavery.

On the eve of the Civil War, education in most of the country, with the exception of the South, had become firmly established. Most communities offered at least some schooling to its children, usually four to eight years. The majority were given the opportunity to earn the equivalent of a high school education. The children of wealthier parents could attend local academies or boarding schools. In the East nearly 80 percent of boys and 70 percent of girls attended school at some point in their lives. In the Midwest and the West, these numbers dropped, though the lag was not because of a resistance to education as much as a lag in implementation as the concept moved from East to West. In the South only 35 percent of school-age white girls and 40 percent of school-age white boys ever saw the inside of a classroom. One consequence was that the rate of illiteracy in the South was higher than in any other section of the nation.

OBERLIN COLLEGE

As far as women were concerned, the educational revolution of the first half of the 19th century was already transforming their lives. The best example of the success of educational reform was Oberlin College, established in 1833. Oberlin was started in response to the suppression of abolitionist activity at the Lane Theology Seminary in Cincinnati. Following the lead of Theodore Weld, most of the students withdrew and moved to Oberlin, Ohio, where Oberlin College had been chartered as the first college that would admit women and African Americans as well as white males. The college played an important role as a liberal center throughout the 19th century. The position of women in the college was not, however, fully equal. Most remained in the "Female Department," where they followed the "Ladies' Course" designed to prepare them for educated motherhood. The first female to finish the "Full Course" graduated in 1841, and by 1857, 279 of the 299 women who had attended the college had opted for the "ladies'" literary program. The differences between the programs were not substantial. All were considered acceptable programs of study for women as preparation for their future roles as wives and mothers. Nevertheless, among the prominent early female graduates of the college were the theologian Antoinette Brown Blackwell, the physician Emeline Horton Cleveland, the feminist Lucy Stone, and Anna Julia Cooper. Cooper was doubly special because she was an African American female graduate. African Americans made up about 5 percent of the student body, and black women a minority of that. Of the 140 who attended between 1835 and 1865, 83 took a preparatory program, 56 opted for the literary course, and only one, Mary Jane Patterson, earned a full bachelor's degree.

Like ripples in a pond, female education spread throughout the nation, expanding horizons, raising expectations, and laying the groundwork for even more accelerated change in the second half of the century.

• • • • •

Prudence Crandall and the Canterbury Female Boarding School
1803–1890

Prudence Crandall never intended to become a champion of civil rights for young African American girls and women seeking to acquire a teacher's education. The Canterbury Female Boarding School, which she opened in 1831, was nothing more controversial than a school for middle-class girls from well-to-do families in the Connecticut area. Crandall enjoyed the support of the townspeople, who considered themselves liberal advocates of equal education for both sexes. All of that changed when Sarah Harris, the 17-year-old daughter of a respectable local African American farmer, applied for admission. Harris had already finished her primary education and wanted to become a teacher and teach other African American children. When Crandall decided to accept Sarah Harris, she did not consider how the community would react. If she thought about it at all, she assumed the residents of Canterbury would consider the woman just another student.

In fact, the community's reaction was swift and unambiguous. Parents threatened to withdraw their daughters if the Harris girl was allowed to remain. The school's financial supporters were also quick to raise objections. A lesser person might have folded under the pressure, particularly one who, like Crandall, was economically dependent on a thriving school, but Crandall did not. Although she was a Quaker and supported abolitionism in a sort of general way, she had never really been committed to the cause. Faced with the racism of her "liberal" neighbors, however, Crandall found that her own thoughts and beliefs crystallized quickly. She had read William Lloyd Garrison's pro-abolition newspaper, the *Liberator*, and wrote to him, stating her intention of doing something worthwhile for African Americans. She also sought out well-to-do African American families from Connecticut, New York, and Massachusetts, soliciting them to support her cause. Garrison and others encouraged her in her plan to close the original school and reopen it as a school for, as she characterized them, "young ladies and little misses of color." Garrison assured Crandall that he would find appropriate students for her.

In April 1833 the new Canterbury School opened as a teacher-training school for African American girls. The now-furious citizens of Canterbury mobilized to close down the school as quickly as possible. Merchants refused to sell supplies to Crandall, threatened to prosecute the students as paupers and vagrants, and refused to allow them to attend the Congregational church. When these sanctions did not work, the townspeople secured passage of a state "black law," which forbade the establishment of any school that taught African American students from out of state and the teaching of any student not a resident of a town in the state. Crandall was arrested and taken to the local jail.

Crandall's abolitionist supporters were not silent during this controversy. Almost overnight, Crandall and her Canterbury School had become a *cause celebre* throughout the country. William Lloyd Garrison publicized the case in the pages of the *Liberator*, and abolitionist Arthur Tappan supplied money for publicity and for Crandall's legal defense. The episode in fact caused some disagreement within the abolitionist ranks between the radicals led by Garrison, who wanted to publicize the event as broadly as possible, and the more conservative abolitionists, who favored colonization of African Americans and, therefore, were not supportive of efforts to establish schools for them. Because the Garrison abolitionists had Crandall's confidence, she did not object when they suggested she spend a night in jail in the very cell that had been previously occupied by a murderer. Such publicity was too good for the cause not to exploit it.

Crandall went through two trials, the first ending in a hung jury. In the second trial, she was convicted under the state law, and it looked as though her school would close down. A higher court overturned the conviction, however, but the reprieve for the school was short-lived. The town turned really nasty, poisoning the well water at the school, breaking windows, and generally terrorizing Crandall and her students. In September 1834 Crandall gave up the fight. Recently married, she closed her school and moved out of state with her husband. She spent the remainder of her life working for the causes of abolition and women's rights. She never returned to Connecticut, but four years before her death, in 1890, the state legislature voted to award her a small pension as an apology for her ordeal.

Although Crandall's ordeal lasted less than two years, it helped bring abolition to the forefront of America's consciousness. The Crandall case was the first one in which national attention was drawn to the still-emerging abolitionist cause.

CHAPTER 4
....

Women's Work: At Home, in the Fields, and in the Factories

W omen have always worked. When men and women worked together in the home, work at home was highly valued regardless of
who did the tasks or what tasks were being done. When, with the
emergence of a market economy, men's work moved away from the home,
and when wages were paid for work done outside of the home, work at home
was devalued. The notion that women who did not work outside the home for
wages did not work at all became a culturally accepted notion only beginning
in the 19th century. With very few exceptions, however, almost all nonwage-
earning women were putting in a full day's work each and every day, and all
wage-earning women were actually working more than one job: their paid job
out of the home and their unpaid job in the home. The exceptions were the
wives of the very wealthy, who could afford one or more servants to do the
physical work of running a home. But even in that circumstance, wives were
responsible for overseeing their servants—what men working on the outside
might have called a managerial position.

WORKING IN THE WEST

The work that a woman did in the first half of the 19th century usually
depended on where, geographically, she lived and her position in society. For
the whole of the 19th century, the majority of women remained at home
maintaining the household and raising the family. This was particularly true
of women in the Midwest and Far West, who settled into new environments
on the edges of the frontier, or worse, pushed the frontier even further afield.

Martha Jane Burke—a 19th-century frontierswoman better known as Calamity Jane—was famous for her riding and shooting skills.

These women, as a part of the western migration that took place throughout the 19th century, had little or no choice about their situation. Their husbands or fathers usually made the decision to move to the West, and the women were expected to go along. Of course, there were women who were eager to move farther and farther west and pioneering women who possessed in full measure the spirit and vitality that helped to civilize the frontier. But the harsh realities of leaving settled areas for unsettled areas cannot be ignored. For most women whatever sense of adventure they started with faded with the reality that they had left behind family, friends, belongings, and community, to begin a new life in a frequently hostile environment that left them overworked and isolated. More than anything, women who journeyed cross-country probably felt an overwhelming sense of loss.

For many women who migrated westward, it was like a move back in time. They were more likely to find their daily lives filled with the same tasks under the same circumstances that colonial women dealt with a hundred years earlier. Living conditions were rudimentary at best, and frontier wives had to tend the animals and garden, run the dairy, and make most of the food, cloth, and clothing for their families. The civilities to which transplanted Easterners had become accustomed were absent. Churches, schools, and associations were entirely lacking and the struggle to recreate them often proved futile, at least during the lifetime of the generation on the edge of the frontier. The farther West they moved, the fewer traces there were of the civilization that most women yearned for. Indeed, the farther West they moved, the fewer women there were. Even at midcentury, only eight percent of the population in California was female. Moreover, the communities into which women moved often seemed rife with lawlessness, vice, and untrustworthy people. One immigrant to the Far West, Eliza Farnham, wrote of seeing youngsters no more than six years old swaggering down streets with "cigars in mouths, uttering huge oaths, and treating men and boys to drinks at bars." Farnham's distress at the open criminality that existed prompted her to warn others before they embarked on the cross-country journey. "There is little in California society . . . to engage the higher order of female intelligence. . . . None but the pure and strong-hearted of my sex should come alone to this land."

WORK OUT OF THE HOME

For most of the 19th century, the vast majority of women who worked for wages were domestic servants, laundresses, and seamstresses, work that remained invisible because it was done in the home. Women who engaged in this work might have been local girls hired to help out housewives, or women who took in ironing, washing, and sewing as a way to supplement the family income. Young, single immigrant women, who in earlier times might have been indentured servants, often went into domestic work because it offered at least a place to live, because room and board were included. Presumably, room and board helped to make up for the extremely low wages, long hours, and lack of personal time and privacy. Although it is hard to calculate exactly how many married women worked for wages in pre–Civil War America, estimates run to about 10 percent. In addition to those women who did domestic work or took in laundry, sewing, and ironing, a few women worked in jobs providing services to other women, including hairdressing, selling handmade goods, and dressmaking. Also, some women took in boarders.

Women and the Garment Industry

Although most women either did not work for wages or worked in some form of domestic service, women were also crucial to the factory system in the early decades of the century. During the War of 1812, when the importation of goods was severely curtailed, American manufacturing began in earnest. Over the course of the next two decades, women were employed in over 100 different industries. For the most part, they were marginal employees in industries, ranging from gunpowder to lumber, which were themselves marginal to the economy in terms of production. The early factory system consisted primarily of textile and textile-related industries, including the garment industry, located primarily in the urban North, and the shoe industry.

The garment industry in Boston, New York, and Philadelphia used the "putting-out" system, whereby seamstresses hired to sew cheap, ready-made men's clothing worked out of their homes. A smaller number worked out of small tailor shops. The cloth was cut by expert cutters, then the women took it and sewed the garments by hand. The pay was extremely low. Women who worked on a piece-work basis—paid by the number of garments they completed—usually earned about the equivalent of what the poorhouses paid to women on relief. Those who were fortunate enough to find regular employment by one manufacturer earned a little more, but still only about half of what women factory workers earned. Mostly, however, women working the garment industry were not regularly employed, but spent most of their time looking for one or two days work. The labor surplus in the cities pitted married and unmarried, immigrant and native, widowed and deserted women against one another for whatever work was available.

Conditions for women in the garment industry became worse after the invention of the sewing machine in 1840. Much of the put-out work was transferred back to factory, where male sewing machine operators did the work. Those women who still took in piece work had to buy a sewing machine to make any money at all. Of course, the sewing machine did the job faster, but the piece-work rate was significantly less than that for hand-sewn garments.

The shoe industry, centered in eastern Massachusetts, followed a similar pattern, though shoemaking was never a home-based industry. Even so, the upper part of the shoes could be farmed out to women and children who worked directly for the factory, but did the sewing work at home. Again, the wages were about half of what the men earned working at the factory. Once the sewing machine was adapted to shoemaking, the home jobs began to disappear. By midcentury, the number of women employed in home work in the shoe industry—15,000 at its peak—had declined markedly.

WOMEN ON THE PLANTATIONS OF THE SOUTH

In both the North and the South, however, textiles dominated the fledgling industrialization revolution, from crop production in the South to final product in the North. In the still-expanding plantation South, the great cotton plantations stretched from the Carolinas as far west as Mississippi. With the invention of the cotton gin in 1793, it was possible to process huge cotton crops. But planting, growing, and harvesting the cotton was still a labor-intensive process requiring many strong hands and backs. To Southerners the logical way to meet this labor need was to maintain at all costs the by-now institutionalized system of slavery. Notwithstanding the commonly held belief in the innate inferiority of those of African descent, slave labor was the only economical option for a lifestyle that required enormous upkeep. At a time when the rest of the country had moved away from slavery or was heading in that direction, the South dug its heels in and made it clear that it intended to keep the system intact.

For white women in the South, the slave system constrained them in a male-dominated culture in which their only right as women was the right to be protected. As George Fitzhugh, a leading southern theorist explained, the right to be protected carried with it the right to obey. While women in the North were beginning to make new claims regarding their rights, women in the South were subjected to greater and greater patriarchy. Indeed, the South had to reject anything that could potentially damage its patriarchal system because the same forces would have the potential to damage the slave system. This was true for women who lived and worked on small family farms with no servants and no slaves as well as those who lived on the large plantations. The entire southern economy depended on the prosperity of the large plantations, so everyone had a vested interest in slavery.

Although many diaries from the era demonstrate that many southern women held the secret belief held that slavery was ultimately harmful to white women, very few of the diarists objected to slavery as a moral issue. The wives and daughters of planters, as disagreeable as they might have found slavery, were still aware that their own welfare depended on the system. The bottom line was that they had more in common with white males than with slaves, even when many of them felt enslaved by the system.

With the growing market for cotton, plantation owners were only too happy to increase production. To do so, they relied heavily on the labor of slave women. Male slaves worked in the fields, but they also filled the jobs on the plantation that required skill, including blacksmithing, stonemasonry, carpentry, and barrel-making, and other trades. Thus it fell mostly to slave women to perform the backbreaking work of planting, tending, and harvesting the cotton.

THE LOWELL MILLS SYSTEM

The first textile factory in America was established by Samuel Slater in Rhode Island in 1791. Slater's factory was rudimentary by comparison to factories established only 20 years later. As new factories sprang up around New England in the 19th century, fully half of them employed the family system of labor that Slater had used in his first factory. Under the family system, whole families were contracted on an annual basis to work for one manufacturer. A competing system, the Lowell system, employed only young women.

The first Lowell factory was established in Waltham, Massachusetts, in 1813 by Frances Cabot Lowell, the founder of the Boston Manufacturing Company. The Lowell mills were the first to hire women in large numbers. In fact, from the beginning the Lowell mills sought local single farm girls to fill their positions. Women were desirable for several reasons, not the least of which was that they would work for relatively cheap wages because they were not the "breadwinners" for their families (though many mill workers sent wages home to supplement the family income). Second, textile work, which often required careful execution, was considered women's work, and the factory managers believed that females made better workers. And last, there was a shortage of male labor because of the westward migration taking place. The willingness of the Lowell workers to accept lower wages, and the perception that this willingness extended to other industries as time went on, also helped to prejudice male workers, and especially many of the early union organizers, against women wage earners.

Throughout the 1820s mill owners and others who agreed with their position, argued that factory work was beneficial for young, single women. Perhaps picking up on the success of those who argued that education would benefit the nation, factory owners claimed that hiring women to work in manufacturing would free men for the more important jobs of farming and business. Moreover, by training them to be prompt, efficient, and industrious, factory work would keep young single women on the right path. All of these characteristics would hold women in good stead when, after a few years of work, they settled down to get married and raise a family.

By the early 1830s, the Lowell mills had refined their recruiting process, targeting young women from rural New England farms to work in the mills. Lowell succeeded in attracting the farm girls because the mills provided a protected, paternalistic environment, a deal maker for parents who would otherwise never allow their unmarried daughters to live away from home. Lowell girls slept in supervised boarding houses, ate family-style meals, and observed strict dress codes and curfews. Lowell girls were expected to keep their rooms clean enough to pass inspection and to attend regular church services. They were also provided with educational and recreational programs, including a library and lecture series within the mill complex, and in all ways were expected to behave with the same decorum that they would have at home. Moreover, they were paid their wages in cash and had the services of a bank to encourage saving.

However, paternalism in the Lowell mills was a double-edged sword. Infractions against the strict rules regarding curfew, dress, moral behavior, and, of course, work performance, could result in immediate dismissal. Youngsters under the age of 14 could have their wages "trusteed" to their families. Married women fleeing abusive husbands had to assume false names to find employment at the mills, and if discovered, their wages also could be trusteed to their husbands. They would probably be fired on the spot, as well. The pre-Revolutionary custom of coverture, wherein a married woman's possessions legally belonged to her husband, applied to wage earnings as well. Consequently, when married women became wage earners, they had no legal claim to their wages.

The work itself was long and hard. Lucy Larcom, who worked for the Lowell mills for ten years, later wrote a memoir about her experiences. Under no circumstances was mill work considered an easy way to earn a living, even by someone like Lucy Larcom, whose memoir tended to be favorable about her experience. Though actual mill work did not start until seven o'clock in the morning, all mill workers were required to rise two hours earlier. Boardinghouse managers were required to report any infractions. From 7:00 to 12:30, the girls worked in the noisy millrooms without respite. After one-half hour for lunch, they returned to the millroom to work until 7:30 in the evening. Larcom also noted that even though the workers had a variety of extracurricular activities to choose from, under no circumstances were they allowed to take a moment off to attend an unusual event. For example, when Charles Dickens visited the mills, no one was allowed even five minutes off to see him.

The Lowell girls, whether in spite of or because of the difficult conditions, developed a remarkable esprit de corps that helped make them excellent workers. Mill girls cherished their sense of community. All of the activities organized for the working girls were well attended, from debating clubs to missionary societies to discussion groups, where the young women could offer their own opinions on subjects as varied as the Mexican War and dress reform. Networks of friends developed that extended beyond the boundaries of the Lowell mills. Many young workers pursued creative interests, writing poetry, plays, and essays for *The Operative Magazine* or the *Lowell Offering*, both published by the mill owners for the benefit of the workers. Lucy Larcom published her first pieces of poetry in the *Lowell Offering*.

More than the sense of community that developed among the female workers at the Lowell mills, the young women enjoyed the autonomy they experienced. For the first time in their young lives, they were free to come and go as they pleased—within the limits of the Lowell rules. They could also spend their money as they wished; attend the classes, lectures, and other activities that appealed to them; and generally participate in a life totally removed from the constraints of even the most well-meaning families. Harriet Robinson, another mill girl whose memoirs reveal the common experiences of hundreds of her female co-workers, conveyed the importance of feeling independent and earning an income: "From a condition approaching pauperism they were at once placed above want; they could earn. . . . For the first time in this country, women's labor had a money value. She had become not only an earner and a producer, but also a spender of money, a recognized factor in the political economy of her time."

Still, for most mill employees, their tenure at the Lowell mills was not much longer than one year. They left for a variety of reasons, from marriage to alternative work situations—usually as domestics. Most of them expected to work for only a short time and that knowledge undoubtedly helped them to endure the long hours at the looms. And they were easily replaced by others eager to gain some sense of their own independence.

The sense of camaraderie, however, worked against the mill owners when the Lowell mill system began to unravel because of increased competition. To meet the competition and retain their profit margins, mill owners began cutting wages and increasing production expectations. These speed-ups and wage cuts significantly lowered the morale of the workers. In some instances, the Lowell managers used devious measures to appear to be making concessions to the workers, increasing wages on the one hand, while increasing rents in the company boarding houses a short time later. The workers, in effect, saw no difference in their paychecks.

Strike!

The first strike action conducted by Lowell workers took place on February 20, 1834, when the company announced intended wage cuts of up to 15 percent in certain departments. Workers from the affected departments held several meetings, deciding to go on strike and to withdraw all their money from the company bank. The strike organizer was promptly fired, but when she left she took with her 800 workers, leading them in a procession around the town. The strikers issued what they called the "Lowell Proclamation," which stated that they would not return to work until wages were restored.

The first Lowell strike, and indeed, many of the strikes attempted by Lowell workers, did not succeed; wages were not restored. On the other hand, the strikers obviously had no intention of remaining off the job for more than a few hours, because they walked out on Saturday and returned to work first thing Monday morning. The wage cuts took place as scheduled about three weeks later, without further protest. The strikes tended to be ill planned or ill timed and often prevented participation by those for whom the wages were a necessary supplement to their families' income. However, the Lowell strike should have been instructive for both mill owners and labor organizers. A few years later in 1836, the Lowell girls again went on strike, again with no real success except to show a willingness to place their jobs on the line. But in 1846 they struck again, and in that strike they succeeded in achieving their goals, limited though they were. Each time they struck, the workers were more and more sophisticated about what they were doing and what they wanted. Eventually, they were at the forefront of women who fought for a ten-hour work day, which they finally secured in 1874.

Labor leaders should have found the Lowell strikes more instructive because the Lowell women proved time and again that women could be as organized and persistent in achieving labor reforms as any group of male workers. In the mid-1840s, the women formed the Lowell Female Labor Reform Association, having learned from previous actions that planning and unity were imperative. When the company withdrew its support from the *Lowell Offering* because workers wanted to publish their complaints, the Reform Association sponsored its own forum, the *Voice of Industry*. Anonymously written articles implored workers to remember that "those who worked here before you, did less work and were better paid for it than you are, and there are others to come after you." In another article an even more dire warning appeared: "Producers of all the luxuries and comforts of life will you not wake up on this subject? Will you sit supinely down and let the drones in society fasten the yoke of tyranny . . . upon you? Now is the time to answer this important question. Shall we not hear the response from every hill and vale, 'Equal Rights, or death to the corporations?' "

The newly expressed militarism of women workers in the mills did not sit well with mill owners. By the mid-1840s, the influx of immigrants—particularly Irish—made a new labor force look more and more attractive to the owners. Gradually, New England women workers were replaced by Irish immigrants of both sexes who, with fewer options available to them, were willing to work under the conditions set by the mill owners. For native New Englanders, temporary mill work as an avenue to the middle class was no longer a viable option, though many of those who worked at the mills did not return to the farms. Many of them moved on and settled in urban areas. Moreover, they tended to marry later than did their counterparts who had remained on the farm and, consequently, had fewer children, which allowed them more opportunity to participate in activities outside of the home after their marriages. Many former mill workers became active in the abolitionist movement and the women's rights movement.

• • • • •

Sarah G. Bagley, Labor Organizer
1806–Date of Death Unknown

Sarah Bagley, of whom very few photographs exist, was born in Meredith, New Hampshire, in 1806. She left her rural farm like hundreds of other young single women in the 1830s, to find employment at one of the Lowell mills. And, like many other of the Lowell girls, Bagley found the experience a heady one at first. Writing for the *Lowell Offering* in December 1840, Bagley described the "Pleasures of Factory Life" for readers. Her common school education was, apparently, more than most of her coworkers had, and Bagley also conducted night classes for awhile. As life in the mills worsened in the 1840s, with wage cuts, deteriorating work conditions, and speed-ups, Bagley became less and less enchanted. The editor of the *Lowell Offering*, who a few years earlier had gladly printed Bagley's laudatory article on mill life, now objected to Bagley's insistence that the workers organize in their own behalf. "It was unfitting," Harriet Farley, the editor, noted, "for mere female employees to question the policies of the Christian gentlemen who owned the mills."

By January 1845 Bagley and some of her coworkers had formed the Lowell Female Labor Reform Association, which soon boasted 500 members. A short time before, the Massachusetts legislature, responding to calls to investigate work conditions at the mills, had set up the first governmental body to investigate labor conditions in the United States. Bagley and the Reform Association quickly gathered 2,000 signatures on a petition to the legislature, describing the conditions that existed in the mills and calling for the establishment of a ten-hour workday for mill employees. In February 1845 Bagley was called before the legislative body to testify about mill conditions. Having taken the bold step of testifying, Bagley's days at the mills were numbered. How much pressure she received to leave is unclear, but she did resign.

For the next few years, Bagley went from mill to mill, organizing chapters of the Labor Reform Associations throughout the region, including in Manchester, Nashua, and Dover, New Hampshire, and Waltham and Fall River, Massachusetts. She also joined the New England Workingmen's Association and was elected corresponding secretary in May 1845. To provide a forum for topics ignored by the regular town lecture series, Bagley organized the Industrial Reform Lyceum of Lowell. Among the speakers she brought to the lyceum were William Lloyd Garrison and Horace Greeley.

Bagley also took on the *Lowell Offering* before an audience of 2,000 workers in Woburn, Massachusetts, on July 4, 1845, denouncing it and the editor as "mouthpieces of the corporations." Apparently, the workers agreed with her, for the readership of the *Lowell Offering* dropped significantly and by the end of 1845 ceased to exist. Bagley was instrumental in bringing the *Voice of Industry* to Lowell in its place. The Lowell Female Labor Reform Association bought the *Voice of Industry*, and for a short time Bagley was the editor-in-chief, making the publication a major forum for the ten-hour movement.

Despite support for a ten-hour day, the labor movement was still too disorganized to manage a lobbying campaign effectively. In March 1846 the Massachusetts senate rejected the petition. Encouraged by this action, the mill owners began a counter campaign, focusing on the personal conduct of a union member to bring discredit on the entire movement. Although Bagley was not directly involved, the attack had a demoralizing effect on her. Her health had also begun to fail. Under those circumstances, Bagley decided that it would be best for the union if she resigned her position. Shortly thereafter, she left union activity behind her, accepting a job in Lowell as the first woman telegraph operator in the United States. Unfortunately, Bagley dropped out of public sight after that. Whether she stayed on in Lowell and when she died is unknown. But her activities as a union organizer helped to advance the ten-hour day movement—which ultimately won acceptance—even though that first battle was not won. Moreover, at a time when very few women spoke out for any reason, Sarah Bagley's public addresses on behalf of women's rights clearly placed her ahead of her time.

CHAPTER 5

• • • • • • • • •

Abolition and Feminism

T he women's rights movement was the result of decades of women's gradual movement from the private to the public sphere. Beginning with the appeal to republican mothers to become the repositories of republican values—the keepers of the flame—women became more and more creative and innovative in dealing with the issues confronting them. Initially steeped in religiosity, women turned to more practical solutions to specific problems and in the process developed their own priorities and their own set of values and goals.

To fully appreciate how women's status changed during the first half of the 19th century, it is important to recognize how cumulative the effects of each individual change were. Republican ideology was the rationale for radical departures from women's pre-Revolutionary role: the gradual shift of power within the home as men moved out into the world and women became the primary transmitters of republican values. In the 1740s a religious revival swept through the colonies. Known as the Great Awakening, it stressed an evangelical or emotional theology as opposed to an intellectual or theoretical theology. The transformation of women's participation in churches, begun during the Great Awakening and reinforced during the Second Great Awakening some 50 years later, resulted in the feminization of religion, with women becoming the backbone of religious communities. As the market economy grew stronger and society adjusted to the change, institutions also began to change. Whereas before when families participated in organized church functions sometimes on a daily basis and with the male head of household as the spiritual leader of the family, men were now more consumed with earning a living outside the home. Women gradually took over as the spiritual leaders of the family. Moreover, ministers quickly recognized that without women standing by their sides, little spiritual growth would take place in the church or in the community. The arguments on behalf of education for women, that it would make them better able to cope with any eventuality, were also being heeded more readily. And women, too, had begun moving out into mills and factories. All these changes had the imprimatur of republican ideology. They were both concurrent and cumulative, each one opening a little wider the doors to a more public life for women, whether or not they chose to move through the door.

VOLUNTARY ASSOCIATIONS

Women also began to take an active interest in voluntary associations and the idea that through a concerted effort they could change some of the negative aspects of society. For most women it was a short step from taking on the mantle of spiritual leader of the family to applying the lessons of Christian doctrine to eradicate social ills.

For many women the stepping stones to participation in public life were the countless female societies founded for religious purposes in the first decades of the century. Because women had been designated the monitors of morality, they felt especially obligated to do something about the potential for a decline in morality. In the wake of the excesses of the French Revolution, and spurred on by the evangelical fervor of the Great Awakening, middle-class women began to dedicate their time and energy to charitable activities. At first the ladies' societies raised money to send preachers to the West or deserving young men to theological school. Gradually, these associations branched out into other, more direct forms of charity, such as collecting food and clothing donations for the poor.

Close contact with poverty and its manifestations, including alcoholism, debt, violence, and prostitution, quickly changed the beliefs that women—and society in general—held about the true nature of the problem. Whereas many people believed that poverty was a crime, closer contact with the poor and the indigent made it clear that the roots of poverty were much less clearly defined than the reformers had previously thought. They also realized that to deal with the problems, their voluntary organizations had to be much more focused and directed. By the 1820s women began organizing voluntary associations aimed at dealing with specific social ills. Alcohol, especially, became a target for reformers.

Temperance Societies

As with many reforms, women played a major role in the rise of temperance societies, organized to curb the excessive use of alcohol that posed not only an immediate threat to countless women and children, but a broader threat to the well-being of the nation. Since colonial days, alcohol consumption had been high, and in the early 19th century, it rose even higher. By the 1820s alcohol consumption was calculated at about ten gallons per person per year (compared to present day per capita consumption of about two gallons). Rum had figured prominently in early colonial trade, and from the organization of the Continental Army through the 19th century, rum rations were routinely allocated. Liquor, in various guises, was the most commonly administered medicine of the day, and even the youngest children were given sweetened liquor as a pacifier. Although it was not unusual for women and children to imbibe, most of the alcohol abuse was by men. Abuse was a problem for families whenever it occurred, especially because there were few, if any, legal restraints that could be imposed upon someone who resorted to violent behavior. Therefore, including society's expectation that women would take up the temperance cause as part of their role as keepers of the moral flame, there were many good reasons for women to become involved to protect themselves and their families.

Several temperance organizations were founded, the first the American Society for the Promotion of Temperance in 1826. Referred to as a "cold water army," the society soon numbered as many as five thousand local affiliates and one million members, mostly women. This significant enrollment suggests the dimensions of the problem and how widespread alcohol abuse was. The attack on alcohol crossed class lines, as both working-class women and middle- and upper-class women had a vested interest in bringing the free flow of liquor to a halt. Ideally, the reformers wanted to see alcohol eliminated entirely. Realistically, given the lack of understanding of the true nature of alcoholism, most reformers would have been equally happy with a decrease in the availability of liquor.

The broad-based support for temperance in the early decades of the 19th century began to dissipate towards midcentury, as middle-class reformers became increasingly involved in both abolitionism and women's rights. Concern about the temperance issue never disappeared entirely, however, and in the late 19th century, temperance once again became one of the chief moral issues.

The American Female Moral Reform Society

There was no dearth of reform issues that concerned women, including prostitution, which spawned a number of moral reform societies. The goal of the women who founded the American Female Moral Reform Society was as simple as it was ambitious: to rid society of prostitution, promiscuity, and all other forms of male-inspired licentiousness. Women throughout New York and New England heard their call, and within 10 years the organization had over 400 chapters.

While the ultimate objective of the society was the thorough reform of America's sexual mores, its particular focus was on prostitution. Prostitutes, of course, had been a part of the New World since the first settlements. Although there were fewer instances of prostitution in the more rigid societies, such as the Puritan communities, the same was not true of the southern colonies, where there was a less fearsome punishment for those found guilty. By the time of the American Revolution, prostitution was so common that Benjamin Franklin remarked dryly that prostitutes used a disproportionate amount of shoe leather.

It was the task of American women, led by the women of the American Female Moral Reform Society, to protect their homes and families from the "predatory nature of the American male," who was "bold," "reckless," and "drenched in sin." That, at least, was the commonly held prevailing view. To some extent the upright matrons most involved in the reform effort also held the view that the prostitutes were the problem, mixing middle-class scorn of the "working girls" into their attempts to provide support to help the prostitutes regain the path of righteousness. But it was not a clear-cut situation, because it was also true that prostitutes were the symptoms rather than the cause of the problem, victims rather than seducers of men.

The society undertook a range of activities to promote its goals. Beyond organizing auxiliary chapters, the society published a newspaper, the *Advocate*, which lasted into the 1850s and both facilitated communications among the group's members and spread its message to the larger society beyond. The society also sought to reform prostitutes by creating a "House of Reception" where they could go to be rehabilitated. The society's most energetic efforts, however, went into direct action to discourage the patrons of sin. Members took up prominent station in front of brothels and wrote down the names of men who ventured in. The *Advocate* published their names, along with those submitted by readers and others supplied by members who actually infiltrated the dens of inequity by posing as domestics.

The impact of the society's actions was mixed. It certainly did not succeed in what it saw as its primary mission, the elimination of prostitution. Ironically, though, it seems to have contributed more to a shift in the mores of mainstream society, for illegitimacy rates fell significantly during the time it was active. And the society certainly contributed to and reflected the cultural trend that portrayed women as the morally superior sex, as the natural guardians of the virtues and values necessary for the health and prosperity of home and family. While the women of the society vehemently rejected explicitly feminist views that included a growing discontent with women's second-class citizen status, they did oppose "the tyranny exercised in the home department, where lordly man . . . rules his trembling subjects with a rod of iron, conscious of entire impunity and exalting in his fancied superiority." Thus, their moralistic understanding of men and women led them in the direction of social and, ultimately, political emancipation, just as their experience in organization and agitation for the benefit of others gave them tools that later women used to gain improvement in their own situation.

WOMEN AND ABOLITION

From 1830 to the Civil War, the reform issue that sparked the most interest and controversy was abolition. What began as a concern of religious reformers over the morality of slavery, by the 1830s evolved into a full-fledged political campaign. Abolitionists opposed the institution of slavery and all trafficking in the slave trade. They sought at first to either confine slavery to those states where it already existed or to abolish it altogether, with emphasis on the latter. The movement attracted some of the most remarkable women of the 19th century, including Sojourner Truth, Lucretia Mott, Lydia Maria Child, Angelina and Sarah Grimké, Elizabeth Cady Stanton, and Maria Weston Chapman. These women became leaders in both the abolitionist movement and the women's rights movement, and were joined by thousands of others who were willing to endure public disapproval.

As far back as 1688, Frances Pastorius and the German Friends Society at Germantown, Pennsylvania, declared that slavery was contrary to Christian principles. At the 1696 yearling meeting, members were cautioned not to import Negro slaves. Fifty years later the Friends ruled that any member who imported slaves would be excluded from the denomination. During the Revolutionary period, antislavery societies continued to spread. The New York Society for Promoting Manumission (the release of slaves), with John Jay at its head, was founded in 1785, with other states following suit. Advocates of abolition were able to get an antislavery clause written into the Constitution. Article I, Section 9 called for a prohibition against the importation of slaves after 1808, and fines or taxes could be levied against those who imported slaves in the meantime, not to exceed 10 dollars per slave. Between 1780 and 1787 slavery was outlawed in Pennsylvania, Connecticut, Rhode Island, New York, New Jersey, Massachusetts, and the Northwest Territory. Thereafter, the sentiment in most of the country was that the South was in charge of its own affairs and the North ought not to interfere.

For nearly 30 years abolitionist activity was low-key. Then William Lloyd Garrison began publishing the *Liberator* in 1831, and attention was drawn once again to the slavery issue with enough force to regenerate the abolitionist movement.

For abolitionism 1833 was a watershed year. In England the British Anti-Slavery Society won a long campaign when Parliament outlawed slavery in the British Empire. Its success inspired American abolitionists to found the American Anti-Slavery Society in Philadelphia. That same year popular author Lydia Maria Child published *Appeal in Favor of That Class of Americans Called Africans*. And one year earlier, just after William Lloyd Garrison formed the New England Anti-Slavery Society, a group of African American women formed the Female Anti-Slavery Society, followed a short time later by Maria Weston Chapman's more aristocratic Boston Female Anti-Slavery Society.

Until her involvement in the abolitionist movement, Lydia Maria Child's writings had all been popular, superficial, and generally undemanding. She began her writing career in 1824, with the publication of *Hobomok*, a fictional account of New England history centering on the relationship between a Native American and a white woman. Its success earned her access to the collection at prestigious Boston Athenaeum Lyceum library. She quickly wrote other books, including *The Rebel, or Boston Before the Revolution* (1825); *The Frugal Housewife* (1829), an advice-to-housewives volume; *The Mother's Book* (1831); and *The Little Girl's Own Book* (1831). She also published the first children's magazine in America, a bimonthly entitled *Juvenile Miscellany*. The income from her writing was enough to support both her and her husband, who devoted his time to various reform causes.

In many ways Child represented countless women of the early 1830s who underwent a political transformation over the issue of slavery. She was not particularly interested in reform causes until her husband persuaded her to attend an abolitionist meeting where Garrison was the main speaker. Garrison, she said later, "got hold of the strings of my conscience." After that Child devoted most of her energies to the abolitionist cause. Her book, *Appeal in Favor of That Class of Americans Called Africans*, condemned the laws against miscegenation and the inhuman treatment accorded African slaves. It drew people like William Ellery Channing, Wendell Phillips, and Charles Sumner into the abolitionist movement. But while some people applauded and were moved by her treatise, Southerners were outraged and, not surprisingly, banned the book in the South. Reaction elsewhere was less predictable. Most Bostonians thought that Child had exceeded the bounds of acceptable opinion and quickly no longer welcomed her into society circles. The Athenaeum revoked her privileges and *Juvenile Miscellany* suddenly failed to sell. Yet, despite this treatment it was too late for Child to turn away, and she continued to work for abolition. Her friendship with Garrison led to her appointment to the executive committee of the American Anti-Slavery Society, and for three years she edited the *National Anti-Slavery Standard*. She eventually returned to writing less political pieces and gradually found reacceptance by the reading public. However, the works that maintained historical significance long after Child died at the age of 78 were her anti-slavery book and several essays on the Fugitive Slave Law, the government's tacit approval of slaves as the property of their owners.

It was in this climate of ferment that reform-minded women in Philadelphia formed their own abolitionist organization. Because the American Anti-Slavery Society, Garrison's organization, was restricted to males, female abolitionists, notably Lucretia Mott, met after one convention to form the Female Anti-Slavery Society. Drawing on the themes and methods of evangelical religion, the women's society undertook a variety of activities to mobilize support against the slave system. For instance, it helped to gather hundreds of thousands of signatures on petitions calling Congress to immediately and unconditionally abolish slavery in the District of Columbia, where it had direct jurisdiction. The original society quickly spawned numerous branches. By 1837, when there were 1,006 anti-slavery groups, over half of their 150,000 total membership was female. In that same year women gathered in New York for their first national anti-slavery convention.

The Grimké Sisters

Most abolitionists were Northerners, but the handful of Southerners who rejected slavery and embraced abolition provided both damning testimony to the evils of slavery and an element of sensationalism. The Grimké sisters of Charleston, South Carolina, led a life so far removed from their genteel southern background of wealth and tradition, that after they left the South in 1829, neither one could ever return, even for a visit. Sarah and her sister Angelina, 13 years her junior, grew up despising their family's connection to slavery. The Grimkés were plantation owners, and the sisters and their 12 siblings witnessed on a daily basis the cruelty of slavery. A Sunday-school teacher, Sarah taught her young charges that preventing slaves from learning to read and write was wrong.

Sarah traveled north for the first time in 1819, accompanying her father to Philadelphia where he sought medical help. Sarah was encouraged to find other white people who agreed with her about slavery and was especially impressed with the Quakers she met. After her father died two years later, Sarah moved permanently to Philadelphia and joined the Quakers, hoping to become a Quaker minister. Angelina, who revealed an equally dim view of the slave system in her diary, joined Sarah in 1829. Both sisters were avid readers of William Lloyd Garrison's abolitionist newspaper, the *Liberator*. In 1835 Angelina wrote a letter to Garrison that was printed in the *Liberator*. Thereafter, the sisters' names were associated with the abolitionist movement.

The Grimkés were unique among abolitionists because they could personally testify about the cruelty of slavery, which no other abolitionist could do because no southern white males had joined the abolitionist movement. Thus, despite the fact that they were women, the Grimkés held a special place in the movement and were encouraged to speak out on behalf of the cause. Angelina left Philadelphia to work with the American Anti-Slavery Society in New York. Sarah, who harbored some hopes of becoming a Quaker minister despite earlier rejection because of poor performance as a preacher, remained in Philadelphia a little longer. In 1836 she attempted to address a Quaker gathering on abolitionism, but was prohibited because the pacifist Quakers believed that abolitionism was too incendiary a topic. After that, Sarah also left Philadelphia and Quakerism and joined Angelina in New York.

Angelina Grimké—and later Sarah as well—also became well-known because of several groundbreaking pamphlets that she wrote on slavery. In 1836 her pamphlet entitled *Appeal to Christian Women of the South* was published by the American Anti-Slavery Society. Although it was intended for southern women, southern postmasters took the liberty of destroying copies that made their way into the postal system. Angelina was warned that she was no longer welcome in the South.

Initially, the Grimkés spoke to small groups of women in private homes. As their fame spread the small presentations grew into public lectures attended by both men and women. As women conducting public lectures, they were the center of an outpouring of criticism from both public and private sources. In July 1837 the ministerial association of Massachusetts issued a pastoral letter that accused the Grimkés of exhibiting behavior totally unbecoming to women. Angelina realized that the criticism placed them in the middle of a conflict that was not about abolition, but rather about their rights as "moral, intelligent, and responsible" women. While some abolitionists hoped that the Grimkés would not let what they considered a secondary issue deter them from speaking, the sisters believed that they had little choice but to assert their rights as women. Garrison encouraged them to face the issue head on. Angelina wrote a series of *Liberator* letters defending her right to speak out and declaring that women ought to have a say in all laws that affected them. Angelina also became the first woman to testify before a committee of the Massachusetts legislature, voicing her views on slavery. Sarah wrote a pamphlet entitled *Letters on the Equality of the Sexes and the Condition of Woman*.

In May 1838 Angelina Grimké and Theodore Weld, a noted abolitionist minister, were married in Philadelphia. Several African Americans attended the ceremony. Philadelphians were outraged over the integrated ceremony. Two days later Angelina Weld delivered a passionate abolitionist speech to an overflow crowd at a Philadelphia anti-slavery convention, while an angry crowd worked itself up outside. The riotous crowd later burned the building down to the ground and set fire to the Shelter for Colored Orphans. This response disheartened the Grimké sisters, and their public-speaking careers were markedly diminished after that. Both continued to write about and speak on behalf of abolition and women's rights, but neither attracted—nor wished to attract—the audiences they had in their early years of public speaking. In 1938 Sarah Grimké and Theodore Weld published a remarkable book entitled *American Slavery as It Is: Testimony of a Thousand Witnesses*, a collection of newspaper articles and editorials published in the South that provided poignant, if unwitting, testimony about slavery. But by 1839, after the difficult births of Angelina's three children had affected her health. The Welds and Sarah Grimké moved to a rural farm and thereafter remained largely out of the public eye. Yet, even in their seventies and eighties the Grimké sisters demonstrated their commitment to their causes. They were among a group of women testing the Fifteenth Amendment by attempting to vote in the election of 1870.

Fanny Kemble

One of the most unusual advocates of abolition was English actress Fanny Kemble, a member of an illustrious acting family in England. Religious disapproval had kept acting and the theater on the margins of American culture for decades. European entertainers had no burning desire to challenge that situation, but regarded tours across the Atlantic about as attractive as tours across Siberia. Only the combined influence of political upheaval and an outbreak of cholera at home inspired the Kemble family to make the trip. The results, however, were sensational for both the Kembles and American culture. Moreover, by her presence in America, Fanny Kemble helped to influence decisions made by the British government during the Civil War.

Kemble's American debut took place in New York on September 18, 1832. Critics and audiences loved her. She united youth, passion, intelligence, and charm and was the main reason for the tour's dramatic impact. The troupe drew crowds of Americans who had never before had the slightest desire to go to the theater. Kemble even inspired the first famous native-born actress, Cora Ogden, and became the standard by which actresses were measured for decades to come. She also introduced Shakespeare to the masses and, to them, remained the one true Juliet whose renown far outlasted that of Ogden and other early American actresses.

Kemble's next move seemed a page out of a contemporary romance: she turned her back on the adulation and fame to marry a Southern gentleman, Pierce Butler. Unfortunately, the marriage was much less happy than Kemble had hoped it would be. For one thing Butler's family disdained her because of her profession, holding the narrow view that acting placed her just slightly above the status of a streetwalker. Their attitude was doubly shocking because the Kembles had always been treated like royalty in England. Kemble's vain hope for happiness turned sour when her husband proved to be a self-centered philanderer. Moreover, Kemble's intimate view of slavery, acquired during the time they spent at Butler's plantation in Georgia, convinced her of the immorality of the system.

Kemble turned to writing with consequential results. In 1863 she published an influential volume entitled *Journal of a Resident on a Georgia Plantation*. It was Kemble's indictment of slavery and it caused an immediate sensation both in America and in Europe. It also caused English sympathizers to rethink their feelings for the Confederacy and, ultimately, withhold support for the South.

Uncle Tom's Cabin

Perhaps the most influential book written by a woman was Harriet Beecher Stowe's *Uncle Tom's Cabin*. Stowe, a member of two of the most illustrious abolitionist families—the Beechers and the Wards—was the sister of Catherine Beecher, the noted educator. She wrote *Uncle Tom's Cabin* in response to passage of the Fugitive Slave Law in 1850. When her brothers, the preachers Edward and Henry Ward Beecher, denounced the law, which said that slaves caught while trying to escape must be returned to their owners, Stowe determined to make her voice heard. She had written other, lighter pieces, and often felt, as she said, divinely inspired. She began writing *Uncle Tom's Cabin* in the spring of 1851, and over the next 40 weeks the book was serialized in abolitionist newspapers. Even so, when the complete book was published, thousands of people were eager to purchase it. The book did so well in the first four months of publication that sales netted its author $10,000 in royalties, an astonishing amount at the time. Indeed, Houghton Mifflin, which acquired the rights to *Uncle Tom's Cabin* in 1862, has never allowed the book to go out of print.

Uncle Tom's Cabin both condemned slavery and made a strong case for family and the harm done to that institution by slavery. Through the voices of the characters in the book, slave and free, young and old, male and female, Stowe drew a portrait of the complexities of slavery. The book was called one of abolition's most valuable weapons against slavery. Whether apocryphal or not, Abraham Lincoln supposedly asked, on meeting Stowe, if she was "the little woman who started this great war?" Henry Wadsworth Longfellow noted in his journal, perhaps a little enviously, "How she is shaking the world with her Uncle Tom's Cabin! . . . At one step she has reached the top of the staircase up which the rest of us climb on our knees year after year." Perhaps the most telling evidence of its influence was the fact that both Stowe and the book were banned in the South.

African American Women in the Abolitionist Movement

African American women were also actively engaged in the abolitionist movement. Obviously, the most involved members lived in the North, but even slaves were able to contribute in a limited way. Resistance to slavery in whatever shape aided the cause. Runaways, work slowdowns, and feigned illnesses, among other things, helped to disrupt plantation life. But even such minor instances could produce dangerous consequences, if their intentional purpose was detected. African Americans less constrained by the immediate bonds of slavery took greater risks. Harriet Tubman, for example, herself a runaway slave, became one of the most important links in the underground railroad—the informal method by which slaves were smuggled out of the South. Time and again, Tubman placed herself in danger of recapture by her former slavemasters. Ultimately, she was responsible for smuggling more than 300 slaves to safety in the North.

Free African American women also played a role in the abolitionist movement. Most were not economically secure and therefore could not engage in voluntary activities, even abolition. Those who could joined abolitionist societies and other voluntary organizations or organized their own societies that mirrored in many respects those formed by middle-class white women. These organizations were not always specifically designated as abolitionist groups. For example, a number of literary societies and benevolent societies eventually turned much of their efforts toward abolition.

One of the earliest free African American women to advocate abolition was Maria Stewart. Though her efforts were not solely dedicated to recruiting African Americans, Stewart was nevertheless responsible for bringing hundreds of new activists into the abolition fold. Other free African American women who played important roles in the movement included Charlotte and Sarah Forten, Harriet Wilson, Frances Harper, and Ann Plato, all of whom were protest writers. In 1853 Mary Ann Shadd Cary founded *The Provincial Freeman*, an anti-slavery newspaper, and, of course, the indefatigable African American preacher and reformer Sojourner Truth (see page 74) passed up no opportunity to speak out against slavery and for women's rights.

Women played a critical role in the mobilization of public opinion in the 1830s that was to make slavery, or rather the abolition of slavery, the foremost public issue in the 1840s and 1850s. But the involvement of women in the abolitionist movement had other effects beyond the immediate objective. Abolitionism was the first overtly political movement that American women participated in, and their experiences in it formed an enduring legacy. On a personal level many of the women who would become leaders of the women's movement met at abolitionist and temperance functions. In fact, the seminal women's rights convention at Seneca Falls in 1848 grew out of connections that were made at the international anti-slavery convention held in London in 1840.

Perhaps most important, on an institutional level, female abolitionists gained experience that they and other women later drew on in mobilizing for other causes, including, of course, their own rights. The anti-slavery societies were where many women learned the basic procedures of political mobilization: drawing up a constitution and bylaws, electing officers, speaking before groups, taking votes, organizing committees, and planning collective actions. Similarly, in speaking out against slavery, they learned the power of speaking out. The lesson was not forgotten when they confronted other injustices and felt their own grievances. And finally, their outrage against slavery made them conscious of other outrages—of the brutality of war, the debilitation of poverty, and the injustice of their own position in society. The latter was most important for women, for it was the first time that a broad-based awareness of their own subordination led women to question their status. It was the beginning of a self-aware feminist movement. In all these ways, women's fight for the rights of African Americans gave birth to their fight for rights of their own.

• • • • •

Fanny Wright and the Nashoba Experiment
1758–1852

Fanny Wright, born in 1758, grew up as an orphaned Scottish heiress, but instead of settling into comfortable indolence, she threw herself into a life of learning and action that blazed the trails that women followed over the next century. She began by studying Greek as a girl and published critically accepted pieces as a teenager. In 1818 she traveled to America, accompanied only by her younger sister Camilla, to see produced a play she had written.

Out of these travels came the first source of her fame, a book entitled *Views of Society and Manners in America*. Published in 1821, more than a decade before the similar travelogues of Alexis de Tocqueville (*Democracy in America*) and Frances Trollope (*Domestic Manners of the Americans*), it was widely read in Europe and established the young woman's reputation as a promising intellectual. The French general and statesman Marquis de Lafayette invited her and Camilla to join him on his 1824 tour in the United States, among the high points of which were meetings with former presidents Thomas Jefferson and James Madison.

The tour also introduced Wright to slavery, which began her lifelong commitment to abolitionism. In 1825 she wrote *A Plan for the Gradual Abolition of Slavery in the United States Without Danger of Loss to the Citizens of the South*. Wright's plan was a well-thought-out solution calling for compensated emancipation—an idea that far predated other abolitionists' similar suggestions. The next year she took more concrete action, buying more than 300 acres of wilderness near Memphis to found a self-help colony, which she called Nashoba, where slaves could learn the skills and attitudes they would need to live free. The idea was that slaves would help to build Nashoba into a viable farm and, at the same time, begin to learn skills that would allow them to find work once they left Nashoba. If the slaves kept their part of the bargain, they could earn their freedom in five years and would have Wright's help in relocating.

Nashoba was going to be Fanny Wright's proof that there was an intelligent solution to the slavery issue if people of good will worked together. She sought "donations" of slaves to populate the farm, which had minimal results. As a consequence, Wright had to purchase slaves with her own money, which limited the number of workers. In addition to the slaves, Wright pulled together a collection of friends and admirers who wanted to see her solution to slavery work.

Though Wright purchased adjoining land on several occasions until Nashoba consisted of over 2,000 acres, the farm had too many strikes against it to succeed. For one thing most of the slaves were children or women, which slowed down considerably the amount of work that could be accomplished. For another thing the environment was less than hospitable. Nashoba was located in what amounted to a swampy wilderness. It required enormous amounts of labor just to clear enough land to plant gardens and one or two staple crops. Moreover, the swamp proved to be a hotbed of illness-inducing mosquito infestation. Time and again, people had to leave Nashoba for long stretches of time to recuperate from illness. Also, Wright's admiration for her friend Robert Owen's utopian community prompted her to apply many of his guidelines at Nashoba. Among them was a green light for free love. There were a host of other problems at Nashoba, but these were the major ingredients for its final defeat.

After leading the initial effort of clearing the site, Fanny became ill and had to return to Europe in 1827. While there she also intended to recruit volunteers and raise money. While she was away a huge scandal blew up involving the Scottish foreman in charge of Nashoba and the women under his charge. The foreman, who kept a fastidious account of the daily happenings at Nashoba, was living with the daughter of a free black woman from New Orleans. Nothing might have come of the episode except that the foreman made a colossal error in judgment when he published his Nashoba book in an abolitionist newspaper, the *Genius of Universal Emancipation.* People reading the account just did not understand why free love was encouraged. The experiment was so controversial to begin with that those concerned should have guessed that there was very little its opponents would not use against it. In any event the colony failed as a business and the conduct of the foreman made Nashoba, and Wright herself, synonymous with scandal. However, Wright made good on her promise to the remaining 30 colonists, and in 1830 she helped them immigrate to Haiti, paying their expenses out of her own pocket.

Changing direction, Wright embarked on a career of publishing and lecturing. She joined with Robert Owen in editing the *Free Enquirer* and began her lecturing with a tour in 1828–1829. She decried the second-class status of women, called for equal education for girls, and advocated equal property rights for women, divorce, and birth control. In a lecture advocating birth control, a taboo subject at the time, Wright said, "Let us inquire not if a mother be a wife, or a father a husband, but if parents can supply, to the creatures they have brought into being, all things requisite to make existence a blessing." While the language is perhaps archaic, the idea is remarkably contemporary.

Wright's public lectures, though delivered to packed audiences, nevertheless made her a target of criticism and scandalous gossip. Her traditional style of dress belied her groundbreaking role as one of the first female public lecturers. Tall and imposing, Wright was both eloquent and effective as a speaker. More often than not, she dressed in white and carried a copy of the Declaration of Independence, to which she frequently referred. However, public speaking was still considered an unnatural activity for a woman. Even her long-time friend, Lafayette, thought her wrong. Ministers denounced her from their pulpits, and the press characterized her as a "female monster whom all decent people ought to avoid." Another newspaper labeled her a "bold blasphemer" seeking to turn the world into a "universal brothel." And even the usually restrained Quakers could not resist branding her as a "fallen and degraded fair one" who would destroy religion, morals, law, and equity, in her misguided quest. In 1829 she founded the Workingmen's Association in New York City, and in the 1830s she became a prominent supporter of Jacksonian democracy. She married a French physician in 1831 and bore two children, but managed to cross the Atlantic five times during the decade and wrote a book calling for world government in 1838. She divorced her husband in 1852, losing custody of the surviving child in the process, and died some months later after a fall on some ice.

Fanny Wright would have been a remarkable woman in any age, but in the context of the early 19th century, her career was truly outstanding. She said and did things decades before others were ready to do or accept them, and her life pointed the way that women would take for the next three generations.

• • • • •

Harriet Tubman, Underground Railroad Conductor
1820–1913

In her short career as a "conductor" for the Underground Railroad, Harriet Tubman helped nearly 1,000 slaves escape from the South to as far north as Canada, where they were not subject to the Fugitive Slave Law. Tubman was born into slavery in Maryland in 1820. Her birth name was Araminta Ross. Her parents, Benjamin Ross and Harriet Greene, had 11 children, of whom young Araminta may have been the most rebellious. Her childhood memories included many whippings at the hands of her white masters because of one or another infraction. One beating was so severe that it left Araminta permanently injured with a deep dent in her forehead. Thereafter, she was determined to extricate herself from slavery if it became possible to do so.

In 1844 Araminta received permission from her owner to marry a free black resident of Maryland, John Tubman. However, her status as a slave was unchanged after her marriage. When her owner died in 1849, Tubman's lifelong fears of being sold south and never seeing her family again took on greater intensity. However, perhaps because her husband was not a slave, she could not persuade him to abandon his life in Maryland and escape with her to the North. That did not deter Tubman, however. Leaving her family, she ran away from Maryland and eventually ended up in Philadelphia where she was able to find employment. By this time Tubman had also abandoned her given name in favor of her mother's. For the remainder of her life she was known as Harriet Tubman.

In Philadelphia, Tubman lost little time in associating herself with abolitionists. She became an active member of the Underground Railroad, a loosely organized network that helped slaves escape from the South by transporting them from contact to contact. After the Fugitive Slave Law of 1850 was enacted, whereby persons in the North who came into knowing contact with escaped slaves were legally obligated to turn them over to the proper authorities, safe haven for runaway slaves could be as far north as Canada. Among the first slaves that Tubman helped lead to safety were members of her own family: sisters, nieces, and nephews.

Tubman knew that she faced great risks each time she returned to the South to gather a new group of slaves. Moreover, at home she ran a risk of being sent back south by the authorities if she were caught breaking the Fugitive Slave Law. For awhile, Southern slaveholders offered a reward for the halt of her activities. When the Civil War began, Tubman took on a further risk when she served as a Union spy, gathering information as she traveled in the South. And for several months she conducted raids on plantations along the Combahee River in South Carolina in an effort to free as many slaves as she could. Yet despite these enormous dangers, Tubman never considered doing less than she could to help bring down the slave system.

Her service to the country was never properly rewarded or acknowledged, despite efforts by the commanding officers under whom she served in the military to secure a pension for her. After the war, Tubman moved to Auburn, New York, where she operated a Home for Indigent and Aged Negroes. She died in 1913.

CHAPTER 6

Beginning the Century of Struggle

L ucretia Mott, a devout Quaker and long-time advocate of abolitionism, had devoted several years to the cause when, in 1840, she was
chosen to attend the World Anti-Slavery Conference in London. Mott
had befriended William Lloyd Garrison in 1831, when Garrison had just
organized the New England Anti-Slavery Society and begun to publish the
Liberator. Garrison had always welcomed women into the movement, though
he bowed to both convention and the strong beliefs held by many abolitionists
and, as in other societies, did not allow women official membership. Female
abolitionists, such as Mott, Lydia Maria Child, and the Grimké sisters, were
willing to form auxiliary organizations so that those who objected to women's
presence in the public sphere would not divert attention away from abolitionism. Indeed, the Grimkés, who were willing to stand up and address "promis-
cuous" audiences—those composed of both men and women—were among
the first with the commitment, daring, and courage to become public speakers. The daughters of a plantation owner, they publicized the slave sytstem as
no other speakers could, and they were willing to risk public indignation to
do so.

Mott attended the organizational meeting of the American Anti-Slavery
Society in Philadelphia (AASS) in 1833, then formed the auxiliary Philadelphia Female Anti-Slavery Society immediately after because the AASS
excluded women. The AASS dropped its restrictions against women members soon after, however, and Mott became an active member of both the
national and the Pennsylvania branch as an executive committee member.
Although all abolitionists sought the eradication of slavery, there was disagreement within the movement regarding whether slavery should be stopped
immediately, phased out over several years, or allowed to die a natural death

by simply prohibiting any further growth in the slave population. Mott remained steadfast in her commitment to Garrisonian—or immediate—abolition, even when she was condemned by members of her church who favored a more conservative approach.

Mott was also instrumental in organizing the Anti-Slavery Convention of American Women held in Philadelphia in 1838. When riotous anti-abolitionists wreaked havoc at the convention, Mott counseled the women delegates to remain calm. The mobs later burned down the convention hall and the Shelter for Colored Orphans, then marched off in search of the Mott home. Fortunately, they were distracted and never arrived there.

When Mott and her husband, James, arrived at the World Anti-Slavery Conference in England, she was distressed to learn that she and the other women delegates would not be seated. The conference was controlled by the more conservative American and Foreign Anti-Slavery Society and its British counterpart, the British and Foreign Anti-Slavery Society, both of which objected to women in the public arena. The male abolitionists who accompanied Mott and the other women tried to persuade the convention organizers to seat them, but the best they could accomplish was a place for the women in the gallery, where they would have no opportunity to participate except as viewers.

Another woman delegate who was refused a seat at the convention, Elizabeth Cady Stanton, made it her business to meet Lucretia Mott as they both sat in the gallery. It struck them both as ironic that the convention, which was billed as a world convention, could begin its proceedings by denying representation to half of the human population. With this observation, both Mott and Stanton experienced a critical transformation. They concluded that they had an obligation to promote women's rights when they returned to the United States. They both continued to campaign against slavery, but never without also placing the rights of women in the forefront.

The fact that the presence of women in the public arena produced reactions that ranged from discomfort to outrage was not lost on the women who were lobbying to rid the nation of a system that enslaved people. It made them question their own status in society, making the obvious comparison between slaves and themselves, for both groups were denied the full benefits of citizenship. Incidents like that experienced by Child, who was ridiculed and criticized when she published *Appeal in Favor of the Class of Americans Called Africans*, led women in the abolitionist movement to raise fundamental questions about their own rights. At the national women's anti-slavery conference in 1838, delegates spent a good deal of time discussing the issue, finally passing a resolution that said, "The time has come for woman to move in that sphere which providence has assigned her, and no longer remain satisfied in the circumscribed limits which corrupt custom and a perverted application of Scripture have encircled her."

Garrison and other radical abolitionists fully supported this position. The more conservative abolitionists, however, were disturbed by this turn of events. When the American Anti-Slavery Society proposed a year earlier that women be hired as anti-slavery agents, it received criticism from a number of quarters, including the clergy, who objected to women assuming "the place and tone of man as public reformer." By the late 1830s, the controversy had caused abolitionists to divide into factions. The still-dominant New England branch of the movement broke into two opposing camps in 1839. And the following year, both the Boston Female Anti-Slavery Society and the American Anti-Slavery Society split. Garrison, certain that the conservatives would attempt to push women into the background by bringing the issue up for a vote at the national convention, quickly appointed Abby Kelley to the business committee and insured the attendance of hundreds of New England women to the convention. When the issue was put to the vote, the Garrisonians had the majority. Shortly after that, the American delegates to the World Anti-Slavery Conference in London arrived in England to discover that the women among them would not be seated.

After 1840 the conservatives walked away from the American Anti-Slavery Society, leaving it in the hands of the Garrisonians. The abolitionist movement proceeded along two separate tracks. Less cohesive than their radical counterparts, the conservatives moved along the more diffuse of the paths. The Tappan brothers, Albert and Lewis, formed their own anti-slavery society, while James Birney became the Liberty Party candidate for president in the 1840 election. Women's rights continued to be a legitimate issue for the Garrisonians and ultimately became the platform from which the women's rights movement was launched. Although it would take another eight years before Mott and Stanton could find the time and opportunity to organize a women's rights convention, the historic meeting they hosted in Seneca Falls in 1848 marked the start of a concentrated feminist movement that would affect the lives of all American women.

A HISTORIC MEETING IN SENECA FALLS

After the London conference, Elizabeth Cady Stanton and her husband, Henry, traveled in England before returning to the United States. Henry began studying law, and Elizabeth bore seven children over the next several years. For awhile the Stantons lived in Boston, which gave Elizabeth the opportunity to meet some of the more liberal thinkers of the day, including Garrison, John Greenleaf Whittier, Maria Weston Chapman, Lydia Maria Child, Abby Kelley Foster, and Frederick Douglass. Stanton's husband had to leave Boston for a drier climate because of health problems, and by 1847 she and her family were living in Seneca Falls, New York. The pace in Seneca

Falls was considerably slower than in Boston, even though Stanton resumed her work in freeing women from their common law bondage. At every opportunity she lobbied state legislators in hopes of changing the law. When, in 1848, the state legislature passed a law granting married women the right to own real estate in their own names, Stanton justifiably felt she had played a part in securing its passage. It was at about this time that Stanton began using her full name—Elizabeth Cady Stanton—rather than Mrs. Henry B. Stanton, convinced that women must retain their own identity even in marriage—or, perhaps, especially in marriage.

When Stanton learned, in July 1848, that her old friend Lucretia Mott was visiting in nearby Waterloo, she immediately went to see her. The visit was a huge success, for Stanton discovered that Mott was as ready as she was to start a campaign for women's rights. Moreover, Mott's sister, Martha Wright, and two friends, Jane Hunt and Mary McClintock, were also ready to join the campaign. Not wanting to let the moment slip, the five women sent out a call to convention to take place on July 19, at the Wesleyan Methodist Church in Seneca Falls. Amazingly, with only a few days lead time and a remote site in rural upper New York State, the meeting attracted 240 women. This factor as much as anything else associated with the convention demonstrated the extent to which women had begun to change their thinking about their place in society.

Drawing on their experience in the abolition and temperance movements, as well as other associations to which the five organizers had belonged, they began to pull together an agenda for the convention. Stanton offered to write a Declaration of Sentiments, using the Declaration of Independence as a model. With a pen as sharp as her mind, Stanton's important document began by declaring, "We hold these truths to be self evident, that all men and women are created equal." She then listed 18 legal grievances under which women suffered and which the convention would address point by point. Women, it was noted, could not legally keep their own wages or their children, nor even retain control over their own lives. They were afforded limited educational and economic opportunity; with few exceptions, they were prohibited from the trades and commerce; they were barred from the pulpit and the professions; and they had to endure a double standard in morals. Moreover, women were not allowed to vote. Stanton also prepared 12 resolutions, each addressing some aspect of the grievances previously discussed.

James Mott actually presided over the convention itself, as it was still considered unseemly for a woman to preside at a public meeting. After discussing each of the resolutions and the issues they represented, the convention delegates voted unanimously to adopt all the resolutions save one—the voting issue. Many of those in attendance, including Mott, believed that asking for woman suffrage was simply too radical a demand at that moment in history and that if pursued the suffrage demand would make the entire women's rights agenda seem ludicrous and irresponsible. Stanton argued in favor of woman suffrage, and in the end a majority of women voted with her. The woman suffrage amendment was passed, but not until the second session of the convention, held in Rochester, New York, two weeks later with an even larger delegation. The Declaration of Sentiments, the first formal statement of women's rights, was signed by 68 women and 32 men.

The convention and the women who organized and attended it—as well as the men in attendance—were roundly criticized by public and press alike. Even before the woman suffrage proposal was ratified at the convention in Rochester, the press was contemptuous of the whole idea. Most of the articles published on the convention either expressed outrage that a group of women would air their discontents in so public a forum as a convention, or the convention was treated as a joke. (The only influential newspaper to regard the convention with respect and seriousness was Horace Greeley's *New York Tribune*.) The press was not alone in denouncing the convention. Ministers throughout the country informed their parishioners that the ideas expressed at the women's rights conventions were unseemly for women and not in keeping with their elevated status as keepers of the nation's moral values.

Stanton and Anthony

Within three years of the women's rights convention, Stanton was introduced to Susan B. Anthony, who had come to Seneca Falls to attend an antislavery meeting. Until her meeting with Stanton, Anthony had not given much thought to women's rights and had never considered changing her life for that cause. Anthony was so impressed with Stanton and the case she made for the importance of woman suffrage that Anthony became a dedicated advocate for the remainder of her life. In the process she and Stanton mobilized thousands of women.

Physically, temperamentally, and even, to some extent, spiritually, Stanton and Anthony were a study in contrasts. Whereas Anthony was tall and austere looking, Stanton was short and jolly looking. Anthony was the more measured and even tempered, while Stanton was more fiery and given to intemperate statements. Finally, Anthony seemed more reserved, while Stanton exuded passion. But they had one great cause in common, and they played off each other's strengths, which made them a formidable team. Stanton, tied more to home because of her growing family, was the nerve center of all activities. She accepted as many speaking engagements as she could, regardless of which organization did the inviting, because, as she noted, the opportunity to gather converts to women's rights could not be overlooked. Anthony, far more organized than Stanton, traveled the country meeting with potential supporters, speaking to small gatherings of women eager to hear her message and gathering the information that Stanton used to bolster their arguments.

If the first advocates for women's rights brought with them to the newly born movement long experience in reform and benevolent associations, they were also ready to jettison some of the baggage associated with other reform movements. The first discard was the religiosity that pervaded them. Many women, especially those with abolition backgrounds, had developed a healthy skepticism of clerical authority, as well as a marked mistrust for the way the clergy interpreted Scripture to justify their views of women's proper place. (Listening to one clergyman interpret the life of Christ in such a way that it upheld in every instance a patriarchal social order, Sojourner Truth [see below] felt compelled to ask pointedly, "Where did your Christ come from? From God and a woman! Man had nothing to do with him.") Stanton believed wholeheartedly that "The Bible and the Church have been the greatest stumbling blocks in the way of woman's emancipation." Lucretia Mott bluntly informed an audience at an 1854 women's rights convention, "The pulpit has been prostituted."

The new movement was also light on organization and relied on spontaneous activity that included informal gatherings, speaking opportunities, and conventions. Nevertheless, women's rights organizations sprang up all over the Northeast and as far west as Wisconsin. In 1850 the first "national" convention was held in Worcester, Massachusetts. Thereafter, annual national conventions marked the movement for its first decade, providing both a forum for publicizing the movement's goals and an opportunity to refine and broaden those goals.

Throughout the first decade of the women's rights movement, the leadership of both women's rights and abolition continued to draw from the same pool. In some ways this proved cumbersome for women's rights because it delayed the opportunity for women to focus all their energies on one singular goal. At the same time, potential supporters of women's rights who were not enamored of abolition used that as an excuse not to support the former cause. This conflict was nowhere made more clear than in the case of Sojourner Truth, the former slave who wanted to address the women's rights convention in Akron, Ohio, in 1851.

SOJOURNER TRUTH

Born a slave with the name Isabella Baumfree, this African American woman became a preacher and changed her name to Sojourner Truth in 1843, at the age of 46. For the next 40 years, she fought against slavery and segregation, and for women's rights.

Truth was born into slavery in Ulster County, New York, in 1797. At age nine, she was sold for the first time, along with a flock of sheep. Ultimately, she was sold to the Dumont family and remained with them for 20 years. The Dumonts were relatively benign, as slave owners went, but they did sell Sojourner's children from her. New York had begun a gradual emancipation plan in 1810 that supposedly insured that all slaves in the state would be freed by 1828. In 1827 Truth ran away from the Dumonts, despite the fact that she would achieve freedom the following year.

A Quaker family, the Van Wageners, took Truth in and supported her petition to get her son Peter back from the Alabama plantation owner who had bought him, illegally under New York law, from the Dumonts. Peter was returned to her, and Isabella Van Wagener (the name she adopted) and her son left for New York City in 1829.

The next years of Truth's life were difficult ones. Her son was of questionable character, and she was frequently victimized by him. Living in a commune in upper New York State in 1835, she was accused of poisoning someone, but was acquitted. After that she began to extricate her life from her son's, and in 1843 she changed her name to Sojourner Truth and began a 40-year career as a public speaker. Her new name accurately foretold how she would spend the rest of her life, as a restless spirit dedicated to exposing falsehoods and hypocrisy.

Truth's first crusade was to join the struggle against slavery. But even at this point, when abolition was still a dream held by a few, she insisted on the importance of emancipating black women not only from their status as slaves, but from their unequal status as women as well. Tall and majestic in appearance, she repeatedly took the podium at abolitionist meetings to argue that for all the concern about the rights of black men there seemed to be little interest in the rights of black women. Yet, she insisted, should black women be emancipated without reform of women's status, they would simply be exchanging white masters for black. Her words stood as a double challenge to abolitionists who ignored women's rights and to feminists who overlooked black women.

In 1851 Truth attended her second women's rights convention and asked to be allowed to speak to the audience. Although many of the delegates raised objections and the presiding officers were a little leery, they nevertheless agreed to let the imposing speaker address the convention. Her demeanor, her words, her delivery mesmerized the audience and moved them first to tears and then to enthusiastic applause. Truth declared to the skeptical audience:

> That man over there says women need to be helped into carriages, and lifted over ditches, and to have the best place everywhere. Nobody ever helps me into carriages or over puddles, or gives me the best place—and

ain't I a woman? Look at my arm! I have plowed and planted and gathered into barns, and no man could head me—and ain't I a woman? I could work as much and eat as much as a man—when I could get it—and bear the lash as well! And ain't I a woman? I have borne thirteen children and seen most of 'em sold into slavery, and when I cried out with my mother's grief, none but Jesus heard me—and ain't I a woman?

Truth's hallmark as a speaker was her ability to captivate her audiences, to make them feel her pain and her pride. However, the ambivalence with which her request to speak had been met was hardly surprising. Ambivalence characterized much of the early women's rights movement, making it at once both tentative and bold. It was clear that women were willing to risk disapproval from both society and family to take their stand on women's rights. Elizabeth Cady Stanton's husband, for instance, was an ardent abolitionist, but he nevertheless disapproved of his wife's constant agitation for women's rights. Advocates of women's rights constituted no more than a small minority of women by 1860, because most women either did not see an expansion of their legal and social rights as benefiting them, they were morally opposed to any change in their status and viewed advocates of women's rights as more of a threat than a salvation, or women's rights was simply not an issue about which they thought. Furthermore, many women still tended to see the fight for their own rights as secondary to the freedom of slaves, which became clear in 1860 when women's rights groups agreed to suspend their activities until such time as African American slaves had been freed. The lessons they learned as a result of that decision helped to shape their priorities in the latter half of the 19th century.

● ● ● ● ●

Susan Brownell Anthony, Women's Rights Activist
1820–1906

Susan B. Anthony (right) with Elizabeth Cady Stanton.

Susan B. Anthony was born in South Adams, Massachusetts, in 1820. One of six children, there was little in her childhood to indicate the path that her life would eventually follow. Her father, a manufacturer, moved the family from Massachusetts to New York, where Anthony grew up. She attended Quaker schools and from an early age taught school, first in New Rochelle, New York, and later in Rochester. Teaching never really inspired her, and Anthony eventually resigned to help manage her father's farm while he was trying to build an insurance business. Her father, quite progressive for the time, always had an open door to people like Frederick Douglass, the orator and former slave; Wendell Phillips; and William Lloyd Garrison, all of whom devoted years to the abolitionist movement, and Anthony soon became an ardent abolitionist.

Anthony was 31 when she met Elizabeth Cady Stanton in 1851. She had already spent several years in the abolitionist and temperance movements, but several conversations with Stanton, as well as her experiences in the temperance movement, persuaded Anthony that the most important cause she could pursue was women's rights. The final straw for Anthony came when she and other women delegates were refused entrance to a session of the World Temperance Convention in New York City in 1853.

Anthony's extraordinary organizational skills soon earned her the respect of the leaders of the women's rights movement. In the years prior to the Civil War, Anthony worked mainly behind the scenes, raising funds, arranging speaking tours, and organizing a series of state and national conventions held in New York. Anthony also organized county-by-county canvassing campaigns, whereby volunteers went door-to-door gathering signatures for petitions to the state legislature on behalf of woman suffrage and to change the Married Women's Property Law. While Anthony was organizing, Stanton was writing, speaking, and winning over legislators with her own exuberant personality, all skills that Anthony lacked and which helped to make Stanton and Anthony such an effective team.

More than any other person in the women's rights movement, Susan B. Anthony was ridiculed in the press, primarily because her severely austere demeanor belied a kindly and even-tempered nature. The *Utica Evening Telegraph* called Anthony "personally repulsive," while the New York *World* characterized her as "lean, cadaverous and intellectual, with the proportions of a file and the voice of a hurdy-gurdy." The fact that she never married allowed many critics to dismiss her feminism as the bitterness of an old maid, despite the fact that in her life she had several suitors.

Anthony, like many women's rights activists who also campaigned for abolitionism, was severely disappointed that the post–Civil War Constitutional amendments, which insured civil and voting rights for former slaves, did not include the same rights for women. It was with renewed vigor that she threw herself into the women's rights movement. With the help of George Train, a liberal Democrat, she and Stanton published a woman suffrage newspaper, the *Revolution*. The *Revolution* was radical for its time, advocating rejection of the Fourteenth and Fifteenth Amendments, an educated suffrage regardless of race or class, equal pay for men and women doing equal work, practical education for girls, the opening of the professions and new occupations to women, liberal divorce laws, and equal property rights.

After the Civil War, both Anthony and Stanton recognized the need for more organization and began a long campaign to formalize women's rights groups in every state and community they could. Their National Woman Suffrage Association became the vehicle for organizing thousands of women across the country, and it inaugurated a long period of time in which Anthony traveled throughout the country. Her travels in the most isolated regions often left her lonely for the companionship and intellectual exchange she enjoyed with Stanton.

Never one to accept the status quo without challenging its precepts, Anthony, in 1870, determined to test the Fifteenth Amendment's applicability to women by voting in a national election. Her attempts to vote in Rochester, New York, led to her arrest, trial, and a short prison sentence, which she never served because the state never forced her to, probably afraid that if they did they would create a martyr. That the government singled out Anthony for this treatment seems certain, because she was the only one arrested out of many who attempted to cast a vote in many areas of the country. Such treatment caused her to press the issue with more vigor. It also further radicalized the once-timid schoolteacher.

Anthony remained the head of the women's rights movement until well into her eighties. By her later years in the movement, she had become a national example to whom other women looked up with respect and inspiration. Ironically, the national press, which had so roundly criticized her in earlier days, now looked upon her as a grandmotherly figure who deserved praise and kind words for her wit and intelligence. Unfortunately, Anthony did not live long enough to see the ratification of the Nineteenth Amendment in 1920, which gave women the long-sought-after vote. She died in 1906, still insisting in her heart of hearts that "failure is impossible."

CHAPTER

. . . .

Industrialization,
Urbanization,
Professionalization

B y the start of the Civil War in 1860, women in general had a significantly different position in society than they did at the start of the
nation. They had more access to education; they had assumed more
control of their traditional domain, the home; they had several decades of
experience in benevolent, charitable, and reform organizations; and they had
begun to move into the work sector as wage earners. Eventually, women had
at least one child-bearing risk lessened when physicians finally accepted the
conclusions arrived at by Dr. Oliver Wendell Holmes in his groundbreaking
study, published as *The Contagiousness of Puerperal Fever* in 1843. The study
was originally rejected by physicians, who scoffed at the idea that washing
hands in an antiseptic solution before delivering a child would dramatically
lower the occurrence of puerperal, or childbed, fever, a usually fatal infection.
Then the book was re-released in 1855 to a much more receptive audience.
Around the same time, the American Medical Association (AMA), in 1859,
announced its opposition to the practice of abortion, and it became harder for
women to get one. Prior to the AMA's opposition, physicians routinely
performed abortions during the first three months of pregnancy. The reasons
for obtaining an abortion were varied. Abortions were performed when the
pregnancy created a health hazard to the mother. But abortions were also
performed because an additional child in a family with several children would
create hardship. While abortion did not have the explicit imprimatur of legal
acceptability, neither was it considered a "sinful" or "criminal" act. Beginning
in the 1860s, male physicians led the crusade to criminalize abortion as part of

the campaign to prohibit all forms of contraception. A personal decision made by a woman in one generation became a criminal act for women in the next.

In 1839 Margaret Fuller, one of the founders of transcendentalism, began the series of "conversations" she had with prominent Boston women and men that would help to shape the women's rights movement. Fuller continued to be an important figure in transcendentalist philosophy, which basically rejected the rationalism of the 18th-century Enlightenment thinkers and embraced the more intuitive moral and intellectual abilities of each human being. In 1843 Dorothea Dix began her life's work, which eventually changed the way in which the mentally ill were treated. Self-taught astronomer Maria Mitchell was the first woman elected to the American Academy of Arts and Sciences in 1848, thanks to her discovery of a new comet. In 1849 Elizabeth Blackwell became the first woman to graduate from medical school. Harriet Beecher Stowe published *Uncle Tom's Cabin* in 1852. By that time Emily Dickinson, who had attended Mount Holyoke College, had begun writing the hundreds of poems, including the only poem published during her lifetime, that would make her one of the most important poets in the 19th century. In 1853 Antoinette Blackwell became the first woman ordained as a minister. Remarkable women such as these continued to make things happen for themselves, for other women, and for the country, even when they faced formidable obstacles. They stepped forward by refusing to take "no" for an answer and were willing to put up with possible ridicule and rejection. The last four decades of the 19th century witnessed even more dramatic change in the status of women.

THE CIVIL WAR

The Civil War helped to advance women's status in two ways. Materially, there were more opportunities for women because of the necessity for goods and services to support the war effort on both sides. Organizationally, the United States Sanitary Commission, under the direction of Clara Barton, provided women with a blueprint for effective large-scale campaigning that was invaluable to them when, after the war, they resumed the fight for their own rights.

With increased business incorporations and manufacturing production supplying the armies with everything from shoes to uniforms to weapons, as well as all the machinery necessary to produce those goods, the labor market also expanded. Though some of these new manufacturing jobs went to women—especially immigrant women—most were filled by male laborers.

It should be pointed out that throughout the 19th century the overwhelming percentage of women wage earners worked as domestics. This was true in both the North and the South. In 1860 females over the age of 10 made up 10.2 percent of the free labor force. Most worked in a narrowly defined range of occupations that included teachers, factory workers, domestics, and seamstresses. Most were single, young, and urban. They were also likely to be immigrants. Married women accounted for less than 5 percent of the work force, while widows accounted for just under 6 percent.

This situation began to change, slowly at first, in the latter decades of the century. By 1900 the shift away from domestic work and into a variety of new opportunities picked up significantly. By the eve of World War I, more women were working in white collar jobs, including teaching, social work, and clerical and secretarial positions, than in domestic jobs. Furthermore, by World War I, nearly 25 percent of all women worked outside the home for wages (Brownlie and Brownlie, *Women in the American Economy: A Documentary History*).

The relative youth and inexperience of the average woman wage earner meant that the lowest-paying jobs fell to them. Having a large labor pool willing to work for less than male workers were paid may have caused resentment on the part of male workers, but employers certainly welcomed and encouraged women, especially in jobs requiring little or no skill. As factories and businesses expanded, it was precisely this unskilled labor category where the jobs were most plentiful. The only thing that kept more women out of the wage-earning work force were the cultural and social constraints that kept most married women, especially those with children, from leaving the home to work for someone else.

Though the influx of married women into the work force was still many years in the future, one group of female workers whose status changed significantly as a result of the Civil War was the former slaves. Despite some cultural conflict, African American women, both married and single, entered the work force in greater numbers than did their white counterparts. For the most part they did so because they had no other choice. To be sure, African American males wanted desperately to take control of their families after having been denied that control for so long. All things being equal, African American women would not have entered the work force in any greater proportion than white women. But, of course, things were not equal. Black families for the most part exchanged their slave status for sharecropper status, often working the same lands that they had worked as slaves. In fact, economically they were not any better off than they had been before emancipation, for now they had to pay their "landlords" to rent the same quarters they had occupied as slaves. Moreover, they had to pay for or raise their own food, and whatever medical care they had received as slaves—however rudimentary—was no longer the responsibility of their employers. Because black males could not, as a rule, find enough work to support a family, women who were not already involved in sharecropping found what paid employment they could—usually domestic service. Approximately 50 percent of all black women over the age of 16 had entered the wage-earning ranks by the end of Reconstruction in 1876. Black women, married and single, were three times more likely than white women to hold paid jobs (Kessler-Harris, *Out to Work*). Furthermore, the average black female worker in the wage-earning work force was more likely to be married than single. Historical evidence regarding African American female workers reveals an interesting parallel with immigrant female workers of the same period. Most women in these categories, black and white, worked with the certainty that their children would have better opportunities to improve their social status in the future, as a direct consequence of their mothers' willingness to become wage laborers.

Clara Barton and the United States Sanitary Commission

Clara Barton was remembered by hundreds of Civil War soldiers as their angel of the battlefield. She was memorialized by generations of school children as a selfless heroine who tended to the wounded on the battlefields and who eventually founded the American Red Cross. While true, such a sketchy outline does not begin to illustrate the enormity of Barton's accomplishments, or how they benefited Americans both in war and in peace.

Barton was a former teacher who started working in the United States Patent Office in 1854. Possibly the first female employee of the federal government, Barton left teaching when she was passed over—in favor of a man—to become head of a New Jersey public school that she had started. Working for the federal government had similar drawbacks, but Barton's organizational skills were much in demand by her superiors. When the Civil War began, she was shocked to learn how ill equipped the government was to properly supply its troops and deal with casualties. On her own initiative, Barton advertised in newspapers for donations in the form of medical supplies and food. She quit her government job and used her home as a storehouse and enlisted the assistance of friends to begin distributing the supplies to the battlefields in Maryland and Virginia. Though she did some battlefield nursing, her forte was in producing the supplies necessary for the military doctors to help the wounded. Though they considered her a nuisance at first, doctors quickly came to appreciate Barton's resourcefulness and dedication. Once the Quartermaster Corps and the Sanitary Commission were organized, Barton became less active.

While Barton was organizing the goods and services to support the troops on the battlefields and to provide relief to the wounded, another woman, Dorothea Dix, was organizing the nursing corps. Theoretically working for the Sanitary Commission, Dix was another individualist who used her own ingenuity to get things accomplished. In all, some 3,000 nurses served on both sides of the war, almost all of them volunteers whose ministrations undoubtedly kept down the already horrific casualty totals. By the end of the war, nursing was on the road to becoming a female profession.

As the war progressed, Barton found herself with less to do, so she found another need to fill. In 1865 Barton opened an agency to locate missing soldiers. The funding for this operation came from both donations and Barton's own resources, which she gladly spent.

Traveling abroad in 1869 to recuperate from her Civil War work, Barton heard for the first time of the International Committee of the Red Cross. Formed in Switzerland in 1863 by Swiss banker Jean Henri Dunant, under the auspices of the Geneva convention, the Red Cross was formalized when 11 nations ratified the Geneva Treaty in 1864. Under the terms of the convention, Red Cross personnel in present and future wars would be allowed to provide relief on the battlefield as neutrals under a white flag with a red cross. Barton was astonished to learn that the United States government refused to ratify the Geneva Treaty, and thus, she began a campaign to persuade the United States to support the organization. It would take her more than a decade.

Barton conducted her Red Cross campaign with the same skill she had used to organize during the Civil War. She toured the country giving speeches, meeting with public officials and private citizens, and granting interviews to acquaint people with the Red Cross. She also lobbied politicians in Washington and sought support from presidential administrations. In 1881 she formed an American Red Cross and was appointed its first president. The following year the Senate finally ratified the Geneva Treaty. Barton remained president of the American Red Cross until 1904, and in that time her agency dealt with 21 disasters, ranging from floods to hurricanes, famines, and a yellow fever epidemic. Refusing to accept government subsidies, probably because of her experiences with government bureaucracies when she was a teacher and at the Patent Office, Barton was forced to be frugal. She determined when a request for assistance merited Red Cross action, and she oversaw the relief efforts. Under her direction Red Cross volunteers entered a disaster area, distributed relief in the form of food, clothing, temporary housing, medical supplies, and whatever else was immediately needed, then evacuated the area as soon as other relief agencies could take over.

The work done by Clara Barton, Dorothea Dix, the more than 3,000 nurse volunteers, and other women during the Civil War provided women with a blueprint for successfully organizing and carrying out a multidimensional task requiring considerable political and diplomatic skills. It showed women how not to take no for an answer, and most importantly, it provided women with a concrete example of their own ability to define a problem, develop a strategy to solve the problem, and successfully implement the plan. If women did not process this experience in a self-conscious fashion, it had nevertheless become a part of their life experience.

THE GRANGE MOVEMENT

The changes that affected the lives of women in general were often not felt as quickly for farm women as they were for women who lived in the cities. The pace of their lives often seemed little different from the pace of their mothers' or grandmothers' lives. Child bearing and rearing and a seasonally determined lifestyle of planting and harvesting left little time for extracurricular activities.

As a inspector for the United States Department of Agriculture, Oliver Hudson Kelley, a Minnesota farmer, traveled extensively through the post–Civil War South and West. He saw firsthand how isolated and impoverished—intellectually and spiritually as well as materially—the lives of farmers and their families had become. In the wide-open spaces of the Great Plains, the nearest neighbor was often miles away, the nearest town dozens of miles away. Even the mail came only infrequently. In these circumstances even prosperous farmers lived meager lives.

Farm wives lived in even greater bleakness. The men at least occasionally traveled to town to buy supplies, sell produce, and negotiate with the bank. While there, they exchanged news and discussed politics with friends. Women, in contrast, were not expected to participate in business or politics, so there was no pressing reason for them to leave the house and children. In fact, their presence was necessary while the husband was away, and few would venture to travel alone. As a consequence, they spent months, or even years, on end in the same small area, bereft of new faces, friends, ideas, or entertainment.

Kelley believed that the farmers had to unite and promote their interests collectively. Through Kelley's efforts, the Order of the Patrons of Husbandry was chartered in Washington, D.C., on December 4, 1867, as a fraternal organization. Better known as the Grange Movement for the local units of organization that called themselves "granges," it offered a framework in which farmers and farm wives could organize regular gatherings for educational programs, discussions, debates, picnics, and dances. The Grange also experimented in cooperative buying and selling of farm supplies and products. Although the society's constitution forebade involvement in politics, once the meetings were over the members would stay and discuss current affairs. The movement never abandoned its cultural and intellectual goal, but it also served as an important outlet for economic discontents and as a collective voice in local, state, and eventually national politics. In the 1870s the Grange Movement became very prominent in securing reforms against monopolistic railroads.

For women the Grange proved to be particularly valuable. Under the terms laid out for establishing a Grange branch, at least four women and nine men had to apply for membership, so women's role in the Grange was institutionalized from the start. Women had full voting rights, they could hold any

Grange office, and there were special posts that were designated to manage female affairs. Most often, in both New England and in the Midwest, the Grange lectures were arranged by women. In the southern Grange branches, women were token members for the most part and were not afforded the opportunity to participate in political affairs. The Grange charter did not cease to exist in the South; rather, it was the weight of cultural bias that relegated women to a peripheral role in that region.

Grange women took to politics quite readily. In the Midwest there is a good deal of evidence suggesting that Grange women were able to persuade many male members to support woman suffrage. By the mid-1870s, there were 750,000 Grange members in 25,000 chapters around the country. Some of the more outspoken, politically radical farmers, the so-called agrarian radicals, came out of the Grange movement, including Mary Lease, who ran for the United States Senate in 1893, and Annie Diggs, a journalist and farmers' advocate who lobbied on behalf of the Populist Party. But the majority of Grange women were not outspoken lecturers. They were dedicated members who worked tirelessly for the agrarian crusade and who brought to it their own talents and interests, from advocating equal education for girls to equal rights for women.

The Grange itself, as it evolved into economic and political organizations, including the Farmers Alliance and the People's Party, did not stand by its original commitment to women's rights, and the latter organizations did not institutionalize women's roles as the Grange had. But having already had the opportunity to shed the isolationism of farm life, women were not ready to take a back seat in the newer organizations. On the local level, women continued to participate and influence events affecting their lives and communities.

NEW LABOR FORCE

Immigration dropped somewhat during the Civil War years, but once the conflict was settled, emigrants from a variety of European communities flooded American shores. Over the course of the next 50 years, nearly 27 million people arrived in the United States. In 1882 alone just under one million immigrants were processed through the nation's largest ports. Most immigrants were willing to leave their homelands because of the perceived opportunities that abounded in America. Immigrants included both skilled and unskilled workers, many from urban regions of Europe, although a significant number came from rural areas. Although opportunity did not always present itself as the immigrants imagined or were led to believe it would, opportunity did exist for upward mobility. Most immigrant families relied on the unmarried female members of the family, whether daughters, sisters, or aunts, to contribute to the family prospects by becoming wage earners in America. Like their American counterparts, married immigrant women were not expected to work outside the home for wages.

Factory work, perhaps the defining experience for many immigrant women, had changed markedly since the first girls arrived at the Lowell mills in the 1820s and 1830s. No longer paternalistic havens for rural farm girls, factories now were simply places where women—and children—workers spent most of their daylight hours, engaged in backbreaking work for very low wages.

The Knights of Labor

At the same time that Oliver Hudson Kelley was organizing American farmers into the vast network of Granges, Uriah Stephens began drawing American workers into what he hoped would be an embracing organization of laborers. If the Grange Movement faced daunting obstacles in the great distances, economic disparities, and traditional individualism that kept American farmers apart, the Knights of Labor faced the equally daunting obstacles of ethnic differences, varying levels of skills, and different ambitions and goals. In the case of the labor organizers, these difficulties were in addition to the inevitable opposition of employers and the hostility of government.

The Knights succeeded in bringing together immigrants and natives, skilled artisans and day laborers, men and women, because they espoused a moderate and practical course of action. In contrast to craft unions, they advocated arbitration over strikes and political agitation over physical violence. The Knights created cooperative stores, which the members hoped would provide better merchandise for less than stores run for profit. Their job-related platform included an eight-hour workday and an end to child labor. Their organization was based on local assemblies that included all of the workers in a shop or neighborhood; their program addressed common problems and offered collective solutions.

Ironically, the high point of the Knights' fortunes followed a series of strikes that local assemblies called against the wishes of the national leaders. Their success brought a rise in membership from 500,000 in 1885 to 700,000 in 1886. But the sudden rise was followed by just as sudden a decline. Further strikes failed miserably, and by 1890 membership had fallen to 100,000. By the end of the decade, the Knights of Labor had disappeared completely.

The failure of the Knights of Labor had particular importance for women, because its successors were the craft unions of the American Federation of Labor (AF of L), which focused on the interests of skilled workers only. These organizations slighted women doubly. To the extent that women were unskilled, the AF of L ignored their needs. To the extent that women competed with skilled men, the AF of L opposed them, because they depressed the wage scales. "Organized labor" agitated for restriction of female (and child) labor on the basis of decency, but the root of its opposition was economic competition. What the history of American women in the workplace would have been had labor organized along the embracing lines of the Knights of Labor rather than the exclusionary basis of the AF of L must remain an open question.

Illinois Women's Alliance

As the 19th century progressed, women's participation in the labor force increased steadily. The majority of female employees were young, single immigrants. Generally relegated to unskilled, machine-tending roles, they rapidly became disillusioned by the indifference and even hostility of the male trade-union movement to women's needs. Yet not everyone was willing to accept conditions as they were. Working women in Illinois created an embracing organization to work for their own interests. Reaching out to existing working- and middle-class women's organization, they forged an unprecedented alliance dedicated to improving the conditions of women and children in the workplace.

The women of the Alliance advanced an ambitious program. They called for factory inspections by women "responsible to women's organizations" and regulation of the sweatshops where so many of them labored. They demanded an end to child labor, the institution of compulsory education, and construction of new schools. In 1892, in cooperation with Hull House, founded in Chicago by Jane Addams (see page 89), and the General Federation of Women's Clubs, they won an eight-hour work day for women and restrictions on the employment of children.

Women's Trade Union League (WTUL)

Despite this significant victory, the Alliance did not long endure. Under the pressure of the depression of 1893–1894, it split apart, no longer able to bridge the gap between middle- and working-class women. The surface issues concerned strategy, but these manifested deeper fissures. Middle-class women regarded work as an object of pride, a source of independence and personal fulfillment. For their less well-to-do sisters, work was just work, nothing more than a source of income that was generally shared with parents, siblings, or spouse. And the endless drudgery was far more often a source of grinding frustration than personal fulfillment.

The Alliance disintegrated in 1894, but its spirit lived on. The influx of young women from southern and eastern Europe around the turn of the century included many who were already politicized and ready to forge a new alliance with the middle-class feminists of America. In 1903 the two groups came together in the Women's Trade Union League, which, from the beginning, had the dual purpose of promoting reforms in the workplace and working for the broader program of women's rights. Their ideology and actions were more militant and their collaboration longer lasting, but they were moving on a trail the members of the Illinois Women's Alliance had already explored. This was particularly evident during the garment workers' strikes of 1909–1911, when women from the financially and socially powerful families of Harriman, Belmont, Morgan, and others, boycotted clothing manufacturers who refused to bargain with the WTUL. Wealthy members of the WTUL provided the strike funds, acted as press liaisons, and even went on the picket line and were arrested with the workers.

The Alliance between upper-, middle-, and working-class women worked better at some times than at other times. Eventually class distinctions once again became seemingly insurmountable, and the alliance disintegrated. But for many years, the only viable union affiliation for women trade unionists was the WTUL. And, just as the Illinois Women's Alliance had demonstrated that class lines could be overcome, the WTUL demonstrated the same point in its heyday, opening the way for similar alliances in other causes.

WHITE COLLAR WORKERS

Before the Civil War, most businesses were small individual proprietorships employing a few dozen workers and needing only a handful of office employees to help the owner. During the 1870s and 1880s, however, the scale of business burgeoned, with corporations and trusts coming to control tens of thousands of workers scattered across the country and eventually around the world. By 1904 just 1 percent of American corporations controlled a full one-third of all manufacturing, and by this time the total value of manufacturing output had increased over 10 times since 1860, while the labor force used to produce it had risen 5 times. To control the operations of these large and scattered corporations, big businesses organized themselves along military lines. They created a carefully designed hierarchy of control, functional divisions within the organization, and corps of middle managers who mediated between top management and labor and coordinated the activities of separate branches of the organization.

Both a prerequisite and result of this growth of bureaucracy was a concomitant growth in paperwork. Consequently, when E. Remington & Sons began selling Christopher Latham Sholes' new invention—the typewriter—it found a ready market for the machine. By 1886 the company was making 1,500 typewriters per month, and a year later a business journal noted that "Five years ago the typewriter was simply a mechanical curiosity. Today its monotonous click can be heard in almost every well-regulated business establishment in the country. A great revolution is taking place, and the typewriter is at the bottom of it."

Although the business journal probably had a revolution in business procedures in mind, the impact of the typewriter, coupled with the growing scale and bureaucratization of enterprise, was revolutionizing the status of its operators as well. Before the Civil War, a clerk in a business was usually a young man at the bottom of the corporate ladder, for what better way was there to learn the business than to keep its records and transcribe its correspondence? With the rise of the typewriter, though, transcribing documents became a task requiring special manual training. These specialists were no longer managers in training but were a new form of skilled worker.

As the status of the clerk changed, so did the characteristics of the stenographer, file clerk, and typist who replaced him. Remarkably quickly, in fact, all three jobs came to be seen as new specialties open to literate, native-born white women with a basic education. As early as 1875, Remington advertised the typewriter as an ideal Christmas present because "no invention has opened for women so broad and easy an avenue to profitable and suitable employment." In 1881, when the New York YWCA offered typing training for women, its classes quickly filled up. If the work was repetitive and limited in its prospects, in the late 19th century it was one of the few occupations available for literate women other than teaching.

DEALING WITH THE CITIES

While industrialization was creating new jobs for men, women, and children, it was also transforming the urban landscape. Of the millions of immigrants, many stayed in the cities through which they entered the country. In a very short period of time, cities such as New York, Boston, and Chicago were literally bursting at the seams. Tenements were thrown up in an effort to capitalize on the housing needs of the immigrants. With very little regulation to observe, apartment builders were constructing little more than structures subdivided to accommodate as many tenants as possible. Most lacked adequate heating, water service, sewers, lighting, and even windows.

Jane Addams and Hull House

Responding to this challenge, the first generation of college-educated, middle-class women stepped into the breach, most inspired by and following the lead of Jane Addams, the principal founder of Hull House. While Hull House was not the first settlement house in America, it did become the prototype for future settlement houses, primarily because of the vision and dedication of Addams. Addams had graduated from prestigious Rockford Seminary in Illinois in 1882. Raised from the age of two by her widowed father, Addams was devastated when, a few weeks after her graduation, he died suddenly. A chronic back problem which required surgery, a period of aimless wandering through Europe, and two years spent in Baltimore with her stepmother—who spent most of her time playing matchmaker on Addams's behalf—persuaded Addams that her life badly needed focus. An effort to find that focus, enrolling in medical school, proved unsuccessful, and after one year she resigned. It was not until she and her college roommate, Ellen Gates Starr, were touring Europe once again, that Addams had what she later described as an epiphany, or revelation. It was suddenly clear that her privileged, middle-class, educated background carried with it a responsibility to help those less fortunate. Ellen Starr held similar views, and together they vowed to do in America what Oxford men had already done at London's Toynbee Hall: open a home where poor people could come to get practical assistance for the problems they struggled with and where immigrants could come to learn how to assimilate into American life and culture.

Within two years, on September 18, 1889, Addams and Starr opened the doors of Hull House, a former suburban mansion built by a wealthy realtor in Chicago. As Chicago grew and expanded in the later 19th century, the once bucolic area around the Hull mansion had turned into one of the city's most populated and crowded districts. Hull House proved to be an enduring and important part of Chicago and American life for two reasons. First, it provided Chicago's most needy and desperate residents with a haven that offered them a variety of programs that not only addressed their immediate concerns, but provided them with cultural enrichment. Within a relatively short period of time, Hull House offered to its constituents medical services, child care, English language classes, legal aid, day nurseries, sewing classes, vocational skills classes, citizenship classes, a cooperative residence for working women, a variety of clubs and activities for children, and rooms where groups such as labor unions could hold their meetings. It also offered or sponsored art exhibits, plays, music, and lectures. By 1893, when the nation was entering a sustained depression, about 2,000 Chicagoans attended one or more Hull House functions every week. It was an invaluable service at a time when the city itself provided little or no services to its residents.

Second, Hull House served a broader function and one which had more profound and further reaching effects for all Americans. It was the genesis of a new profession—social work—that attracted some of the best minds of the Progressive Era. Hull House was an on-going experiment in social services that led naturally to pressure for social legislation. Activists including Julia Lathrop, Florence Kelley, Edith and Grace Abbott, Sophonisba Breckinridge, Alice Hamilton, George Mead, Charles Beard, and John Dewey were all involved in Hull House at one time or another. They, along with Jane Addams and the residents themselves, became advocates and activists working for reforms in child labor, sanitation, housing and work conditions, and city services. Taking aim at the causes of poverty, the reformers worked first on the local level, and they persuaded the Illinois legislature to enact legislation mandating factory inspection and to establish the nation's first juvenile court system. They also advocated required schooling for all children, recognition of labor unions, industrial safety laws, and protection for immigrants against exploitation. Such reforms did not long remain only a concern for Chicagoans. Quickly, reformers across the nation were seeking similar redress in their own communities, as well as on the national level.

• • • • •

Charlotte Perkins Gilman Studies the Effects of Industrialization 1860–1935

Born into the prominent Beecher family in 1860, Charlotte Perkins Gilman learned early about the drawbacks of women's economic dependency. Her father neglected his wife and children, and they were forced to live off the generosity of their relatives. From this childhood experience came a life-long emphasis on economic self-sufficiency.

Charlotte's concern for self-sufficiency was coupled with a creative talent, possibly inherited from her great aunts, Catherine Beecher and Harriet Beecher Stowe, which showed itself first in artistic ways. She attended the Rhode Island School of Design and went on to work as a commercial artist and art teacher before marrying Walter Stetson at age 24. She bore a daughter, but then fell into a profound postpartum depression that only lifted when she separated from her overprotective husband and moved to California. Eventually, Gilman divorced Stetson and sent her then nine-year-old daughter to live with him and his new wife, an action that scandalized most of Gilman's friends, because women did not relinquish their children under any circumstances in those days.

In California Gilman turned her creative energies to speaking and writing. Her first novel, *The Yellow Wallpaper*, published in 1892, was a powerful portrayal of the onset of insanity based on her own experience of depression. Its radical feminist thesis, essentially a demand for equality and independence, and its surreal style put it decades ahead of its time, a prescience that was to characterize much of Gilman's later work.

In 1895 Gilman moved to Chicago and lived for a time at Hull House. Here she gained an appreciation of economics on the social rather than personal level. Over the next year, her appreciation was heightened when she attended the International Socialist and Labor Congress in London, and it bore fruit in 1898 with the publication of her most famous work, *Women and Economics*. In it she advocated economic independence for women and also called for communal solutions to individual needs. The book was translated into seven languages and brought Gilman both widespread recognition and the financial security that she had so desperately searched for since her childhood. Lauded at the time of its publication, *Women and Economics* became almost instantly an important contribution to women's rights. A review in the *Nation* called it the "most significant utterance on the subject since Mills's *Subjugation of Women.*"

In 1900 Gilman married her younger cousin, and in the following decades she continued to write both fiction and nonfiction works. Adding to both her body of work and her reputation, Gilman wrote *Concerning Children* (1900), *The Home* (1903), *Pure Sociology* (1903), *Human Work* (1904), and *Man-Made World* (1911). From 1909 to 1916, she published the aptly named *Forerunner* magazine, which she financed largely by herself. She used it as a platform to publicize her progressive ideas, including things like communal child care and communal kitchens, which, many years later, would become reality as day-care centers and take-out restaurants (although few were conscious of the connection at the time).

After World War I, Gilman appeared to lose her place in the forefront of American society. Her social activism and feminism seemed outdated to the new generation of women, as did her resistance to the loose sexual mores of the "Roaring Twenties," which she argued would end up emphasizing women's sexuality and contributing to their further dependency. Her husband died in 1934, and the following year, Gilman took her own life after being diagnosed with breast cancer, but not before she published her autobiography, *The Living of Charlotte Perkins Gilman*.

CHAPTER 8

Getting the Vote

B oth Elizabeth Cady Stanton and Susan B. Anthony were involved in abolition and women's rights long before the outbreak of the Civil War. Though they never denied the importance of women's rights, once the war began they, like all other women, were willing to suspend activities until the conflict was successfully concluded. As early as 1861, Stanton began advocating emancipation for slaves, but when President Abraham Lincoln delivered his Emancipation Proclamation to take effect on January 1, 1863, Stanton and other abolitionists were somewhat disappointed. The proclamation really only affected slaves in the Confederate states, where there was little anyone could do to enforce the edict until the Confederacy was defeated. Slaves residing in the so-called border states were not affected by the Emancipation Proclamation.

Despite this disappointment, Stanton sought ways in which women could express their support for the aims of the Union and for full emancipation. Public affirmations of any kind by women were still unusual, but Stanton and Anthony wanted to do more than knit garments to support the war effort. By then a resident of New York City, Stanton, with her colleague, issued a call for women to meet on May 14th to join an organization that would take a more active role, the National Women's Loyal League. Several hundred women responded.

THE NATIONAL WOMEN'S LOYAL LEAGUE

At the initial meeting, the members adopted several resolutions. Hoping to keep either women's rights or abolition from becoming the domain of the League, some members supported resolutions that would have confined the

League's movement to only those issues that addressed Lincoln's conduct of the war. This conservative faction was voted down, however, and the most significant resolution adopted was to mount a petition campaign urging Congress to vote for immediate emancipation of all slaves in the Union. The League also passed a resolution supporting the government for as long as it continued to wage a war for freedom. Finally, the members voted to attempt to collect one million signatures in support of passage of the Thirteenth Amendment, which would abolish slavery.

The League remained in existence for only a little over a year, disbanding in August 1864. At its height the League counted nearly 5,000 women as members. Operating on a shoestring budget, volunteers fanned out, eventually collecting almost 400,000 names in support of their petition. Their success at collecting signatures was only slightly hampered by the one penny that they also collected with each signature, as a means of financing their organization. In its short lifetime, the League was an invaluable educational experience for thousands of women who, after the Civil War, turned their energies to other reform causes.

THE AMERICAN EQUAL RIGHTS ASSOCIATION

If women's rights advocates thought that they would be justly rewarded for their support of the Union and their willingness to suspend their own interests for those of the slaves, they were bitterly disappointed. Eighteen years after the first historic women's rights convention in Seneca Falls, New York, suffragists founded the first national suffrage organization. The American Equal Rights Association, founded in 1866, was intended to reconcile the American women's movements that had run on two increasingly divergent paths ever since the World Anti-Slavery Conference in London in 1840, when women delegates from the United States were refused seats. The new organization hoped to bring together the anti-slavery and women's rights movements to work simultaneously for legal rights for both former slaves and women. The slate of officers included Lucretia Mott, president; Susan B. Anthony, secretary; and Elizabeth Cady Stanton, vice president. Their combined credentials seemed to ensure that the organization would remain on track with its dual goals. But die-hard abolitionists, mostly men, had other agendas. Wendell Phillips and Frederick Douglass were among the biggest critics of pursuing women's rights at what they considered a crucial time for African Americans. The feminists argued that women had deferred their suffrage quest for the duration of the war, which was long enough.

The Thirteenth Amendment, which ensured emancipation for all slaves and the abolition of all slavery, had the unqualified support of all abolitionists. But when the Fourteenth Amendment was introduced, feminists were more than a little concerned. For the first time in the history of the Constitution, the word "male" was inserted to define precisely whose right to vote was ensured and protected by the government: males who had reached the age of 21 or over.

Not all women were upset by the Fourteenth Amendment. The more conservative women's rights advocates insisted that this was the "Negro's hour," and refused to engage in any activity that might jeopardize their long-awaited freedom. They supported the male abolitionists, like Douglass, who cautioned restraint.

The final straw for more radical feminists came when abolitionists insisted that the reform agenda had to be, in the words of Wendell Phillips, "Negro suffrage, then temperance, then the eight-hour movement, then woman suffrage." These feminists, already outraged when the Fourteenth and Fifteenth Amendments did not include the women's right to vote, were further disillusioned when they received no support from abolitionists within the American Equal Rights Association for inclusion of women's rights. In their view, women had set aside their own issues to support the abolitionists. Now the abolitionists were turning their back on women's rights.

THE NATIONAL WOMAN'S SUFFRAGE ASSOCIATION (NWSA)

In May 1869, at the New York Women's Bureau, Anthony and Stanton organized the National Woman Suffrage Association, with 118 women signing up on the spot. Among the initial joiners were Lucretia Mott, Martha Wright, and Paulina Wright Davis, all noted feminists and former members of the American Equal Rights Association. From the start the NWSA excluded men from leadership positions and elected offices, and emphasized the necessity of securing an amendment to the United States Constitution that would guarantee to women the right to vote. Stanton was elected the first president of NWSA, and Anthony served first on the executive committee and then as vice president. Eventually, Anthony became president of the organization. Stanton, as president, did not mask her radical feminist views, the most radical of which were her belief in equality and her views regarding married women (see page 72), and NWSA tended to reflect her position. Cross-country lecture tours, discussions, and rallies helped to ignite the still-fledgling women's rights movement, and NWSA chapters sprang up, especially in the East and Midwest.

In the meantime a second organization, the American Woman Suffrage Association (AWSA), was founded in Cleveland, Ohio, in November 1869 by Lucy Stone. Stone, whose abolitionist roots ran deeper than her feminist roots, disagreed with what she perceived as the radicalism of Stanton and Anthony. She stood with other abolitionists who feared that an insistence on women's rights could very well jeopardize the rights of former slaves. AWSA expressed a willingness to defer woman suffrage, and it also prominently featured male office holders. The first AWSA president was Henry Ward Beecher. AWSA also undertook a nationwide lecture tour in an effort to build a national audience. Although AWSA also advocated a national suffrage amendment, its advocacy was somewhat diluted by the organization's concentration on changing individual state constitutions.

While AWSA claimed to represent the views of the majority of women, they really represented only a hard-core group of New Englanders, most of whom were former abolitionists. Almost from the start, NWSA far out-stripped AWSA in its ability to attract members and money. Interestingly, NWSA's publication, called appropriately, the *Revolution*, was much shorter lived than AWSA's weekly, *The Woman's Journal*. *The Woman's Journal* attracted a wide audience and became one of the more influential publica-tions of the 19th-century women's movement.

With the establishment of the two major suffrage organizations of the 19th century, the women's movement itself had identified the two strains that would continue to separate women well into the 20th century, despite apparent reconciliations from time to time. Feminists placed the rights of women on a level equal to all other current issues, reasoning that as long as half the population was denied its rights, all other issues had to be secondary. The moderates, on the other hand, viewed women's rights as only one component of a series of desired reforms—not all of which dealt with women's issues—including political reform, temperance, civil rights, and problems associated with rapid urban growth.

Attempting to Vote

In the first election after the ratification of the Fourteenth Amendment, a number of women attempted to force the women's rights issue. Influenced by the NWSA, an extraordinary example of civil disobedience occurred, with hundreds of women across the country breaking the law by attempting to register to vote or voting. The intent was to force the issue in the courts, then hope that it would be taken all the way to the Supreme Court, where many feminists believed there might be a decision in their favor.

The actions did result in many court cases, including the trial of Susan B. Anthony. Anthony had led a small delegation of women to the polls in Rochester, New York, determined to test the validity of the contention that women, as citizens, were entitled to vote under the Fifteenth Amendment. Anthony was convicted of civil disobedience at a trial without a jury and by a judge who had written his opinion before the trial even started.

In St. Louis, Missouri, another officer of the NWSA, Virginia Minor, also attempted to register to vote. When Reese Happersett, the registrar of voters, refused her, Minor brought suit against him, asking for $10,000 in damages. Minor contended that, while states could regulate suffrage, the Constitution "nowhere gives them the power to prevent" (Zophy, ed., *Handbook of American Women's History*). Her husband, Francis Minor, an attorney, acted as his wife's lawyer. Not suprisingly, Minor lost her case in both the St. Louis circuit court and the Missouri Court of Appeals. But the Minors pressed on, bringing the case to the United States Supreme Court. In 1874 Chief Justice Morrison R. Waite handed down the unanimous opinion denying Minor's appeal, stating that "the Constitution of the United States does not confer the right of suffrage upon anyone," because suffrage was not coexistent with citizenship.

The court's decision dashed suffragists' hopes for a judicial solution to the woman suffrage question. Instead, they turned full force towards the alternatives, campaigning state-by-state to change individual state constitutions or seeking a federal woman suffrage amendment to the Constitution.

A Woman Suffrage Amendment

In 1875, still smarting over the passage of the Fourteenth and Fifteenth Amendments, Susan B. Anthony penned a woman suffrage amendment modeled on the Fifteenth Amendment. Just two sentences long, it was simple and to the point: "The right of citizens of the United States to vote shall not be denied or abridged by the United States or by any State on account of sex. Congress shall have the power, by appropriate legislation, to enforce the provisions of this article." Three years later Anthony and Elizabeth Cady Stanton were able to persuade Senator Arlen A. Sargent of California to introduce the legislation in the United States Senate. For a time the amendment was referred to as the Sargent Amendment, and it was reintroduced in each succeeding Congress until its final passage 45 years later.

When Sargent introduced the legislation for the first time, some members of Congress were openly derisive, others were supportive, indifferent, or even amused. But no one believed then, or for many years after that, that the legislation would either be reported out of committee favorably or find sufficient support for passage by the full House and Senate. Over the course of 45 years, the amendment was reported out of committee for a full floor vote 12 times by the Senate and 10 times by the House.

THE NATIONAL AMERICAN WOMAN SUFFRAGE ASSOCIATION (NAWSA)

By 1890, with the trend in the women's movement pointing toward unification and confederation, leaders in both major suffrage groups announced the formation of the National American Woman Suffrage Association. The impetus for the merger came, interestingly enough, from the daughters of the original founders, Harriot Stanton Blatch, the daughter of Elizabeth Cady

Stanton, and Alice Stone Blackwell, the daughter of Lucy Stone. At the time of the merger, Stanton and Susan B. Anthony were still very involved in suffrage, and Stanton especially had to be won over to the unification because of her lingering suspicions about how committed the moderates were to a federal suffrage amendment. But the advances made by women in the post–Civil War decades had wrought changes that made a merger desirable for suffragists in general.

By 1890 there were more women in high schools than there were men, and women were attending the majority of colleges. Nearly one-third of college students were women, and one-third of all professional workers, including doctors, lawyers, and teachers, were women. The women's club movement had united under the banner of the General Federation of Women's Clubs, and the Women's Christian Temperance Union was moving into its most powerful phase. Suffrage, no longer an isolated vehicle for change, was now part of a larger women's movement. The new, educated, younger, more active constituents of the women's movement began to exert an increasingly more dominant influence over the suffrage movement. Though Stanton and Anthony were elected the first and second presidents of the NAWSA, their influence was clearly on the wane and would quickly be replaced by the new generation.

Anthony, in particular, found much of the new direction that NAWSA was taking to be a bitter pill to swallow. After years of working for the federal amendment, the new emphasis on changing state constitutions seemed like a step backward. Nevertheless, Anthony succeeded Stanton as president in 1892. The very next year, however, she was forced to bow to the influence of the NAWSA members who wanted to hold the annual conventions in places other than the nation's capital. Anthony knew that by removing the central activity of NAWSA to a venue outside of Washington, D.C., the organization was going to abandon altogether the federal amendment as its primary goal. Then when Colorado granted women suffrage in 1893, it encouraged those who favored a state-by-state approach. For the next quarter century, NAWSA pursued hundreds of state campaigns, with less than a handful of successes in that time.

Anthony remained president of NAWSA until 1900, when she was 80 years old. In the final years of her presidency, when she had little ability to stem the new tide, she watched NAWSA become more and more conservative. There was an increasingly nativist slant to the speeches and resolutions that encouraged toning down civil rights to cultivate southern membership, favored educational requirements for suffrage, and advocated immigration restriction.

In 1896, after a bitter and prolonged internal struggle, NAWSA formally disassociated itself from Elizabeth Cady Stanton's *Woman's Bible*, an annotated exposition of the Bible. Stanton argued, in this radical critique, that the Bible's interpretation and language had aided in the oppression of women over the centuries. When it was published in 1895, NAWSA officials, including Anna Howard Shaw, moved immediately that NAWSA disassociate itself from the book. Shaw, a long-time women's rights activist who was both a physician and a minister, as well as an orator of unparalleled skill, considered Anthony her mentor. But despite Anthony's impassioned pleas, the majority voted with Shaw.

After Anthony stepped down as president, Carrie Chapman Catt stepped into the post and remained president for almost all of the organization's remaining years. Catt, whose reputation for administration was sterling, was very much an advocate of challenging state constitutions rather than seeking a federal amendment. Catt was more than adept at developing personal relationships with politicians, but under her leadership, NAWSA began to stagnate as the frustration of losing campaign after campaign began to wear on the membership. For her part Catt had always professed that she expected to be in the fight for suffrage for the rest of her life—a pronouncement that suggested she had little hope that suffrage would be achieved in her lifetime.

ALICE PAUL

By 1917 Catt had reversed herself, announcing what she called her "Winning Plan" for suffrage—a return to the pursuit of a federal suffrage amendment. In large part Catt and NAWSA changed directions because of a challenge from the younger, more activist National Woman's Party. The Woman's Party was founded by Alice Paul, a young veteran of the English suffrage movement, who was the psychological heir of the Stanton-Anthony wing of the suffrage movement. Whereas NAWSA attracted hundreds of thousands of members, most of whom were inactive, the Woman's Party, a far smaller organization, tended to attract members who were committed to active participation. NAWSA also tended to attract members who favored carefully orchestrated cooperation between suffragists and government whenever possible, to initiate change from within. The Woman's Party had no qualms about engaging in activities that would place pressure on the government.

Alice Paul, whose experiences with the English suffrage movement persuaded her that a federal amendment was the quickest way for American women to get the vote, took over NAWSA's Congressional Committee in January 1913. Paul also believed that, to succeed, federal suffragism required the support of the president of the United States. Over the objections of some of NAWSA's more conservative members, Paul scheduled the great Washington suffrage parade for March 3, 1912, the day before Woodrow Wilson would take the oath of office. In addition to serving notice on Wilson that the suffragists would have to be reckoned with, the timing of the parade was selected to ensure the maximum audience and maximum press coverage.

The parade was testament to Paul's organizational abilities: 8,000 marchers, 26 floats, 10 bands, six chariots, and five units of cavalry (for crowd control) participated in the parade. The 8,000 marchers included representatives from every occupation and profession that women were engaged in; every local, state, and national suffrage organization; most of the voluntary and women's club associations; and several prosuffrage congressmen and senators.

On March 1 Congress had passed a special resolution instructing the Washington superintendent of police to "prevent any interference with the suffrage marchers." The superintendent, who did not approve of the parade, insisted that the matter should be handled by the War Department, though the War Department denied responsibility. Paul contacted Secretary of War Henry L. Stimson through his sister-in-law, suffragist Elizabeth Rogers, and Stimson agreed to position the Fifteenth Cavalry on the city's western perimeter, in the event that they might be needed. It proved to be a prescient move on Paul's part.

An estimated half-million people lined Pennsylvania Avenue for the suffrage parade. Quickly, the crowd became uncontrollable, as disinterested police failed to stop the ill-behaved among the spectators. Within a half hour, crowds had spilled out into the line of march until it was virtually impossible to distinguish marchers from spectators. A near-riot broke out, with sporadic acts of violence against the suffragists. When Genevieve Stone, the wife of Congressman Claudius Stone, appealed to the police for help, a nearby officer responded by saying, "If my wife were where you are, I'd break her head." A contingent of Boy Scouts from Philadelphia tried to assist the beleaguered suffragists, but order was not restored until the Fifteenth Cavalry arrived. In all, 175 calls for ambulances were made, and over 200 people, mostly suffragists, were treated at local hospitals. Fortunately, no one was seriously injured.

The parade accomplished its goals. When Wilson arrived at Union Station as the parade was underway, he was somewhat surprised that no welcoming crowd had gathered for his arrival. Indeed, from where his party stood, the streets of Washington looked deserted. When one of his people asked where everyone was, he was told, "Over on the avenue, watching the suffrage parade." It was, as Paul had hoped, the first issue confronting Wilson on his arrival in Washington. Within days of the parade, a delegation of suffragists was able to secure their first meeting with the new president. Secondly, the publicity that was generated as a result of the riot led to an outpouring of public sympathy for the suffragists and, by extension, for their cause. Contributions to the suffrage movement increased markedly, including a $1,000 donation from the editor of the *Washington Post*. A special Senate investigation was held to determine why the riot had occurred, resulting in the firing of the superintendent of police. Finally, the suffrage parade was the first shot fired in the final suffrage battle that would culminate in 1919 with passage of the Nineteenth Amendment. It was also recognition that a new generation of suffragists, much more willing to take direct aggressive action to secure a federal amendment, had arrived on the scene.

In 1916 Paul founded the National Woman's Party and mounted an anti-Democratic Party campaign. The Woman's Party lobbied especially hard in the western states where women already had the vote, urging them to cast their votes for Wilson's opponent, Charles Evans Hughes. Paul believed that the only way to make politicians sit up and take notice of women was to consistently vote against the party in power, if that party had done nothing to secure the vote for women. It was a controversial tactic that garnered for Paul a great deal of criticism from women who argued that the Woman's Party was jeopardizing the support of prosuffrage Democrats. But there is substantial evidence to suggest that Paul's tactics had the desired effect, as politicians began expressing concerns over the possibility of the Woman's Party campaigning against them in their districts.

The Woman's Party also picketed the White House, the Congress, and the Supreme Court on a daily basis. When President Wilson announced that he was seeking a declaration of war against Germany, after Germany had resumed submarine warfare in early 1917, everyone expected the Woman's Party to suspend their picketing. But Paul, a student of history, knew all too well what had happened to women when they had suspended their women's rights campaign during the Civil War. As a consequence, she announced that while individuals in the Woman's Party were free to pursue their own course of action, as an organization, the Women's Party would continue to picket until women had the vote.

The picketing policy certainly embarrassed the Wilson administration. While professing to be in a war to make the world safe for democracy, foreign delegations going into the White House were confronted with women holding signs asking when that same democracy would be implemented at home. Over a period of several months, hundreds of arrests were made. Women were sent to jail, at first for two or three days, but later, as the Administration attempted to bring pressure on the women to stop the picketing, the sentences ran to several months in Occoquan Workhouse, a particularly vile women's correctional facility across the Potomac River in Virginia.

Ultimately, the picketing campaign wore the administration down. When members of Wilson's own administration began to question the government's position on suffrage, Wilson took matter into his own hands. In September 1918 Wilson made a dramatic appearance before the Congress, announcing that suffrage would now be considered an emergency war measure, which the administration had refused to do earlier. Wilson made an impassioned plea for Congress to pass the suffrage legislation, without which, he said, he would not be able to construct an effective world peace. With Wilson now supporting suffrage, it was simply a matter of time before it became the law of the land. Women, both the radical feminists of Paul's National Woman's Party and the social feminists of Catt's NAWSA, had forced the issue and ensured that the amendment would be passed by Congress.

THE NINETEENTH AMENDMENT PASSES

Between 1887 and 1919, the amendment had been brought to a vote before the Senate or the House a total of eight times, with the last five of those votes taking place between January 1918 and June 1919. Clearly, most of the congressional support for a woman suffrage amendment did not come until the last three years before its passage. In the final two votes, the House passed what had become known as the Susan B. Anthony Amendment, on May 21, 1919, by a vote of 304 in favor to 89 opposed. And on June 4, 1919, the Senate passed the Anthony Amendment by a vote of 56 in favor to 25 opposed. Within a year after that, the Anthony Amendment officially became the law of the land as the Nineteenth Amendment to the Constitution. The wording of the amendment remained as Susan B. Anthony had composed it 45 years earlier.

Theoretically, at least, the Nineteenth Amendment represented a moral and legal victory for all women. In actuality, however, both American Indian and African American women did not have free and easy access to the vote for years after the amendment was ratified. It would take massive attitudinal, as well as legal, changes, both of which followed on the heels of national civil rights and American Indian movements, before the socially accepted prejudices that kept Native Americans and African Americans away from the polls could be set aside.

THE LEAGUE OF WOMEN VOTERS (LWV)

The League of Women Voters evolved directly from the National American Woman Suffrage Association. When Carrie Chapman Catt addressed the NAWSA delegates at its final meeting in March 1919, she was able to persuade enough delegates to reconvene as the LWV. Initially, however, about 90 percent of NAWSA's membership felt that the LWV was unnecessary and would serve little purpose now that the Nineteenth Amendment was just about in place. Catt was elected president-for-life, an honor bestowed upon her by the grateful NAWSA members who believed that she was largely responsible for securing woman suffrage. But the actual first-term president was Maud Wood Park, a long-time member of NAWSA's leadership.

Catt outlined three goals that she believed the LWV needed to pursue. First, they had to guarantee that all women would be enfranchised by continuing to press for state ratification of the Nineteenth Amendment. Second, the LWV had to take the lead in eliminating any remaining legal discrimination against women. And third, the LWV had to be involved in making sure that democracy was secure enough to take the lead in providing for a secure world.

During the conservative 1920s, the LWV lobbied for a variety of legislation focusing on protection for women and children and on good government. In all, the LWV lobbied for 38 separate pieces of legislation, but saw success on only two issues because of the increasing conservatism. In 1922 Congress passed the Cable Citizenship Act. Prior to passage of the Cable Act, American women who married noncitizens could conceivably lose their own citizenship if their husbands were deported. The Cable Act guaranteed independent citizenship for married women. And in 1924 the Sheppard-Towner Act was passed, which provided medical care to women and children.

Alice Paul and the National Woman's Party, immediately after the ratification, began to lay plans for an equal rights campaign. To Paul, the vote was only one step in the pursuit of full equality. Until the nation was willing to proclaim in the Constitution that men and women were equal in all matters, women would not be truly equal. Paul wrote an Equal Rights Amendment (ERA) in 1922. Neither she, nor the members of the Woman's Party who vowed to work for an ERA, were quite prepared for the level of opposition they met. The greatest impediment was from women who for years had worked to secure protective legislation for women and children in the workplace and who were fearful that an ERA would, with one blow, wipe out all their hard work. In many ways the division between the goals of the League of Women Voters and the goals of the Woman's Party were simply a restatement of the same issues that had earlier divided the women's rights movements and that would continue to divide the women's movement until women found a way to resolve their differences.

• • • • •

Jeannette Rankin, First Woman Elected to Congress
1880–1973

Jeannette Pickering Rankin served two terms in the Congress of the United States. On each occasion she had to choose whether to stand on principle in support of her long-held conviction that pacifism was the only true road to peace, or to make a popular choice and vote with the majority. In each instance Rankin stood on principle.

Rankin began working on behalf of woman suffrage in her home state of Montana in 1910. She had graduated from the University of Montana in 1902, taught for several years before furthering her education in New York, and then did social work in Seattle. While a graduate student at the University of Washington, Rankin became a suffragist. From 1910 to 1914, she worked full time for the suffrage movement. In 1914, the year Montana enfranchised women, she was elected legislative secretary for the National American Woman Suffrage Association.

As a candidate to fill one of Montana's two at-large congressional seats, Rankin ran as a Progressive Republican. She was well-known and respected throughout the state. The women of Montana owed a great deal to Rankin for her efforts in securing the vote there. When she announced her candidacy, therefore, she had the support of women from both political parties. Even so, the campaign required her to travel hundreds of miles to remote towns in Montana, persuading women not only to vote for the first time, but to vote for a woman as well.

Much of Rankin's first term in Congress was spent on legislation affecting the lives of women. She was a member of the committee charged with writing a constitutional amendment that would give women the vote. Rankin was more than diligent in her work for health reform legislation for women, aimed at lowering the infant mortality rate. She was an effective backer of the Sheppard-Towner Act, eventually passed in 1921, which appropriated matching funds for states that wished to participate in building clinics that would provide prenatal and infant care.

Within days of being sworn in as a congresswoman in 1917, however, Rankin was faced with a conscience vote. President Woodrow Wilson asked for a declaration of war on Germany. Part of Rankin's campaign pledge had been to keep America out of war. It was not an idle pledge, for Rankin was an avowed pacifist. Moreover, Wilson himself had campaigned on a peace platform. But as events in Europe went from bad to worse, Wilson's opinion changed, as did the opinion of the general public. Rankin had to choose to stand on principle as a pacifist or support the president. In the hours before the vote, several suffrage delegations appealed to her to support Wilson, for fear that Rankin would harm the suffrage cause with a negative vote. Carrie Chapman Catt, the president of NAWSA, put as much pressure on Rankin as she could, arguing that, because the president had more than enough votes to win the declaration of war, Rankin's negative vote would not help her cause. Catt warned that Rankin could only hurt suffrage, and it would cause Rankin to lose her congressional seat in the next election. Alice Paul was the only suffrage leader who counseled Rankin to vote her conscience regardless of the consequences. When the vote was finally taken, Rankin was one of 50 members of Congress who voted against the declaration of war. And, as Carrie Chapman Catt predicted, Rankin lost her congressional seat as well as a bid for a Senate seat.

For nearly 20 years thereafter, Rankin stayed out of the political limelight. As World War II approached, she ran for Congress once again in 1940. Running on a pacifist platform, Rankin garnered the benefit of the isolationist feelings that still ran high in the Great Plains states. Once again, she was elected. And once again, quickly after taking her seat, she was confronted with a conscience vote. On December 8, 1941, President Franklin Delano Roosevelt asked Congress to declare war in the wake of Japan's attack on Pearl Harbor. The attack had immediately wiped away any isolationist thoughts as far as most Americans were concerned. Rankin, however, as despicable as she thought the attack had been, could not renounce her pacifism. She was the lone opponent of Roosevelt's request for a declaration of war. Her Montana constituents neither understood nor condoned her vote. Knowing that she stood no chance for election in 1942, Rankin chose not to run. Her political career was over. Whether one agreed with Rankin's votes against war, no one could deny that America's first female congresswoman had placed principle above career on two important occasions.

CHAPTER 9

· · · · · · · · ·

The Reform Impulse

S hortly after the Civil War, women across the country began organizing local clubs. The models for the first clubs were Sorosis, a club for journalists and professional women started by Jane Cunningham Croly in New York in 1869 to protest the exclusion of women from the National Press Club, and the New England Women's Club, organized in the same year by several upper-class Bostonians. At first the club movement focused more on cultural affairs, with clubs dedicated to weekly lectures, book discussions, and other similar pursuits. For many women the clubs were a form of higher education. The members tended to be middle and upper class, and the club to be fairly exclusionary. But gradually, many clubs took on more concern for civic as well as cultural events.

As the requirements of family life changed with technological developments, industrialization, urbanization, and immigration, middle-class women in the late 19th century had more opportunity to concern themselves with issues beyond the immediate family. Indeed, many women felt compelled to help find solutions to the entirely new set of problems caused by the profound changes in society. These social feminists, who favored more opportunity for women in society but drew the line at full equality, were concerned with issues that dealt primarily with social justice and social reform. These were issues that settlement houses, such as Hull House, had been dealing with for nearly two decades. By 1900 the settlement people had spread out, forming a variety of associations that created a dynamic reform network that included the Association of Collegiate Alumnae, the General Federation of Women's Clubs, the Women's Christian Temperance Union, the National American Woman Suffrage Association, the National Consumer's League, and the

National Women's Trade Union League, among others. The suffrage movement itself, which did not necessarily attract reform-minded women, owed some of its resurgence to the social feminists, many of whom held overlapping memberships in two or more associations. Operating almost like an interlocking directory, the women's associations supported each other's causes to secure support for their own.

By the late 1880s, there were literally thousands of local women's clubs operating across the nation. For women of the late 19th century who did not necessarily advocate the agendas of either the enormous temperance movement or the ever-growing suffrage movement, women's clubs represented an opportunity to participate in public affairs without abandoning their traditional values.

When Jane Cunningham Croly invited women's clubs to join the General Federation of Women's Clubs (GFWC) in 1890, it marked a turning point for thousands of middle-class women who, thereafter, had a respectable alternative for expressing their views on social issues. Croly believed that, through the GFWC, women could apply their influence through the club structure to effect a variety of social reforms. Croly's vision was quickly realized when the GFWC became involved in improving public education and expanding public libraries. These and other noncontroversial activities, including beautification of the environment, building of hospitals and playgrounds, and support of women's colleges and social settlement houses led to a national agenda that eventually embraced woman suffrage, temperance, and support of the progressive movement agenda. Regarding the latter, the GFWC in 1899 was responsible for establishing a national model for juvenile courts, and in 1906 it was an important factor in the passage of the Pure Food and Drug Act that led to establishment of the Pure Food and Drug Administration. Local clubs were also involved in factory inspection, control of child labor conditions, improvement of tenement housing, availability of municipal services, elimination of graft, and conservation. Thus, the middle and upper classes moved from weekly book reviews into social activism almost seamlessly and without feeling as though they had abandoned traditional values.

The social feminists, sometimes referred to as the New Women, tended to be educated and members of either the middle or upper-middle class. Their particular status gave them more influence than they might otherwise have had. Their concern for achieving the social reforms they believed were necessary for the good of society caused many of them to endorse the suffrage movement. In the eyes of the social reformers, the tradeoff for supporting suffrage was the greater ease with which social reforms could be enacted when women had political power. For the most part, the radical feminists, such as those who belonged to the National Woman's Party, were the only suffragists who spoke about demanding woman suffrage simply because women were citizens and were, therefore, entitled to the vote regardless of how they intended to use it. The social feminists, on the other hand, needed the feeling of usefulness and accomplishment that would go along with securing reforms. Thus, NAWSA experienced an increase in its membership from less than 13,000 recorded members in the late 19th century, to more than 75,000 NAWSA members in 1910.

The club movement and the subsequent reformism that emerged was by no means isolated or confined to only middle-class women. Working-class women, like those in the WTUL, had long allied with club women to secure reforms, and African American women had also started organizations that mirrored those in which white women participated. The reform impulse, which came to fruition in the years between the late 19th century and World War I, had been building in society along with the growth of cities and rampant industrialization. There were really two distinct strains of progressive reform, one focusing on political and legislative reforms, and the other on social justice. Women reformers, like those involved in the various clubs and voluntary associations, tended to be more intimately involved in the social justice movement, but in general women played a pivotal role in the Progressive Era.

In the progressive struggle for the nation's soul, the reformers generally found the national level a difficult forum. On the national level, the reformers' fragmented coalition opposed the wealth of vested interests from across the country. Consequently, the reformers won many of their early victories on the state level. Because of Hull House and the enormous range of activity being encouraged by Jane Addams, Illinois became in some ways a proving ground for progressive reform efforts. With the able assistance of Governor John Peter Altgeld, himself a liberal reformer, the state legislature often led the way in passing legislation, particularly legislation affecting women and children. In 1892 Illinois became the first state to pass laws limiting to 10 the number of hours women could be required to work per day. Massachusetts and New York quickly adopted similar statutes, and by 1917, 39 states had adopted or strengthened laws protecting women. This pattern became a common one during the Progressive Era, as what began as a daring experiment in one state soon became the norm for the rest of the country.

FLORENCE KELLEY

Not only did some of the most prominent women reformers come out of the Hull House experiment, they in turn influenced the direction that Hull House followed. Florence Kelley, who later achieved national recognition as head of the National Consumer's League, began her reform career in Illinois. A chance meeting in Europe in 1883 with M. Carey Thomas, the president of Bryn Mawr College, changed the direction of Kelley's life and indirectly contributed to some of the most far-reaching social reforms of the Progressive Era.

Kelley, the product of an upper-class Philadelphia family, graduated from Cornell University in 1882. After being refused admission to the University of Pennsylvania law school because she was a woman, Kelley left on an extended tour of Europe. It was there that she met M. Carey Thomas, who told Kelley about her own experiences in being denied entrance to a university because of her gender. Thomas had then gone to the University of Zurich, which accepted women, and Kelley determined to enroll there also. In Zurich Kelley became a convert to socialism, primarily because to her it explained why working women and children were subjected to so much abuse and why nonwhites were subjected to racial bias. Kelley married a fellow socialist, a young Russian medical student, and the couple and their first child moved to New York in 1886. After two more children and a disappointing association with the Socialist Labor Party because the European-oriented leadership did not trust the eager young American, Kelley left her husband and took her three children to Illinois. Divorce laws were much more permissive there than in many other states. By 1891 Kelley and her children were residents of Hull House, where Kelley struck up lasting friendships with Jane Addams, Julia Lathrop, and Alice Hamilton, all of whom were involved in the sweeping social reforms taking place in the late 19th century. Kelley's growing interest in child labor led to her appointment as factory inspector by the Illinois Bureau of Labor Statistics. She was also asked to conduct a survey of city slums. The results of her combined efforts galvanized Hull House workers, including Jane Addams, to a greater awareness of the industrial conditions within the city. In 1892 the Illinois legislature passed significant reform legislation that limited the hours that women could work, prohibited child labor, and placed controls on tenement sweat shops. Governor John Peter Altgeld appointed Kelley chief factory inspector, with a staff of 12 and a budget of $12,000, responsible for enforcement of the new legislation.

Kelley finally earned her law degree in 1894, graduating from Northwestern University. She might have remained in Illinois had Altgeld's successor reappointed Kelley. Instead, she decided to move with her three children to New York. Long a believer in controlling child labor through the buying public, Kelley jumped at the chance to work as general secretary for the newly organized National Consumer's League (NCL). For nearly 30 years, Kelley *was* the NCL. Her program targeted middle- and upper-class women consumers, educating them to boycott products made with child labor. The NCL published a "White List" of companies whose production methods met the NCL "Standard of a Fair House." By 1907 the program was successful enough that manufacturers vied for the privilege of issuing their goods under a "white label" that consumers were educated to seek when making purchases.

In addition to her service with the NCL, Kelley was instrumental in the successful prosecution to *Muller v. Oregon* in 1908, which regulated working hours for women. With her good friend Julia Lathrop, she lobbied as well for creation of the federal Children's Bureau and continued to lobby for factory inspection and minimum wage laws, which several states ultimately adopted. Kelley was also an advocate of woman suffrage, though she withheld her support for an equal rights amendment in the 1920s, fearing that an ERA would undercut the protective legislation that she had worked her entire life to help secure. She did attempt to secure support for a federal child labor amendment to the Constitution and, never one to pull punches, characterized those who opposed her as "rabbit hearted," angrily demanding to know why "seals, bears, reindeer, fish, wild game in the national parks, buffalo, migratory birds, [are] all found suitable for federal protection; but not the children of our race and their mothers?"

Kelley's enduring legacy, however, remained her advocacy of intelligent purchasing and the use of the boycott by consumers, and her contribution to the ferment that led to so much New Deal legislation, especially protective legislation.

ALICE HAMILTON

Alice Hamilton and Julia Lathrop were also influential reformers who were associated with Hull House. Alice Hamilton fulfilled a long-time dream when she, in 1897, became a resident of Jane Addams' Hull House, then a center of groundbreaking research and social reform. Hamilton, who was born in 1869 in Indiana, received her early schooling at home before spending two years at the prestigious Miss Porter's School, a finishing school in Connecticut. Despite the overwhelming concentration on acquiring the requisite skills to become a middle-class homemaker, Hamilton knew she wanted to study medicine. Elizabeth Blackwell, the first woman who graduated from medical school, had received her M.D. nearly 40 years earlier, but little had been done since then to encourage women to go into medicine. Following Blackwell's trail, Hamilton applied to several medical schools before settling for, as she described it, "a little third-rate medical school" in Indiana. Shortly thereafter, the University of Michigan accepted her application to enroll at its coeducational medical school, and she jumped at the opportunity. With her M.D. in hand in 1893, Hamilton went to Europe to study bacteriology at the Universities of Leipzig and Munich.

In 1897 Hamilton was appointed as a professor at the Women's Medical School of Northwestern University. As a resident of Hull House, she was able to draw on her training as a bacteriologist, reaching the conclusion that many of Hull House's constituents were contracting diseases from the noxious chemicals they were exposed to at work. It was standard practice at the time, when there were no workmen's compensation laws or safety standards to protect employees, to fire employees whose productivity was hampered by illness and replace them with any of the thousands of workers looking for jobs. Responding to the situation, the governor of Illinois appointed an Occupational Disease Commission in 1910, with Hamilton as its director. Her 1911 report, focusing in part on the effects of lead poisoning on the factory workers, quickly became a model for future investigations. At once, Hamilton was established as one of—if not *the*—leading toxicologists in the United States. It also led directly to enactment of workmen's compensation legislation in Illinois, establishing a precedent that illness resulting from work entitled an employee to some compensation from the employer.

The work that Alice Hamilton did in the field of toxicology helped to establish it as an important medical specialty. Hamilton's studies in industrial toxicology and the seminal contributions they made in helping to secure legislation protecting workers both from exposure to harmful chemicals and from the economic hardships of enduring industrially caused diseases, remain a lasting contribution to a still-controversial subject.

CHILDREN'S BUREAU

Julia Lathrop, a graduate of Vassar College in 1880, had been a member of Jane Addams' inner circle at Hull House for more than 20 years when President William Howard Taft appointed the well-known sociologist as the first head of the Children's Bureau. Lathrop's friendship with Florence Kelley had ignited her interest in children's welfare and her desire to promote restrictions that would eliminate child labor. Under Lathrop's direction, a primary focus of the Children's Bureau was the crusade against child labor. But the Children's Bureau pursued a broad range of interests on behalf of children, including infant mortality. With a staff of 15 and a budget of $25,000, Lathrop investigated infant mortality in selected cities across the country. The investigations led to appeals for uniform birth registration procedures, previously lacking, and to the initiation of bureau-sponsored maternal education programs that offered instruction and advice in prenatal care, infant feeding and care, and medical consultation for women who had little or no access to such care.

When Taft was succeeded as president by Woodrow Wilson, the new president reappointed Lathrop, enabling her to continue her work. She published additional studies on maternal mortality, the effects of nutrition on child development, juvenile delinquency and juvenile courts, illegitimacy, child labor, and mother's pensions, providing a wealth of information for reformers, agencies, and citizens alike. In 1916 the first National Baby Week was held, with the goal of getting information into the hands of parents. In that same year, Congress passed the first child labor law, the Keating-Owen Child Labor Act, which forbade interstate shipment of goods produced by child labor. Enforcement of the new law fell to the Children's Bureau. Lathrop immediately established the Child Labor Division and sought another Hull House colleague, Grace Abbott, to head the new division. Although the Supreme Court struck down the Federal Child Labor Law in 1918 (*Hammer v. Dagenhart*), Abbott remained at the Children's Bureau as Lathrop's assistant. In May 1919 Lathrop and the Children's Bureau held a national conference on child welfare standards, in conjunction with the "Children's Year" activities. Two years later the enormous amount of research conducted by Lathrop and others, as well as their active campaign on behalf of federal aid to states for maternal and infant care, led to passage of the Sheppard-Towner Act, a measure intended to reduce the rate of childbirth-related mortality and infant mortality.

When Lathrop resigned as head of the Children's Bureau in 1921, she was succeeded by Grace Abbott. Abbott continued the programs set in place by Lathrop. In this way she preserved much of the groundwork that allowed the Roosevelt Administration to enact a variety of health and welfare programs under the New Deal, including the Social Security Act. During World War II, the Emergency Maternity and Infant Care Program insured departing servicemen that their pregnant wives and newborn children would be provided with the best medical care available.

MOTHERS' PENSION LAW

For years a major concern of both the protective legislationists and the progressive reformers was who was responsible for widows with young children, deserted wives and mothers, and other single mothers with no means of support. In 1909 these concerns were formalized at a conference on the care of dependent children, held at the White House in Washington, D.C. Called by President Theodore Roosevelt, the conference discussed the social consequences of paying mothers a pension so that they could keep their children at home rather than having to institutionalize them. Most of the supporters of the mother's pension considered it an entitlement, not a charity. Common to the approach to social problems of the time, a coalition of women's organizations, clubs, social workers, politicians, and trade unionists lobbied legislators for appropriate legislation.

In 1911 Kansas City, Missouri, became the first city in the nation to make provisions for those eventualities. Illinois followed later that year, passing a statewide mother's pension provision. By 1919, 39 states had enacted some kind of mothers' pension law. In all states that had mother's pension laws, eligibility extended to widowed mothers with children 14 years of age and under. Because in most states children over 14 years old were considered capable of holding a job, no provisions were made for older children. In some states, but not all, divorced mothers, women whose husbands had deserted them, and women whose husbands were in prison were also eligible for pensions.

Despite efforts to persuade politicians and the public that pensions should be considered an entitlement, most people looked upon them as charity. Women who applied for funds often had to endure the close scrutiny of city and state employees whose goal it was to disallow anyone who did not precisely fit the designated criteria. Thus, recipients were constantly harassed by investigators, who were constantly checking to make sure the home environment was satisfactory and that no other source of income was available to the recipient. These constraints were imposed despite the reality that mother's pensions were usually not enough to maintain a home without supplemental income. Moreover, many southern states would not even entertain applications from African American women.

Even with all of the drawbacks associated with the mother's pension programs, they still constituted the best hope for women left alone to care for their children. And until the enactment of the Social Security Act of 1935, it was the first and only acknowledgment from governments at various levels that the government did have some responsibility for the well-being of its citizens.

THE LITERATURE OF REFORM: *SISTER CARRIE*

Another influential motivator for reformers was the popular literature of the day. Literature, such as Theodore Dreiser's turn-of-the-century novel, *Sister Carrie*, made people aware of conditions requiring some action by public or private sources. The initial response to Dreiser's novel was condemnatory and defensive, as the reading public and critics alike refused to accept Dreiser's portrayal of Sister Carrie as an average young woman who discards conventional morality to gain financial advantage. Dreiser's Sister Carrie, based loosely on the experiences of his own sister Emma, arrives in Chicago in 1889, determined to make a life for herself. Her initial experiences and appearance, as Dreiser describes them, mirror those of most late 19th-century urban working women. At the time there was a good deal of fluidity in what eventually became categorized as blue collar and white collar work. A young working woman like Sister Carrie might move from factory work to mill work to shop clerk to piece work, almost interchangeably and with little change in status. She was recognizable in her "course woolen garments, . . . shabby felt sailor hat, . . . cheap piece of fur, . . . knitted shawl, and gloves." Sister Carrie, tiring quickly of the low wages and the drabness of her life, seeks to change all that by entering into liaisons with a series of men, each of whom offers more than the last. Her success in the theater, still considered a bastion of immorality in the 19th century, leaves her at last wealthy but no happier in her personal life.

Dreiser, the first of the American naturalist school of writers that included Jack London, Upton Sinclair, John Dos Passos, and Ernest Hemingway, refused to condemn Sister Carrie for abandoning conventional morality, a factor that did not sit well with critics. Instead of meeting with disaster, as Victorian morality demanded, Carrie continued to rise up the ladder of success. Dreiser challenged norms of the day, refusing to accept that the same set of moral standards could be applied to all circumstances. He also challenged society's views about women like Carrie. Always fascinated by the uses and abuses of wealth and power, Dreiser wanted to expose the hypocrisy with which society viewed women of a certain class. He also wanted to show how cruel and demeaning urban life, with all its rough edges, could be for those who lived on the edge of poverty.

The first edition of Sister Carrie was heavily expurgated before it was published. Sister Carrie sold less than 500 copies when, stung by the critics' lash, the publisher recalled the book, claiming that the public was simply not ready to read about urban life with its lack of morals. Although subsequent editions of Sister Carrie were released in the meantime, it took 81 years for Dreiser's novel to be published in the form he intended.

Sister Carrie was one of several books that caused people to look more critically at a number of issues, including the status of women in society, and helped to create an atmosphere of change that was characteristic of the Progressive Era.

Ida Tarbell and Standard Oil

Ida Tarbell did the research and much of the writing that went into her famous exposé for a series of articles for McClure's Magazine, for which she worked as an editor. McClure's was the first and most influential of the muckraking journals that appeared around the turn of the century. These magazines found a lucrative market in showing the sordid side of the Gilded Age, combining thorough investigations with sensationalistic presentation that contrasted the ideology of human progress through capitalist competition with what seemed to be the realities of human misery and monopolistic practices. They found a ready audience in the new middle-class readers, who were concerned about the social welfare of the masses and their own quality of life. Both appeared threatened by the dark manipulations of the great monopolists.

Tarbell went to work alongside many more prominent muckrakers, but she benefited both from her obscurity and from the fact that she was a woman. Presenting herself as a naive female desiring only to publicize the achievements of Standard Oil, she gained access to records that revealed special favors from the railroad companies and from politicians. Her exposé, published in book form in 1904, was entitled *The History of the Standard Oil Company*. She so effectively showed the monopolistic practices of John D. Rockefeller's company that her work led to more official investigations, the application of the Sherman Anti-Trust Act, and the breakup of the Standard Oil Company. Tarbell's work, as much as any other's, vindicated the muckrakers' faith that public exposure could promote public good.

Tarbell herself had a strong background for the project. Her family made its fortune from the Pennsylvania oil fields discovered in 1859, and she graduated from a coed college in 1880. She worked briefly as a teacher and then for eight years as editor of a monthly magazine, after which she studied history at the Sorbonne in Paris. She began writing for *McClure's* upon her return in 1894 and published her first book, a biography of Napoleon that sold more than 100,000 copies, in 1895. She drew on both her family's experience in business and her scholarly studies to prepare her *History* and subsequent works. She published eight books about Abraham Lincoln alone, as well as more contemporary studies of tariffs and scientific management, and did significant primary research on women in the American Revolution.

Two years after her success with Standard Oil, Tarbell, along with several of her colleagues, left *McClure's* to purchase the *American Magazine*. She served as coeditor until 1915, then traveled on the lecture circuit. During World War I, she served on the Women's Committee of the Council of National Defense. After the war she covered the Versailles peace conference as a reporter, and in 1919 President Woodrow Wilson appointed her as a delegate to an International Industrial Conference.

Although Tarbell had been an early supporter of women's rights, her growing ambivalence about women choosing public life over marriage and motherhood gradually led her to oppose woman suffrage, a position she defended in books published in 1912 and 1915. Nevertheless, her life stands as an example of the dedicated public service made possible by the women's education movement of the late 19th century and nurtured by the champions of reform during the Progressive Era.

Sinclair's *The Jungle*

Food processing reforms were also influenced by literature, in this case Upton Sinclair's *The Jungle*, a graphic exposé of meat-packing factories. But the efforts to regulate food industries began long before Sinclair's novel. Ever since the Civil War, when nurse Annie Whittenmyer began arguing for better

and more varied diets for the patients in hospitals, the public became aware
that regulating the production of foods and medicines was a necessary social
reform. Harvey Wiley, who eventually became the chief chemist of the
United States Department of Agriculture, credited Whittenmyer for his
decision to make the study of food additives and food production his life's
work. When Wiley became the chief chemist his campaign for pure food and
drug regulations began to build momentum. Turning to the women of the
United States, Wiley cast the problem as one of family safety, requesting their
assistance in forcing legislation that would make food processing and the
production of medicines safer for American families.

Women responded with enthusiasm. The Food Consumer's League, organized in the 1890s, appointed Alice Lakey as chair of the food investigation
committee, charged with arousing public opposition to aniline, a coal by-
product commonly used in making food dyes. Following another avenue,
Florence Kelley, as the head of the National Consumer's League and a former
state factories inspector in Illinois, spoke on behalf of increased food and drug
legislation at the city, state, and federal levels. She continued her campaign,
on and off, for the next 25 years. Even after passage of the Pure Food Act,
Kelley sought to bring more and more products within the scope of the
legislation.

The Women's Christian Temperance Union (WCTU) came into the fight
in 1902, responding angrily to the accusation of Wesleyan University professors that the WCTU consistently lobbied against beer but said nothing about
medicines containing 10 times more alcohol than beer. The WCTU quickly
began an information education campaign against the use of medicines
containing alcohol and the mislabeling of patent medicines. Between 1903
and 1906, the WCTU's campaign was helped along by a number of women's
magazines, including *The Ladies' Home Journal* and *Collier's*, which began
publishing numerous articles relating the dangers of patent medicines, un-
tested home remedies, and medicines containing large amounts of alcohol.

By 1905 advocates of food and drug regulation had picked up political
support in both the House and the Senate. Senator Porter McCumber
sponsored the first bill calling for regulation, but when the Senate session
ended before action was taken, the bill died. Coincidentally, in 1906 Sinclair
published *The Jungle*, relating the horrific practices employed at Chicago
slaughterhouses on beef products intended for human consumption. Public
concern for regulation now became a groundswell of demands for instant
reform. Three separate bills were immediately introduced into Congress.
Senator Albert Beveridge of Indiana supported legislation for government
meat inspection that was passed and signed into law by June 30, 1906. At the
same time, Senator Weldon Heyburn of Idaho and Congressman William
Hepburn of Iowa both introduced strong food and drug bills. Congress passed

a combined version of the Heyburn and Hepburn bills on June 29, 1906. Little persuasion had to be exerted to get President Theodore Roosevelt to sign the bill into law immediately, because Roosevelt had also read Sinclair's account of meat processing. Though it is certain that a Pure Food and Drug Act was inevitable, it is probable that even with Sinclair's exposé of the slaughter-houses, legislation might have taken considerably longer had it not been for the widespread grassroots movement that began with Annie Whittenmyer during the Civil War.

REFORMING THE WORK PLACE

By the mid-1880s, social reformers had begun advocating and working for enactment of protective legislation that insured the welfare and safety of women and children working in factories. With a few minor exceptions, unions had failed to take women into the fold in any meaningful way. Therefore, female workers had no institutionalized method of securing safety and fairness. Moreover, protective legislation served the purpose of organized labor because it offered a way to prohibit the infiltration of women into skilled jobs. By designating certain jobs as dangerous to a woman's health and safety, unions could preserve those jobs for male union members.

At the same time, the social reformers were acting in what they sincerely considered the best interests of women and children. As more and more information came forth regarding unsafe working conditions and long hours for low wages, social reformers met with greater and greater success in securing protective legislation. Massachusetts passed a 10-hour work day law in 1887, and by 1914, 27 other states had enacted similar legislation. In addition, many states passed legislation establishing minimum wages.

The state of Oregon passed 10-hour-day legislation and, when a laundry owner forced his female employee to work longer than 10 hours, he was arrested for violation of the law. The laundry owner sought to challenge the state's right to prevent women from working as many hours as they wished, bringing suit in the case of *Muller v. Oregon*. The suit worked its way through the lower courts and finally up to the Supreme Court, which handed down its decision in 1908.

The Court's decision in *Muller v. Oregon* was a landmark decision for two reasons. First, in upholding the right of the state of Oregon to pass legislation regulating the number of hours women could work, proclaiming that "sex is a valid basis for classification," the Court was, in effect, endorsing the concept of protective legislation. This was a clear victory for social reformers because, in most cases, protective legislation did what the reformers intended it to do—it provided protection for the health of female employees, improved the conditions under which they worked, limited their hours, and raised their wages. Though future Court decisions would invalidate some protective legislation, for the moment, the social reformers had won.

The second reason that *Muller v. Oregon* constituted a landmark decision was that it was the first instance of so-called sociological jurisprudence. Florence Kelley worked closely with the counsel for the state of Oregon, Oliver Wendell Holmes, in preparing the case. Holmes, soon to be sitting on the Court himself and destined to become one of the Court's ablest and most influential chief justices, gathered data from a variety of sources to demonstrate how vulnerable female employees were. Holmes argued his case using the statistics to demonstrate the relationship between long work hours and the declining health and morals of female employees. The Court was receptive to Holmes's line of argument, declaring that women's physical well-being "becomes an object of public interest and care in order to preserve the strength and vigor of the race." A precedent had been set in allowing the introduction of sociological data to support or refute a piece of legislation and, for the first time, real world experience won over disconnected legal dogma.

Women's Trade Union League (WTUL)

Mary Kenney O'Sullivan and Leonora O'Reilly were separated by hundreds of miles, but united in a common goal of bringing relief to working women. O'Sullivan, from Chicago, organized the Woman's Bookbinder Union #1 in the 1880s. Even after her marriage to a Boston labor activist, she lived at Hull House with Jane Addams. Eventually, she and her husband moved to Boston. When her husband was killed in an accident, and with three children to support, O'Sullivan returned to union work. O'Reilly, a native New Yorker who had worked in the garment industry from early childhood, was a member of the Knights of Labor in the 1880s and one of the organizers of the United Garment Workers in 1897. The two came together as members of the American Federation of Labor at its annual meeting in 1903. Disillusioned at the AF of L's lack of commitment to women, O'Sullivan and O'Reilly organized the National Women's Trade Union League.

The WTUL, whose motto was "The Eight Hour Day; A Living Wage; To Guard the Home," embraced both women in the work force and middle- and upper-class women whose sympathies lay with working women. These so-called allies to the WTUL proved to be valuable especially during strikes because they had the resources and the desire to support the efforts of strikers, providing both personal and financial contributions. Moreover, the allies tended to be better educated and better able to communicate the ideas of the WTUL to the public. At the same time, the allies educated working members of the WTUL for leadership roles. (Leonora O'Reilly was responsible for bringing Mary Elizabeth Dreier and Margaret Dreier Robbins into the trade union movement. Margaret Robbins eventually established an annuity for

O'Reilly so that the latter could quit her 10-hour-a-day factory job and devote full time to union activity.) The allies were particularly important during the garment industry strikes from 1909 to 1911. The Dreiers, Alva Belmont, and other influential women led the effort to provide the necessary support for the striking women.

At its first convention, the WTUL proposed six primary goals, including equal pay for equal work, woman suffrage, full unionization, an eight-hour work day, a required minimum wage, and all of the benefits subscribed to in the AF of L's economic program. By 1911 WTUL chapters were organized in 11 cities, from Boston to Denver, Colorado. After the Triangle Shirtwaist Company fire (see page 120), the WTUL took the forefront in conducting investigations into the conditions that led to the fire, resulting in legislation requiring corporations to maintain minimum safety precautions.

After World War I, with the postwar conservatism adversely affecting labor unions, the WTUL never again achieved the kind of influence it enjoyed during the Progressive Era with Rose Schneiderman at its helm. It continued to exist until just after World War II as an organization dedicated to improving working conditions for women.

The workers who created ladies' garments, mostly men, began to organize into small, informal groups in the late 19th century. They came together in June 1900, spurred on by the United Brotherhood of Cloak Makers' Union in New York, with the immediate purpose of forming a national union to promote a national union label and to find a way to resist injunctions against striking garment workers. Garment workers were also concerned about finding a way to end the "home contract" system of production. In this system independent contractors, usually women, worked at home for a pittance, about 30 cents a day. The women and men, who held the preferred positions as workers in the shops, opposed the contract system because the owner's exploitation of the "home contract" women facilitated the exploitation of those who worked in factories.

With 2,000 delegates meeting in New York on June 3, 1900, the AF of L issued a charter to the new International Ladies' Garment Workers' Union (ILGWU). The union leadership remained predominantly male during its first decade, even though most garment workers were women. Like most union officials, the AF of L and the male unionists believed that women were incapable of handling union hierarchy. Moreover, the belief persisted that women would not support union actions because their primary career was marriage and not industrial work. Then the increase of young, radical, immigrant Jewish women began to exert an influence. Typical of them was Clara Lemlich, a refugee from Russia who came to New York at age 15 in 1903 and became a founding member of ILGWU's Local 25 in 1906. She participated in innumerable strikes and demonstrations, and was arrested 17 times in 1909 alone. When, on November 22, 1909, she joined several thousand other young women at the Cooper Union meeting hall, she listened to several hours of boring speeches calling for a general strike. Able to endure them no longer, Lemlich marched to the front of the hall, boldly took the podium, and eloquently spoke in favor of the general strike. The crowd roared its agreement, and 30,000 garment workers walked off their jobs.

In the days that followed, the Women's Trade Union League and the women of the Socialist Party came to the strikers' aid. They established 20 strike halls and helped with organizing picketing, strike support, and dealing with police brutality. At first the enthusiasm and dedication of the strikers appeared unstoppable, but the solidarity of the Jewish immigrants did not extend to Italian, native-born, or African American women. Without total cooperation, the strike failed. However, it did succeed in establishing the ILGWU as a major union, and, as a result, more women in the United States were unionized than ever before.

Triangle Shirtwaist Fire

The infamous Triangle Shirtwaist Company fire, in which 147 New York City garment workers—mostly young Italian and Jewish immigrants—died because of the total lack of regulations governing workplace safety, drove even more women into the union the next year. The ILGWU won a 14-week strike in 1916 and went on to pioneer union-sponsored health centers and other benefits. It gained from the prosperity of the war years, and though it languished (like other unions) in the 1920s and 1930s, it revived in succeeding decades. The proportion of women remained high, around 75 percent of the rank and file, although the leadership reverted to predominantly male. Nonetheless, the union had provided an important impetus to the organization of women in labor.

Only a year before the disastrous Triangle fire, employees at the dress factory returned to work after a strike called to protest both low wages and dangerous conditions had failed. The Triangle strike, part of an industrywide walkout of 18,000 workers from over 500 shirtwaist factories, had begun in November 1909 and ended in February 1910, when workers returned to their 59-hour work weeks, the same low wages, and the same dangerous conditions. Some of the striking women were not allowed to return to the Triangle Company. As it turned out, they were the lucky ones. On March 25, 1911, a cigarette that one of the few male employees dropped in a pile of trash set off a rapidly expanding blaze that quickly tore through the several floors of the Triangle Shirtwaist Company, located on the upper floors of the Asch Building in New York's Washington Square Park. Because it was Saturday, payday at the Triangle, all but one of the exit doors was locked because management did not want workers leaving a few minutes early to get a jump on their one day off. As the employees became aware of the fire, some were fortunate enough to get to elevators that were still operating, and a few managed to get out of the unlocked door before fire blocked that exit. Others were able to jump to a building across the alley, and some escaped to an enclosed courtyard below. Those in the courtyard survived only because firemen chopped through locked doors on the street level. But for 146 young women, there was no escape. More than 50 bodies were found piled behind locked doors. And scores of desperate girls and women chose to jump from the upper windows rather than succumb to the flames which by then had become an inferno. No one who jumped from the building survived the fall to the sidewalk below, and some were impaled on iron fences surrounding the Asch Building.

Despite the irresponsible locking of exit doors by the company managers and owners, a subsequent trial exonerated all concerned from any wrongful death charges. A member of the all-male jury later explained that there was a feeling among the jury that the young women, who they deemed to have less intelligence than people in other occupations, probably panicked and therefore caused their own deaths. Little consideration was given to the locked doors and dangerous working conditions that had been allowed to flourish.

Devastated by the loss of life, Rose Schneiderman and other Women's Trade Union League members dispatched a committee of 50 garment workers to the state legislature in Albany, to present a petition asking for an investigation into the fire and for new laws regulating safety conditions. Responding to the petition, Senator Robert F. Wagner, who later helped to write the Wagner Labor Act during the New Deal, and Alfred E. Smith, the future mayor of New York and presidential candidate, proposed the formation of the New York State Factory Investigating Commission, commonly referred to as the Triangle Fire Commission. After a four-year investigation, Chairman Wagner and Vice Chairman Smith, along with the field investigators, one of whom was future Secretary of Labor Frances Perkins, called for a series of new regulations governing factory safety. The 13-volume report included recommendations for 60 separate laws, 56 of which were enacted by the legislature. Out of the Triangle Shirtwaist Company fire, New York emerged as the state with the most comprehensive laws governing factory safety standards of any state in the union.

REFORMERS AND PEACE

With greater and greater influence placed upon international peace as a goal of the women's movement in the early 20th century, nearly every significant woman's organization had a "peace department." The issue attracted the most notable of women reformers. Among the founders of the Women's Peace Party (WPP) were Jane Addams and Alice Hamilton from Hull House; Charlotte Perkins Gilman, author of *Women and Economics*; Florence Kelley of the National Consumer's League; and Crystal Eastman, a radical young lawyer who authored New York state's first workmen's compensation law. In January 1915, 86 delegates representing nearly every major woman's organization in the country, convened for the first WPP meeting. The delegates wrote a pacifist platform that represented, as they said, "the mother half of humanity." From its inception the slogan of the WPP was "Listen to the Women for a Change."

The WPP was the first major all-female United States peace organization. Its members, most of whom could not yet vote, advocated woman suffrage and an equal right to participate in government. The war in Europe seemed to these women to underline the failure of government policies enacted by male leaders only. A number of women, led by Jane Addams, went to the International Women Suffrage Association conference at The Hague in April 1915, meeting with women leaders from other nations. Delegates to the conference included those from nearly all the belligerent countries. A peace committee then began a round of visits to the capitals of Europe, where they met with various governments, pleading with them to enter into negotiations to bring the hostilities to an end. Addams also called upon United States President Woodrow Wilson to mediate an end to the war.

Once the United States entered the war, the WPP nearly faltered. Suffragists, like Carrie Chapman Catt, did not want to jeopardize suffrage to openly oppose government policy. Others, like Jane Addams, remained adamantly pacifist despite the fact that her reputation suffered greatly for it. In an atmosphere of "100 percent Americanism," initiated to solidify support for the war, neither the government nor the public was willing to suffer quietly those whom they considered traitors, even someone as illustrious as Jane Addams. In the end most WPP members followed their consciences in deciding whether to oppose the war, but formally the organization worked to bring an end to the "war to end all wars" without criticizing government policy. Instead, they supported efforts to negotiate an end to the war and petitioned for peace.

When the war finally ended, the American WPP joined with its European counterparts to form the Women's International League for Peace and Freedom (WILPF), a name that it still retains. Over the decades of its existence, the WILPF has been involved in an unremitting campaign to bring about peace and justice. The WILPF has been influential in a variety of peace campaigns, including securing a nuclear test ban (1963) and organizing a protest against United States involvement in the Vietnam War (1964), as well as numerous other campaigns, protests, and awareness movements: the Nuclear Weapons Freeze campaign (1979), a conference on racism (1979), the Stop the Arms Race campaign (1980), the March for Jobs, Peace, and Freedom (1983), Listen to Women for a Change (1983), the Campaign for a

Comprehensive Test Ban (1984), the International Cruise Missile Alert (1985), and the Campaign to Stop Star Wars (1987). As a tribute to its most illustrious founder, the educational affiliate of the WILPF is the Jane Addams Peace Association.

Women and World War I

The war brought some opportunities to women that they did not have before. Many women went to work for the first time, while others found it easier to advance in the jobs they held. The work force increased by about 400,000, with many women going into occupations previously denied them. For example, the government informally organized the "women's land army," a voluntary force of about 20,000 women from both urban and rural areas, who were to fill in for men from the Midwest and the Great Plains areas who had been mobilized by the military. These women picked up the slack in jobs related to farming, law enforcement, and railway operation, among other things. The Navy employed women, classified as "yeomen," to take over clerical duties. The female yeomen did not have real military status; they were classified militarily to give the Navy more leverage over their conduct. Apparently, Navy personnel feared that women engaged in war work would be flighty enough to quit their jobs or to engage in delinquent habits if the military could not order the women to perform. Women also served on government boards related to the war effort, for example, the Women's Committee of the Council for National Defense. Women were also employed in munitions factories. Indeed, the first American casualties of the war were the women who died in an explosion at a munitions factory in Pennsylvania in 1917.

Approximately 25,000 women served overseas in a variety of capacities, mostly as nurses, but also in service organizations, including the American Red Cross and the Young Women's Christian Association. Many of these women actually served in combat areas, but with the exception of military nurses, they were considered volunteers in their various capacities.

Despite their desire to contribute their professional services during World War I, women physicians were prohibited from serving in the United States military. Shortly after the United States entered the war in April 1917, the American Medical Women's Association (AMWA) held its second annual convention from June 5–7, 1917. The focus of discussion for women who wanted to contribute to the war effort, or who simply wanted to donate their professional services in an emergency, was how best to circumvent the current government policy to preclude women physicians from military service. The doctors voted to establish a committee of the AMWA, the American Women's Hospitals Service (AWHS), whose mandate was be to organize an all-female force of doctors, nurses, and ambulance drivers who would set

A woman war worker drives a truck in a munitions factory, 1917.

up and service dispensaries to serve the civilian population in outlying areas along the French war zone.

The AWHS barely had time to organize and establish a few dispensaries when the war ended in November 1918. It quickly changed its mission to helping with the reconstruction of Europe following the war, maintaining the dispensaries and providing needed medical care for the civilian population throughout the continent. It expanded its scope of operation, and in 1923, at the height of its overseas service, the AWHS provided medical care to more than 12,000 Turkish refugees in a clinic set up on a Greek island. Despite the years of service, both overseas during wartime and at home, that the women physicians had provided under the auspices of the AWHS, when World War II broke out, the same military restrictions were imposed. Women doctors were not allowed in the regular military services until 1943, and when the war ended, the restrictions were once again imposed. It took another decade before women physicians were allowed to join the military with commissions and full rank.

THE FIGHT FOR A MINIMUM WAGE

In the postsuffrage conservatism of the 1920s, social feminists found that few of the reforms they envisioned were accomplished as a consequence of having the right to vote. Without the unifying and underlying cause that had held them together despite their disparate goals and causes, the apparent unity they had briefly enjoyed before suffrage was secured fell apart. Politicians in the early 1920s reacted to their fear that women would vote as a bloc and passed legislation such as the Sheppard-Towner Act of 1921. But when it became apparent that the threat of a solid voting bloc would not materialize, the politicians stopped paying attention. The irony of the social feminists' willingness to support suffrage to achieve their goals was that without the suffrage cause, there was no unity and little reform.

Minimum wage laws were a crucial part of efforts to enact protective legislation since the early 20th century. Rooted in the shockingly low wages paid to women and children in some factories and in the so-called sweated trades, the minimum wage laws were an effort to eliminate the exploitation of workers largely unprotected by any other means. Labor unions, for example, routinely ignored women workers. When protective legislation advocates, like Florence Kelley of the National Consumer's League, succeeded in securing at least lukewarm union support for minimum wages for women and children, it was not because the unions had a true change of heart. Rather, organizations like the American Federation of Labor decided that supporting protective legislation only for women and children would eliminate the need for unions to accommodate women while at the same time protecting jobs for male union members.

In 1908 the courts ruled that imposing regulations governing women's work was allowable because of their unique vulnerability. Between 1912 and 1919, 14 states, primarily in the Midwest and Far West, and the District of Columbia passed minimum wage laws for women. Employers continued to oppose minimum wage laws in the courts, with mixed results initially. They used the argument that, while women might be considered a vulnerable segment of the working population, the imposition of minimum wages unfairly prohibited women from freely negotiating their own work contracts. In 1917, in the case of *Stettler v. O'Hara*, the Supreme Court upheld the minimum wage law by a narrow margin. But five years later, in the case of *Adkins v. Children's Hospital*, the Court, by a five-to-three margin, struck down the minimum wage law that had been passed for the District of Columbia in 1918. In the *Adkins* case, the Court ruled that the recent suffrage victory had made special protective legislation for women unnecessary. Surprisingly, Justice Oliver Wendell Holmes, who earlier had proclaimed that the Court had an obligation to give protective legislation the benefit of the doubt, sided with the opposition in *Adkins v. Children's Hospital*. Adopting a strict-constructionist point of view, Holmes argued that "the criterion for constitutionality is not whether we view the law to be for the public good."

When Florence Kelley heard, in 1923, that the United States Supreme Court had struck down minimum wage laws for women, she noted somewhat bitterly that the Court had proclaimed "the inalienable right of women to starve."

The *Adkins* decision effectively overturned all of the minimum wage laws that had been enacted in the previous decade. Efforts to formulate a minimum wage law for women that would stand up to constitutional scrutiny continued to prove futile for protective legislationists throughout the 1920s and 1930s. The *Adkins* decision also stands as a model for what happened generally in progressive reform in the post–World War I years. Much of the conservative reaction to the years of liberal reform was influenced by the general disillusionment with the consequences of the war itself. Disappointment over the failure to achieve a lasting peace in the wake of such a bloody conflict translated into a cynicism towards liberal reform in general.

• • • • •

Margaret Sanger and the Fight for Birth Control
1883–1966

When Margaret Sanger and her sister, Ethel Byrne, opened the first birth control clinic in the Brownsville section of Brooklyn in 1916, they anticipated being closed down by the police and being brought to trial and possibly imprisoned for violating the Comstock Law. Passed in 1873 largely through the zealous efforts of moral purity crusader Anthony Comstock, the law made it illegal to disseminate contraceptives and contraceptive information using the services of the United States mail. The Comstock Law strengthened a law passed a year earlier that prohibited sending obscene literature through the mail by designating birth control information as obscene.

What Sanger and Byrne did not know was how many women would take advantage of the window of opportunity they were offering to get advice on birth control and contraceptives. The response was overwhelming. In the 10 days that the clinic remained open, nearly 500 women came in looking for information. That turnout, as much as anything else, convinced Sanger that she was correct in her long-held conviction that women wanted to be able to control their own reproductive capabilities.

Sanger's experiences growing up in an Irish Catholic family in New York were the motivating forces behind her lifelong crusade for birth control. Her mother, Anne Purcell Higgins, had 11 children and several miscarriages, and the toll on her health led to her death at the early age of 49. Sanger's older sisters were expected to, and did, sacrifice their own dreams to step in and provide the physical and financial support necessary to keep the family going.

Sanger escaped the same fate by accepting her sister's offer to pay for college teacher training. She quickly discovered, however, that teaching was not her desire, so she enrolled in nursing school. While there, she met and married William Sanger, an architect and artist. Although she knew that she did not want to emulate her mother's life, Sanger was not yet at the point where she could break away from a lifetime of learned middle-class values. She moved to Westchester with her husband and had three children. A fire that destroyed their newly built home caused Sanger to recognize how precarious was a life built on acquiring things. Her urgent need to be involved in activities that would make a difference was so great that Sanger's husband agreed to move to New York with her to save their marriage. The marriage did not hold together after all, but Sanger had saved herself.

From 1910 to 1914, she threw herself into a series of radical causes, working with people like the labor leaders Elizabeth Gurly Flynn and Big Bill Hayward. She also discovered her own capacity for sexual expression, much of which occurred outside of the bonds of marriage. The discovery provided Sanger with a profound sense of personal power and convinced her that women needed to achieve sexual liberation before anything else because that alone would release repressed or misdirected energy. At the same time, Sanger worked as a visiting nurse on New York's Lower East Side. Confronted with case after case of abortions gone awry because there was no information and no help available, Sanger found her life's work. She was also incensed at the medical professionals who dismissed womens' concerns about multiple childbirths. Sanger often told the story of a woman from the Lower East Side who queried her doctor about how she and her husband Jake might avoid additional pregnancies, because they already had several children. The doctor coldly advised her to tell Jake to "sleep on the roof." It was exactly this attitude that Sanger believed had driven her own mother to an early grave and that she was now determined to fight.

Sanger first ran afoul of the Comstock Law in 1912 when she wrote an article on syphilis for the socialist periodical, *The Call*, and the Post Office ruled that that issue could not be mailed because the article was obscene.

Sanger was determined to remove any association with obscenity from birth control and contraception. She began publishing a distinctly feminist newspaper called *The Woman Rebel*. The Post Office refused to mail it even though the paper contained no explicit advice on birth control. After being indicted in 1914 for violating the Comstock Law, Sanger left for Europe. While there she investigated various methods of birth control and contraceptive devices, which, at the time, consisted primarily of spermicidal douches, diaphragms, condoms, and of course abstinence. Several months into her European sojourn in 1915, Sanger learned that her five-year-old daughter had died of pneumonia. Her sense of guilt was profound, and she returned to the United States. Unlike the authorities who continued to make moral purity a priority, the public was much more sympathetic to Sanger's efforts (because they clearly would be the beneficiaries). Listening to public opinion, the authorities dropped the pending charges against her.

Undaunted and ever more determined to pursue her crusade, in part to commemorate her daughter, Sanger and her sister opened the first birth control clinic. Sanger was convicted of violating the Comstock Law and sentenced to 30 days in jail. Her conviction was not without victory, however. Judge Frederick Crane, while upholding the Comstock Law, acknowledged that doctors need not prescribe condoms only to prevent pregnancy. Crane broadened the interpretation of the law, giving doctors the right to prescribe contraceptives to women to prevent disease as well.

After that Sanger changed her strategy, seeking to elicit the support of the medical profession. The new strategy meant leaving behind her radical feminist beliefs and associates. But in moving towards a middle-class constituency, Sanger was able to garner badly needed financial support from socialites and philanthropists. This infusion of money allowed her to establish the American Birth Control League, the forerunner to Planned Parenthood. Her new support network allowed Sanger to keep open the Birth Control Clinical Research Bureau in New York, the first doctor-staffed birth control clinic in the United States. The clinic kept fastidious records demonstrating the safety of contraceptives and refuting the contention of some medical experts that certain contraceptives caused diseases such as cancer.

By 1938, after the obscenity definitions in the Comstock Law had been altered by federal courts, Sanger and her associates had succeeded in opening a network of 300 birth control clinics nationwide. It was a phenomenal achievement. Sanger retired with her then-husband, Noah Slee, shortly thereafter. Her successors, in an effort to gain even more middle-class support, gradually phased out birth control in favor of the softer and broader concept of family planning, and in 1942 the Birth Control League officially became the Planned Parenthood Association.

Margaret Sanger did more than almost any other American to open the way for women to determine their own destiny by having the option of choosing how many children they would bear, and at what point. Although Sanger herself got sidetracked into the eugenics movement in the 1920s, which proposed that genetic defects could be bred out of the human race, she nevertheless did a tremendous service to women in particular and to society in general with her groundbreaking work in birth control and family planning.

CHAPTER

Between the Wars

T he 1920s should have been a period of significant change for American women. After nearly a century of concentrated effort on behalf of securing the vote, women had won. Hundreds of thousands of women, past and present, could rightfully feel a sense of victory and satisfaction for all the time they had devoted to the cause. Most women had looked to ratification as the end of a long and costly, but ultimately rewarding, campaign. For the majority of women, the ballot was seen more and more as a cure-all for society's, as well as women's ills. However, the differences between the social feminists and the radical feminists continued to divide the women's movement. Moreover, the differences among the social feminists and among the radical feminists became more obvious after the vote was won. Everyone, it seemed, had a different agenda.

The differences did not become immediately clear, however, and until the latter part of the decade, most people held on to the belief that having the vote was going to significantly affect American life. In fact, there were some immediate changes that supported that expectation. For one thing the polling places were changed. Prior to women voters, polling places tended to be located where men congregated: saloons, bars, and barber shops. The new polling places were located at schools and churches. Of course, if the temperance movement had not already secured the prohibition amendment, there might have been much more objection to moving the polling booths to locales where the atmosphere tended to be more wholesome. Many state legislatures began to pass laws favorable to or supported by women, in an effort to appear cooperative. In many states, for the first time, women were allowed to serve on juries. A considerable number of states passed various protective legislation for which social reformers and progressives had lobbied for years. On the congressional level, Congress also responded to the anticipated woman vote. A child labor amendment to the Constitution was passed quickly, although it was never ratified by more than six states. Perhaps the biggest legislative success was passage of the Sheppard-Towner Act of 1921.

THE SHEPPARD-TOWNER ACT

The Sheppard-Towner Act was the first federally funded health care legislation ever passed by Congress. Under the terms of the act, Congress appropriated $1.25 million to establish prenatal clinics and public health centers in any community for which the state was willing to pledge matching funds. The legislation had enormous support among the various women's groups. Mary Anderson and Julia Lathrop of the Children's Bureau, both active supporters of the law, pointed out that infant mortality in the United States had reached 250,000 per year. Florence Kelley, who also fought hard for passage of the bill, considered it a culmination of 40 years work on behalf of women. Several national women's magazines ran a series of timely articles that helped to generate support and keep the issue in the eyes of the public. And, in the event that any congressman did not understand the ramifications of opposing the Sheppard-Towner Act, Harriet Upton, the vice-chairperson of the Republican Party, made it clear that women would not forget who opposed the bill when it came time to cast their ballots. An overwhelmingly large vote in favor of the legislation in both the House and the Senate indicated that congressmen heard and understood the message.

The Sheppard-Towner Act was not without its critics. The National Woman's Party considered it special interest legislation that would perpetuate women's second-class status. Birth control advocate Margaret Sanger found it inadequate because it did not provide for the dissemination of birth control information. As Sanger noted disdainfully, the clinics would teach a woman how to take care of her seventh child, but not how to prevent an eighth. The strongest opposition came from the American Medical Association. Prior to 1921 the idea of well-patient doctor visits—check-ups to prevent medical problems from developing—were not considered part of physicians' medical responsibility. The clinics were mandated to correct this for mothers and their children, but physicians worried that health care was being removed from their control and taken over by the government.

The clinics that were established because of the Sheppard-Towner Act provided information and health care to hundreds of thousands of mothers and their young children. They were generally staffed by women doctors and nurses, and most were located in rural areas where there was little access to health care on a regular basis. Ironically, the success of the clinics and the lucrative potential of well-care service if it was provided by private physicians, also brought the demise of the Sheppard-Towner funding. By 1929 Congress, under continued pressure from the AMA and by then less fearful that women would retaliate in any organized fashion, voted to terminate the program. The program nevertheless caused physicians to absorb preventive health care and well-baby office visits into their private practices. Medical practices expanded thereafter to include office visits for well patients of all ages. But the termination of funding meant that medical care was no longer as widely available in many of the rural communities that had come to depend on it.

AFTER THE VOTE

The major assumption shared by almost everyone—suffragists, antisuffragists, social feminists, radical feminists, politicians—that women would vote as a bloc to effect the changes they desired, proved to be unfounded. In contrast to the fight for the vote, there was no longer one unifying issue that could hold the coalition together. Instead, difference in class, race, ethnicity, philosophy, politics, values, and prejudices made it virtually impossible for women to vote as a bloc. For those women who remained politically active in trying to advance their agenda, the 1920s would be characterized by an ongoing struggle between advocates of protective legislation, who wanted to protect the legal advances made on behalf of women, and advocates of an equal rights amendment, who were willing to forego special protective legislation to secure an equal rights amendment to the Constitution. Though the basic disagreement was not resolved for many years, it provided the proponents on both sides of the question with a new focus, but one that was being argued within the women's movement and not between the women's movement and the rest of society. Thus, it made for a very different kind of struggle than suffrage had been. Instead of one overarching umbrella under which many issues were huddled, there were now many different umbrellas.

In fairness, the burden upon women voters to cure the ills of the world had largely been placed there by women themselves. All of the rhetoric of the suffrage campaign focused on what women would be able to accomplish once they had secured the vote. As more than one historian has pointed out, the success of the suffrage movement was not so much in getting the vote, but in taking a proactive part in their own destiny and changing the course of events. Women had reached out to become part of a larger life than the one confined by the four walls of their homes. Whether the vote accomplished what it was supposed to, the process itself permanently changed the way in which men and women interacted in society.

It is equally true, however, that suffrage came at a time when good will towards reform and reformers was already on the wane. The Progressive Era ended with World War I. The war, in some ways, could be considered the most ambitious and far-reaching effort at reform: to make the world safe for democracy, Americans were constantly reminded, took reform to its farthest reaches. And while the intentions of those who advocated American partici- pation in the war were by no means devious or less honorable than they claimed, the results were nevertheless disappointing. The cynicism over the results of a demanding war, particularly one that claimed so many American lives in so short a time, left most people with a sour taste for more reform. The mood of the country had definitely become politically conservative, and the fact that women were no less subject to the intellectual and emotional currents sweeping the nation is not often acknowledged in assessing the so- called failure of suffragism in the 1920s.

Then too, the leadership that had been able to rally so many women for so long on so many diverse issues seemed incapable of making an effective appeal to the next generation—young women who were just coming of age in the 1920s. There were no up-and-coming Stantons, Anthonys, Kelleys, Lathrops, Catts, Gilmans, Addamses, Pauls, or any of the other luminaries of the women's movement, standing in the wings waiting to take on the mantle of leadership—or, at least, they were not readily apparent. The new genera- tion expressed little interest in women's issues, causes, or institutions. Indeed, the younger generation seemed much more affected by a live-for-the-moment materialism than they were by long-term improvements in the general status of women.

THE FLAPPER

Regardless of how many of their generation actually fit the parameters, the prevailing image of young women in the 1920s was that of the flapper. The flapper represented a new freedom, a willingness to try anything, to flout old social and sexual behavior codes, to dress in a style that her mother might have considered risqué, to frequent speakeasies, to smoke in public, and generally to establish her independence as an individual. The flapper was a natural constituent for the new mass advertising of the era. Cosmetics and clothing in particular became important consumer items.

Perhaps nothing epitomized the image so much as the bathing beauty contests that became popular in the 1920s, most notably the Miss America Pageant. Hoping to keep tourists in Atlantic City beyond the normal end-of- summer Labor Day weekend, the city organized a Rolling Chairs Pageant in 1920. The chairs, decorated much like floats in a parade, rolled along the boardwalk in a long line, with prizes awarded to the most creative. The following year, organizers decided to include a beauty pageant in the Rolling Chairs Pageant. Thus, the Miss American Pageant was born.

A reporter for the *Atlantic City Press*, Herb Test, hired to publicize the event, invited city newspapers to ask their readers to send photos for consid- eration. The winner of each city contest was brought to Atlantic City, all expenses paid, to participate in the pageant—to become, as Test titled it, Miss America. On September 6, 1921, 16-year-old Margaret Gorman of Washington, D.C. became the first Miss America, picked from hundreds of finalists from all over the country. In addition to her title, Gorman was awarded a statuette valued at $5,000.

The pageant was held yearly after that, with the exception of the years between 1927 and 1933, when pageant officials gave in to critics who called it "an immoral display." Pageant officials raised the level of the competition after 1933, hoping to remove from it some of the carnival atmosphere. In 1938 a talent aspect to the contest was introduced. And in 1939 only states, cities, and recognized regions could send contestants to the pageant. Moreover, contestants had to be at least 18 years old and swear to the fact that they had never been married. The whole image of the beauty contest had changed to reflect the seriousness of the times by the late 1930s. The flapper image itself faded into obscurity with the onset of the Great Depression.

The Technological Revolution in the Home

The fact that the flapper image was so popular tended to make people overlook the other images of women that were a part of the 1920s, from the college coed to the professional woman to the political activist to the housewife/consumer. The 1920s ushered in a new age of consumerism that affected everyone, including the housewife, whose range of options now added a new role to her list of duties—that of intelligent consumer. Technological developments of the previous two or three decades were now finding their way into American households. One example was the washing machine.

Laundry was "the white woman's burden . . . the bane of American housemother's professional life," according to Marion Harland, a prolific writer of household advice around the turn of the century. Washing clothes took up as much as one-third of a woman's time if she had no servants, and most women had none. The electric washing machine changed profoundly the way that middle-class American women spent their time.

The invention of the washing machine was one example among many of the technological changes that revolutionized women's lives between 1870 and 1920 and that have continued to simplify them. Small electric water pumps made possible the introduction of running water, while small electric heaters meant that the water could be hot or cold, which made possible kitchen sinks, toilets, bathtubs, and showers, as well as washing machines and ultimately dishwashers. Small electric motors powered vacuum cleaners, ventilation fans, sewing machines, compressors in refrigerators, and eventually electric appliances like can openers, bread makers, juicers, and food processors. Electric heaters ironed clothes and cooked food both as burners and as ovens. Rubber tile floors made kitchen clean up easier, along with white tile walls (along the lower portion) and chemical cleaners. Commercial canning and refrigeration made preserved, processed foods and fresh meats available in all seasons, while modern transport and industrial marketing replaced the weekly baking day with packaged breads. Chores that had once taken hours were now done in minutes; tasks that had once left women drained were now incidental.

Technology meant that wealthy women needed fewer servants at a time when help was getting harder and harder to find, while women of lesser means were freed from many of the jobs that had previously defined their existence. In the first case, machinery caused social distinctions to be relaxed, as wealthy women no longer had to maintain the air of authority over a staff of dozens. In the second case, machinery led women to widen their horizons, participate in leisure and social activities, and study. Technological change made possible the "New Woman" of the 1890s as well as the "Flapper" of the 1920s; it released women into the work force and set the basic conditions of modern life.

The Industrial Revolution occurred in two phases. The first, from 1760 to roughly 1870, was the age of coal and iron, factories and railroads. It revolutionized production, but left daily life in most ways unchanged. In contrast, the second Industrial Revolution, which lasted well into the 20th century and in some respects is still in effect, brought steel and electricity, oil and chemicals, and it profoundly altered the most fundamental aspects of human life. The impact of apparently minor technological innovations on women's lives and opportunities, their behaviors and attitudes, has been so huge that it is almost impossible to perceive. Women's lives are today more different in their most basic conditions from those of their grandmothers than between any three generations in history. All of these developments began to filter down into private homes in the 1920s, aided and abetted by mass production and mass advertising, both of which were necessary to bring products to the individual. But if the new technology freed women from some of the drudgery of everyday household chores, it also established a higher standard of housekeeping that quickly became accepted in middle-class homes.

WOMEN IN THE WORK FORCE

Minority women saw very little change as a result of either suffrage or progressive reform. During World War I, large numbers of African Americans left the rural South for the urban North, intent on becoming part of the war-related work force. Though a few African American women were able to find work in factories or in other occupations, most continued to go into domestic service. After World War I, domestic service in big cities became more and more dominated by African American women. Nearly 75 percent of the domestic servants and laundresses were black. White collar work, where many more opportunities existed, was off limits to African Americans, with a few exceptions.

A new range of clerical and secretarial jobs, however, began to absorb the supply of young, white, middle-class women eager to establish their independence as wage earners. Between 1920 and 1930, two million women found employment as secretaries, clerks, telephone operators, typists, and stenographers—20 percent of the female labor force. Professional women increased their presence in the work force as well. By 1930 nearly 15 percent of the female work force was engaged in professional occupations, and some professions were dominated by women. Ninety-eight percent of all nurses, 91 percent of all librarians, and 68 percent of all social workers were women. In addition, 30 percent of all college professors and instructors were women. Even dominating or having significant representation in these fields, however, still left women with only 11 percent of all professional jobs.

As for working-class women, the vast majority still tended to fill the lowest-paid unskilled work category. Housewife, childbearer, and child rearer remained the occupational category for 75 percent of all women. Of the 25 percent of adult women in the work force, women were represented most heavily in the service work category—for example, commercial cleaning and food preparation. Fully 88 percent of all service work was done by women.

Working-class women were still not welcomed into labor unions, most of which were having their own problems in the 1920s. But a series of experimental schools for working women started up during and after the war, not to provide women with an education that would allow them to move into white collar or professional work, but rather to expose them to some of the broader issues affecting their lives. The University of Wisconsin ran one such school, and there were others that operated for limited periods in other parts of the country. Perhaps the best known of these schools was the Bryn Mawr Summer School for Women in Industry.

The Bryn Mawr Summer School for Women in Industry

M. Carey Thomas, educator, feminist, and president of Bryn Mawr College, brought to that institution her own personal standard of excellence that she expected everyone else associated with the college to strive for, whether faculty, student, or support personnel. Thomas shaped Bryn Mawr in an effort to make it the elite of the elite women's schools. In her view Bryn Mawr had to maintain standards equal to or better than those of the most demanding men's colleges. Few women who passed through Bryn Mawr's halls denied that the Thomas stamp remained on them long after they left.

Between 1921 and 1938, hundreds of working women who passed through Bryn Mawr, however briefly, were also touched by the forceful and often

controversial Thomas. Thomas, along with Professor of Social Welfare Hilda
Smith, organized the Bryn Mawr Summer School for Women in Industry in
an effort to bring to working women some of the education that they were not
privy to because of their economic backgrounds. The hope was that a summer
of instruction in a variety of fields, including economics, history, and politics,
would help prepare the participants to step into leadership roles in organizing
and sustaining unions.

Though women workers were never well represented by established unions,
in the post–World War I era, their participation plummeted to new lows. To
be sure, all unions were experiencing drastic declines during the new conservatism of the 1920s, but women's unionization dropped to less than 3 percent,
with only one woman in 34 protected by union membership. At the same
time, the Women's Trade Union League had begun to shift its focus from
organization to education, so the prospects of women becoming unionized
were dimmer than they had been in several decades. Moreover, the protective legislation laws enacted under the aegis of the progressives tended to
segregate women further, prohibiting them from many jobs that required
night work, for example. In trades where few women worked anyway, protective legislation tended to favor male employees, because there were fewer
restrictions placed on them.

The Bryn Mawr program was financed by union funds, which enabled
approximately 60 women workers to spend between six and eight weeks each
summer on the Bryn Mawr campus. The program mirrored the Brookwood
Labor College program, which also began in 1921. While Brookwood concentrated on training its coeducational classes on union activism, Bryn Mawr's
focus was more humanistic. For most of the women who participated in the
summer school program, their lives were changed immutably, as were the
lives of the faculty members with whom they came in contact, perhaps just as
significantly. The summer school, in many ways, was a politicizing experience
for faculty members previously insulated from the reality of working-class
lives and work. Many of the women workers who participated did move into
union leadership roles, with several becoming vice presidents of national
unions. And many of the faculty members turned to public service careers,
either in addition to or in place of their academic careers. Notable in the
latter category was Esther Peterson who, years later as the head of the
Women's Bureau, would be instrumental in the establishment of the President's
Commission on the Status of Women in the Kennedy Administration.

The Bryn Mawr Summer School for Women in Industry continued until
1938. As the depression deepened and less funding was available for nones-
sential programs, programs like Bryn Mawr's began to close down. Yet, the
impact that the summer school program had upon women who attended
remained with them for decades. Surveys conducted in the mid-1980s, in

which both workers and faculty were interviewed, revealed that the program affected their lives and their self-images positively. For them, the school was a profound experience that changed not only their lives but the lives of many working women.

THE DEPRESSION

Just as the depression of the 1930s affected the Bryn Mawr summer school, so did it affect everything else. Unemployment reached an all-time high of 25 percent. In occupations where both men and women were employed, women were let go first, on the grounds that working women did not really need to work because they were not the heads of household. It was an absurd assumption because, as is the overwhelming case today, the majority of women who worked for wages did so because their income was necessary to the family's survival, because they had to support themselves, or, in some cases, because they were the heads of household. Because most married women did not work outside of the home, women workers tended to fall mostly into the latter two categories.

In some important ways, women bore the brunt of the depression. If they were married and their husbands lost their jobs, women had the burden of finding ways to make do in the emergency. They still had to run their households and feed and clothe their children, but they had to do so without an income. Moreover, there was enormous social pressure on women who held jobs to give up their job so that an unemployed man could find work. The notion that women worked only for "pin money" was so widely held that even someone who should have known better—Secretary of Labor Frances Perkins, the first woman cabinet officer—chastised women workers as "selfish and short-sighted." Between 1932 and 1937, Section 213 of the National Economy Act prohibited more than one family member from holding a civil service job with the federal government. Although Section 213 was opposed by most women's groups, the only government representative who opposed it was First Lady Eleanor Roosevelt. The prohibition remained in force, and two-thirds of the federal employees dismissed under this regulation were women.

Another barometer of the depression, besides loss of jobs, was a drop in marriage and birth rates. With the uncertainty of a prolonged economic depression looming over them, marriage-aged young adults tended to put that decision on hold. Between 1929 and 1934, the marriage rate dropped precipitously. In some instances eligible men just disappeared because they were so devastated. Many men felt that they had lost control over all aspects of their lives. Never before had they gone through long periods when there was no work to be found anywhere and no prospects in the foreseeable future. With such dire prospects, how could they marry and support a spouse?

Not only were couples delaying marriage, but married couples were beginning to think for the first time about the consequences of having additional children. For more than 60 years prior to the depression, most couples, with no real access to birth control information because of the restrictions imposed by the Comstock Law, practiced only rudimentary birth control, if any. Without a pressing economic deterrent, there was little difference between one or two children and several children, at least in the minds of most people.

Numerous people had been prosecuted under the Comstock Law, including the radical Emma Goldman and, of course, Margaret Sanger, by zealous enforcers who equated birth control with obscenity. When the Comstock Law was passed, physicians and the American Medical Association were in the forefront of those who supported the legislation. Yet, by the 1930s, because of people like Sanger, physicians favored the dissemination of such information. So it was something of an irony that physicians' hands were tied because of a law that the AMA had endorsed more than half a century before.

For years Sanger had been conducting guerrilla warfare against the legal system in an effort to overturn the most harmful impediments to establishing a meaningful birth control movement. From smuggling illegal diaphragms into the United States to testing the constitutionality of laws outlawing contraceptives, Sanger campaigned vigorously to put reproductive control in the hands of women. Sanger's Committee on Federal Legislation for Birth Control initiated a legal suit to test the Comstock Law when it sent contraceptive material through the mail, confident that the material would be seized by the Post Office. The resultant suit, *United States v. One Package*, was decided by a federal court in 1936. In its decision the court ruled that new clinical information regarding contraceptives forced a reinterpretation of the Comstock Law. Birth control, the court declared, was not synonymous with obscenity and henceforth mailing contraceptive information intended for use by physicians would no longer be illegal.

The court's reversal of Comstock Law interpretation and its new ruling regarding appropriate birth control materials for physicians cleared the way for a resolution passed the following year by the American Medical Association. In 1937 the AMA voted to recognize contraception as a legitimate medical service that should be taught in medical schools. Sanger's goal of winning professional medical support for birth control had been achieved. The legitimacy necessary for the success of birth control had been established. Ironically, although this legal reversal of a punitive law was certainly welcome, individuals on their own had been seriously engaging in birth control for several years. Much like the decline in the marriage rate from the late 1920s to the mid-1930s, the birth rate declined also, although at a much steeper rate. Births per 1,000 women dropped from 97.4 to 75.7 by 1933.

Not all families were so harshly affected by the depression. Very poor families, such as tenant farmers in the South, who had always worked and lived on the margins, did not necessarily notice a substantial difference in their condition. On the other hand, farm families from the Midwest and Southwest were hit hard, suffering first through several years of drought and crop failure, and then losing their farms to the banks for failure to meet mortgage payments. Many of these families became migrants, packing belongings and family in available vehicles and following the latest rumor of work.

Social Security

New Deal efforts to provide relief for American families were not necessarily directed at particular groups and, in many instances, left certain groups out of the relief loop. African Americans, for example, received very little aide from New Deal agencies. People who worked in certain occupations, such as domestic workers, tended to be exempted from any benefits. But in other respects, the New Deal was the culmination of what many progressives had worked for for decades. For instance, child labor was eliminated under the National Recovery Act in 1933. Perhaps the most far-reaching New Deal legislation were the Social Security Act and the Fair Labor Standards Act, both of which benefited women. Prior to passage of the Social Security Act of 1935, the government failed to acknowledge that the country had long before outgrown the idealized concept of Jeffersonian agricultural self-sufficiency. In an industrial society that periodically fell victim to the vagaries of severe market fluctuations, and whose workers had only rented apartments or mortgaged homes rather than family farms to see them through economic difficulties, social reformers had long argued that some kind of government-guaranteed security was crucial. Indeed, the New Deal, mandated to reform a crippled system that had been devastated by depression, represented an opportunity to insure that future generations would not be left unprotected when disaster struck.

The primary provision of the Social Security Act was retirement pensions for workers, both male and female, who had reached age 65 or older. In addition, it provided coverage for dependent wives and mothers with young children, which was a victory for the protective legislationists, like Florence Kelley, Mary Anderson, and Mary Elizabeth Dreier, who had worked for decades trying to protect women and children. These women, close colleagues of First Lady Eleanor Roosevelt, had worked with the administration to secure these provisions. Next to the dramatic decrease in the number of women workers over the age of 65, the greatest impact of Social Security on the lives of Americans was the support of dependent widows and children, and the educational benefits that these children had access to. But it took another 40 years and the renewed feminist movement of the 1970s for the government to make changes in the Social Security Act that afforded protection for homemakers who had spent years, sometimes decades, raising children and maintaining a home, only to be left without retirement protection when they were involved in a divorce. Despite the criticisms of the system in its current form, Social Security has probably had as significant an economic impact on the lives of women as any other social reform enacted in the 20th century.

The depression years were particularly difficult for most people who normally held industrial jobs. Working women, as we have seen, were caught in the double bind of needing to work more than ever because of the overall state of the economy and the probability that one or more contributors to the family income was unemployed, and a public perception that a woman should not be taking a job that a man could do. Those women who found themselves employed during the depression were likely to be working for seriously reduced wages. In some textile mills in the South, women worked for five cents an hour, and some unscrupulous manufacturers hired women apprentices with the provision that they would not begin earning wages until the apprenticeship was completed. When that time approached, the apprentices were fired. For these and other reasons, advocates of protective legislation and minimum wage laws continued, even at the height of the depression, to lobby for reforms.

The Fair Labor Standards Act

Minimum wage laws had been on the protectionists' agenda since the turn of the century. Indeed, many states had passed minimum wage laws, and sometimes 10-hour-workday laws, only to have the Supreme Court rule them unconstitutional. As late as 1935, the Supreme Court was still finding fault with establishing wages and hours when it struck down the National Industrial Recovery Act (IRA), a New Deal effort to revive the economy that included establishing wage and hour guidelines according to industry. Almost immediately, the Roosevelt administration responded with new legislation to take the place of the IRA. The Fair Labor Standards Act (FLSA) was passed by Congress in 1938.

Under the terms of the FLSA, which applied to all workers in specified industries, regardless of sex or age, a minimum wage of 25 cents per hour was established. Over a seven-year period, this was to increase to 40 cents per hour. At the same time, a maximum work week of 44 hours was imposed, which was to eventually decrease to 40 hours. The FLSA prohibited the employment of children under the age of 16. Of course, the administration and everyone else waited for the Supreme Court to rule on the constitutionality of the new legislation before relying on its permanency (though the FLSA had to be observed by all parties in the meantime). As everyone expected, the wait was relatively short. In 1941 the Court ruled, in the case of *United States v. Darby*, that the FLSA did not violate the constitution.

After nearly four decades of effort, a minimum wage law protecting women and men was in place. The FLSA was not without some flaws, however. It did not cover, for example, domestic work or farm work, which meant that African American women were largely unaffected. In 1930, 90 percent of employed African American women worked either as domestics or as farm laborers. Most African American women spent the 1930s unemployed. Moreover, they were least likely to be included in federal relief programs. On the plus side, whereas previous wage and hour restrictions applied only to women and only covered about 12 percent of the adult female work force, the FLSA covered 57 percent of women workers and 38 percent of male workers. And, of course, the elimination of child labor, which had been fought for so long, was finally accomplished.

The FLSA also made moot an issue that had long divided the women's movement. Ever since 1921, the equal rights advocates had argued that protection should apply to everyone, otherwise women would always remain second-class citizens. Protectionists, fearful of losing all the ground they had gained since the late 19th century, argued that the laws were necessary to protect women who otherwise would be at the mercy of unscrupulous employers. Overnight, the FLSA had eliminated that whole argument on both sides. Passage of the new legislation, then, helped to pave the way for eventual reconciliation of the opposing camps of the women's movement.

The years between World War I and World War II tested women's capacity to survive and grow. Whereas the suffrage years had been more of a collective experience, the 1920s and the depression were very much a backdrop for individual experience. From the flapper's frantic insistence on living life her own way, to the depression-era housewife who became the glue that held the family together in whatever way presented itself, women in the pre–World War II era demonstrated a resourcefulness and a tenacity of will that was not fully recognized as such. Heroines of the era tended to be women who pursued an individual goal rather than a cause: aviator Amelia Earhart; painter Grandma Moses; singer Marian Anderson; First Lady Eleanor Roosevelt; photographers Dorothea Lange and Margaret Bourke-White; novelist Pearl Buck; actors Bette Davis and Katharine Hepburn; and the nameless women refugees from Appalachia and the drought-ridden Great Plains, whose faces said volumes about what hard times were really like.

● ● ● ● ●

Margaret Bourke-White (1906–1971) and Dorothea Lange (1895–1965) Photograph the Faces of the Depression

From the "Migrant Mother" series, photo by Dorothea Lange.

For almost four decades, from the late 1920s through the 1960s, two of the world's best photographers were American women. Dorothea Lange and Margaret Bourke-White created brilliant photographs that captured the pain, despair, hope, determination, and humanity in the faces of Americans during two of the most trying experiences of the 20th century: the Great Depression and World War II. Both women were frequent contributors to *Life* magazine's pictorial cavalcade. As a consequence, hundreds of millions of people around the world have seen one or more photographs taken by Lange and Bourke-White.

Dorothea Lange wanted to be a photographer from the time she was a child growing up in New York City. She completed a degree in teacher training, though she never taught, and she very briefly studied photography at Columbia University. But a move to San Francisco, marriage, and two children ended her formal training. In San Francisco, Lange gained a reputation as a portrait photographer. Her success did not insulate her from the misery of others, and as the depression deepened in the early 1930s, Lange began photographing the faces of white-collar workers who, for the first time in their lives, were unemployed. A 1934 exhibit of those photographs led to a job with the Farm Security Administration. Given the task of putting the lives of farm workers on film, she helped the rest of America see how bleak farm life had become. Her 1939 book of photographs, entitled *American Exodus: A Record of Human Erosion*, won critical acclaim as well as popular success.

Lange, the first woman to win a Guggenheim Fellowship, turned her camera towards another subject shortly after World War II began. As a photographer for the War Relocation Authority (WRA), she recorded the internment of Japanese Americans in detention camps. While the WRA expected her photos to reflect their point of view, Lange chose instead to record from the point of view of those imprisoned. As a result, she left the WRA and went on to another agency for the duration of the war. After the war Lange's work appeared regularly in *Life* magazine, and she spent the final few years of her life pulling together an exhibit for the Museum of Modern Art. She was the first woman to be so honored. Lange died in 1965, five years after one of her most poignant photographs from the depression years—

Migrant Mother—was chosen as one of the 50 best photographs of the century.

Margaret Bourke-White helped to invent the genre of photographic essay. Also a native New Yorker, she graduated from Rutgers University in New Jersey, then pursued her interest in photography in a graduate program at Columbia University. As one of *Life* magazine's original staff, not only was her photograph chosen for the cover of the magazine's first issue, but her photos were regularly featured thereafter. As a young photojournalist, Bourke-White focused on an area generally considered to belong to men: industry. In 1929 *Fortune* magazine hired Bourke-White as a staff photographer. A self-proclaimed feminist from her early youth on, Bourke-White never refused a job because it was inappropriate for a woman. She traveled to Russia several times, and in 1931 her first book, *Eyes on Russia,* was well received by many Americans suffering the ravages of the depression. Eventually, Bourke-White published two more collections of photographs focusing on the Russian people. Not yet in her mid-thirties, Bourke-White could already claim a solid reputation with a number of publishers.

Like Lange, Bourke-White spent part of the depression years traveling America, especially the South, recording the lives of the desperately poor. For her this sojourn was more than a journalistic exercise, for it opened her eyes to subjects far more interesting than the dispassionate industrial photographs with which she had earlier been preoccupied. Bourke-White's depression coverage was influenced by her association with writer Erskine Caldwell, with whom she collaborated on several projects and whom she eventually married. They did two subsequent depression books, including the remarkable *Have You Seen Their Faces?*, published in 1937, which elevated Bourke-White's photography to new heights.

When World War II began, Bourke-White immediately began lobbying for a war correspondent slot, and in 1942 she became the first woman provided with army credentials as a war correspondent. As with everything she did, Bourke-White threw herself wholly into covering the war, bringing back the faces of American servicemen, sometimes at the risk of her life. During the North African invasion in 1942, she was on board a ship that was torpedoed, and when Patton's army crossed the German border, Bourke-White crossed with them. When Bourke-White sent back extraordinary photos of Buchenwald, *Life*'s editors had to decide whether to go with long-standing tradition not to print the most excruciating scenes of battle or to print what they knew to be the most compelling photos of the war. Bourke-White's photos ran in *Life* magazine.

After the war Bourke-White continued her quest for photos that told entire stories. In India she took the last photo of Gandhi before his assassination, she covered rebellion in South Africa, and she captured scenes from the Korean War. All together, before her retirement Bourke-White spent 33 years as *Life*'s leading photographer.

Hattie McDaniel, African American Actress
1895–1952

As an actress, Hattie McDaniel immortalized herself in the role of Mammy, the memorable house slave in *Gone With the Wind*, the 1939 movie based on Margaret Mitchell's novel. McDaniel also won an Oscar as Best Supporting Actress, the first time the award was won by an African American actor or actress. Ironically, the Mammy role was also a metaphor for McDaniel's career as an actress, for she received her greatest recognition when she was playing either slave or servant roles that reflected not so much her acting abilities as Hollywood's inability to see her in anything other than servile parts.

McDaniel, born in Wichita, Kansas, in 1895 and raised in Colorado, was one of 13 children of Henry and Susan McDaniel. She began her career alongside her father in the Henry McDaniel Minstrel Show. By her teen years, she had moved into a tentative career as a blues singer.

In 1931, McDaniel relocated to Los Angeles and there began her film career, moving from bit parts to more substantive roles, but always as a servant of one kind or another. Although McDaniel became associated with the South, she actually had to teach herself a southern dialect for her roles. McDaniel was part of a small coterie of African American actresses, including Ethel Waters and Louise Beavers, who dominated the available roles. She was not even credited for many of her earliest parts, and it was not until her 1932 performances in *Blonde Venus* and *I'm No Angel* that McDaniel did receive credit. For the next several years McDaniel appeared in virtually all films featuring a black maid or a Mammy. By the end of the decade, McDaniel boasted nearly 50 credits, including *Show Boat*, *Alice Adams*, *The Mad Miss Manton*, and several *Our Gang* shorts.

McDaniel's breakthrough performance came when David Selznick cast her as Mammy. Her discomfort with playing servant roles was offset by her desire to remain employed in a severely limited profession. That reluctance did not save her from coming under attack in the 1940s by the National Association for the Advancement of Colored People (NAACP), who said she perpetuated stereotypes of black Americans.

Although she continued to take similar types of roles, for example, as Beulah the maid in a popular 1940s radio program, McDaniel did portray at least one multidimensional African American woman. In her performance in the 1941 production of *In This Our Life*, she presented to the movie-going public the dilemma of being black in America. McDaniel played a mother, Minerva Clay, whose son is unjustly accused of murder. The film, which also starred Bette Davis and Olivia DeHaviland, another alumna of *Gone With the Wind*, in some ways was far more of a breakthrough for African American actresses than McDaniel's Academy Award-winning role. Audiences, who knew that Minerva's son was innocent, were confronted with the reality of racism when Minerva observed resignedly that the police always assumed blacks were lying.

Increasingly criticized for her persistent desire to act regardless of the roles available to her, happiness also seemed to elude McDaniel in her personal life. She had several failed marriages, complicated undoubtedly by the criticisms of her success that came from fellow African Americans. Ill health plagued her final years, and in 1952 McDaniel died after an unsuccessful bout with cancer.

CHAPTER 11

Going to War, Coming Home

B y the late 1930s, after nearly a decade of depression, the economy was still only sluggish at best. The nation seemed to have reached an economic plateau for which there was no apparent or easily implemented solution. With political conditions in Europe worsening by the day because of the fascist policies of Hitler and Mussolini, and with discomfort building over Japan's military buildup, President Franklin Roosevelt, from 1937 on, tried to prepare America for the possibility of war. Resistance from the isolationists, still bitter over the World War I experience, made it difficult for Roosevelt to make much headway until the long-time ally, England, appeared to be faltering under the onslaught from Hitler's aggressively advancing army and bombing campaign. By 1940 Roosevelt was able at least to authorize military aid to European allies, and industrial production in the United States began to pick up. When Roosevelt announced in 1940 that he wanted the United States to produce 50,000 airplanes a year, as well as other heavy armaments, people thought he was being far too optimistic about productive capacity of the United States. Actually, because industry had been operating so far below capacity for so long, it was the industrialists, economists, and other experts who were underestimating its capabilities.

With starts and fits, the economy began to move back into full production, but it was not until after December 7, 1941, that everyone seemed to be reading from the same page. After the Japanese attack on America's principal naval base at Pearl Harbor, Hawaii, opposition to American entry into the war disappeared. With only one dissenting vote, that of Representative Jeannette Rankin, the pacifist congresswoman from Montana, Congress voted a declaration of war.

AMERICA AT WAR

Many of the new opportunities opened up to women as a result of United States entry into World War II turned out to be temporary. But in profound ways, the war initiated changes in the American work force and in the lives of women from which there was no going back.

The immediate problem facing the American government was that of quickly producing the tools necessary to challenge effectively the German and Japanese armies, both of which had been stockpiling weapons and supplies for years. Everything from uniforms to bombers had to be produced. The attack on Pearl Harbor had destroyed a significant portion of the American navy. Battleships, destroyers, troop ships, aircraft carriers, supply ships—the necessity for more of everything to fight a war was daunting, to say the least.

To accomplish the monumental production task, industrialists turned to a heretofore untapped labor source: middle-class women. The desire to contribute to the war effort and a reasonable compensation attracted hundreds of thousands of women who had never before been involved in the industrial work force. Between 1940 and 1945, the number of women in the American work force increased from 12 million to 19 million. Former barriers to employment, including marital status and age, were removed from many jobs, including teaching. While "Rosie the Riveter" was a highly publicized icon symbolizing the willingness of women to participate in the war effort, women were entering a number of previously restricted jobs, and in some cases, by the war's end, the job category had been transferred from male to female. During the depression, white collar jobs including bank tellers, cashiers, and office clerks were considered male jobs. By the end of the war, these jobs had become female jobs. One of the biggest changes came about in government employment. Previously, most government employees were men. Over the course of the war, women moved into government jobs in unprecedented numbers, and the government became the single biggest employer of female workers.

Domestic service largely disappeared during the war as thousands of African Americans, who had made up the vast majority of domestic servants, left these jobs to work in other areas, particularly defense factories. Fully half of the African Americans who had held domestic service jobs quit to take more lucrative and higher status jobs. As a consequence, the remaining domestic servants could ask for higher wages and better work conditions.

Professional women also found themselves in demand for the first time. Military commissions for female physicians who wanted to enter the service, lawyer jobs for degreed women who previously find only legal secretary work, administrators, teachers, and journalists—in all these professional occupations, women found themselves able to move beyond levels at which they were previously underemployed because of the vacancies left by newly mobilized men.

The shape of the work force and its impact on women was felt in other ways as well. The percentage of married women entering the work force increased by more than one-third, from just under 15 percent of all women workers to almost 23 percent. At the same time, the age of women in the work force increased sharply, and for the first time, women in the 35- to 44-year-old age bracket were represented in large numbers. Between 1940 and 1944, the total number of women in the work force rose from 25 percent to 35 percent, and the number of married women from 800,000 to three million. The war emergency transformed women from a marginal to a basic labor supply. This trend continued even after the war ended.

The single greatest area where women workers were needed was in industry. A massive government campaign urged women to do their patriotic duty by joining the labor force. "Rosie the Riveter" and "Winnie the Welder" became national heroines, the symbols of women's willingness to do whatever had to be done to bring the war to a speedy and victorious conclusion. Defense plants absorbed two million women workers almost overnight, putting them to work doing everything from making airplanes to assembling machine guns and building ships. Many of the restrictions placed against women by protective legislation were either abandoned entirely or temporarily suspended, so that women could now work overtime, work different shifts, and engage in types of heavy labor previously prohibited.

With more married women in the work force, more mothers with children under the age of 14 were now working. One area that remained off-limits, insofar as politicians and the government was concerned, was that of child care. Moreover, the upper-level women in the administration concurred. Both Frances Perkins, FDR's secretary of labor, and Mary Anderson, head of the Women's Bureau, believed fervently that, regardless of the emergency, a woman's first job was still to care for her children, and women had to figure out how to do both. Consequently, for the most part there were no provisions for child care. Women associated public child care with welfare, so there was no overwhelmingly demand for government intervention from them, either. While other countries, England for example, had instituted programs to assist mothers during the emergency, no such help was forthcoming from the government until 1943, when the Lanham Act, containing a provision for government-sponsored child care centers, was passed. Very few centers were opened, however, because several agencies had to be involved in each center and the various chiefs responsible for making decisions had difficulty seeing eye-to-eye. By 1946 the funding for such centers was suspended entirely.

Most of the women who went into the work force wanted to go into defense work because the wages were significantly higher than that in factories producing commercial goods. Women in low-paying jobs, such as waitressing and laundressing, quickly shifted over to higher-paying jobs and many low-wage jobs went unfilled. Women were still earning less than men doing comparable work, but equal pay or equal rights was not an issue for most women at the time. A few of the old-time reformers, like Mary Anderson of the Women's Bureau, complained that women were not being adequately consulted about job allocation and related war work and needs, but their voices went largely unheeded except for lip-service responses. For the most part, upper-level planning on both the war front and the domestic front was still considered men's work.

As an example of how capable the new labor force was, by 1944 industry was turning out 120,000 new airplanes every year, far exceeding the initial requests that everyone assumed would be impossible to fulfill. Moreover, by 1944 ships were being turned out from keel laying to launching in a record 10 to 11 days. If executives were nervous about taking in so many women to perform what they considered male jobs, their fears soon evaporated, as women responded to the demands placed upon them admirably.

At the same time, working women were experiencing, on a large scale, the double phenomenon of taking sole responsibility for making family decisions regarding everything, including the allocation of financial resources, and earning a paycheck over which they had sole discretion. Before the war most women said they wanted to work outside the home only until the war was over and the soldiers returned home. By the end of the war, their lives and sensibilities had changed so markedly that more than half wanted to remain in the work force for both personal fulfillment and the opportunity to earn their own money. For young, single women, work was also changed immutably. Many of them traveled away from home for the first time to take advantage of job opportunities. The whole notion of delaying marriage and family to have a career, however brief, also took hold among many women.

In many significant ways, then, the war changed a number of American women: in their outlook towards family issues, in their desire to earn their own way, in their willingness to take advantage of new opportunities, and in their refusal to return to prewar sensibilities. At the same time, some things in the area of employment did not change in any fundamental way. Job categories tended to still move along two tracks, with some jobs classified as male and others as female, with little opportunity for women to cross over these lines. And wages for male workers in equivalent jobs continued to be higher than wages for female workers. By and large, however, it is hard to argue that working women did not make significant gains as a consequence of the war.

Women in the Military

Since the turn of the century, women have served in the military as nurses in formally organized permanent military units. In 1901 the Army Nurse Corps was established, followed in 1908 by the Navy Nurse Corps. For the next 30 years, with one brief exception, women were allowed to serve in the military only as nurses. During World War I, a loophole in the legislation affecting military personnel allowed the government to enlist women as navy yeomen, filling jobs as telephone operators and clerks in order to relieve male personnel for active duty. Despite the outstanding service performed by these female yeomen, that loophole was soon closed. Unofficially, of course, women have served the nation in a variety of military capacities as far back as the Revolutionary War, when they traveled with Washington's army as nurses and quartermasters. In that war and in the Civil War, numerous instances have been recorded of women disguising themselves as men in order to join combat units.

When the United States entered World War II, women began to be officially accepted into military units in other than nursing roles. Representative Edith Nourse Rogers of Massachusetts sponsored legislation to establish a women's army corps, and on May 15, 1942, President Franklin Roosevelt signed Public Law 554, creating the Women's Auxiliary Army Corps (WAAC), which had partial military status. In 1943 Congress abolished the WAAC in favor of the Women's Army Corps (WAC), which gave women personnel full military status with rank and benefits equal to those of male personnel. On July 30, 1942, Public Law 689 created the WAVES (Women Accepted for Volunteer Emergency Service). The WAVES had the status of male reservists. Mildred McAfee, the president of Wellesley College, became the first director of the WAVES, with the rank of navy captain. Later in 1942 women in the United States Coast Guard, called SPARS, from *Semper Paratus* (Always Prepared), the Coast Guard motto, were also accepted on the same basis as male reservists. The Marines did not create a women's corps until February 1943, nor did they assign a distinctive name to their female marines. Marines were simply marines.

Most African American women who served in the military belonged to the WAC. The WAC accepted both white and black enlistees, although, like the men's service, there was segregation within the corps and, of course, discrimination. In the navy, plans to increase African American enrollment to 10 percent never reached fruition, and by 1945 there were still less than 50 African American WAVES. Even fewer African Americans served with either the SPARS or the marines.

In all of the women's branches of the military service, women freed up men for combat posts during World War II. Women performed a variety of jobs, including telephone operators, clerks, supply clerks, machinists, mechanics, drivers, intelligence gatherers, carpenters, cooks—virtually any job that was not classified as combat. Although there was considerable doubt in the beginning regarding women's ability to perform military jobs, when the military brass discovered how efficiently they performed, generals were asking for more women to take the place of men who could be freed up for combat.

Dwight Eisenhower, as Supreme Allied Commander, asked for more WACs than belonged to the entire corps. Over the course of the war, approximately 350,000 women joined various branches of the service. At peak strength 271,000 women were members of the military. Of this number approximately 4,000 were African Americans, not because they were any less patriotic but because there was simply less opportunity.

In June 1948 Congress passed the Women's Armed Services Integration Act, which made women's corps a permanent part of the military. It was another 20 years before women's corps were abolished altogether and women were accepted directly into various military branches. Women have continued to serve in all branches of the military, making up about 10 percent of the total personnel. The controversy over whether women should be allowed to take on combat roles continues, although there are signs that even those barriers are crumbling. In 1993 women aviators were given permission to fly fighter jets. Breaking down the combat job barrier is considered important because top-level command posts in the military have always gone to individuals with combat experience.

Women Pilots

Women were flying airplanes decades before World War II began. In 1911, seven years after the historic flight at Kitty Hawk, the first American woman, Harriet Quimby, earned her pilot's license. By the time America entered the first world war, 11 women held pilot's licenses, but many more were flying without licenses. Women pilots were prominent during the barnstorming 1920s, and at least one woman, Mabel Cody, owned her own flying circus. In 1929 women pilots organized a group called the Ninety-Nines. By 1929 the first women pilots' air race had been established, attracting some women who wanted the prize money, but many more who wanted to demonstrate their skills. Perhaps the most famous woman pilot, Amelia Earhart, made her historic solo flight across the Atlantic in 1932.

Another female pilot, Jackie Cochran, won 17 speed races by 1940, including beating a field of male aviators in the 1936 Bendix Transcontinental Air Race. When World War II erupted in Europe, Cochran immediately began thinking about a women's air force and enlisted Eleanor Roosevelt's support in bringing the idea to fruition. For two years Cochran lobbied politicians to no avail. Finally, in the summer of 1941, frustrated with the American neutrality that kept it on the sidelines while nations fell to fascism, Cochran contracted to fly a bomber from Canada to England, then joined the British Air Transport Authority as a captain. She then began recruiting other American women pilots. Until December 1941 they flew all types of military aircraft, from the giant bombers to small experimental fighters. When Pearl Harbor was attacked, bringing the United States into the war, Cochran returned to the United States. With the help of Air Corps General Hap

Arnold, she created the Women's Air Service Pilots (WASPs), based in Sweetwater, Texas.

The WASPs was not a military organization. Women who wanted to join had to have their own pilot's license and at least 200 hours of flying time. They had to pay their own way to Sweetwater, and initially, they had to supply their own wardrobe because uniforms were not issued until the lack of them created problems for the pilots. Their lack of recognizable uniforms made them appear to be interlopers, trespassers, or—worse yet—spies on the airfields. They also had to undergo a six-month-long training program. As civilians contracting with the Army Air Corps, the WASPs lived in military housing and followed military orders. But they had no military rank and no benefits, including insurance. When a WASP died in the line of duty, as 38 of them did, their families were expected to pay for their funerals. In one instance a WASP head-of-household supporting several children died in a plane crash. Although she had over 2,500 hours of flying time with the WASPs, her comrades had to take up a collection to send her body back home.

For nearly three years, the WASPs flew every type of military aircraft that male pilots flew. Primary tasks included breaking in and delivering new planes, towing glider planes for the male cadets learning to fly, towing target for gunnery practice, and flying tracking planes for artillery students learning to follow planes at night. WASPs also had to test planes that cadets reported as having mechanical problems. In an effort to reproduce the reported problems, the WASPs put the planes through dangerous maneuvers, obviously at the risk of their lives.

Toward the end of 1944, Cochran, believing that the WASPs had more than proved their value to the war effort, appeared before Congress to demand that it either make the organization a military branch or disband it. Already under pressure from male pilots looking ahead to flying jobs in the postwar years, Congress refused to upgrade the WASPs to military status. By Christmas 1944 the over 1,000 WASPs were on their way home.

It is safe to say that most Americans did not know—and still do not know—that the WASPs ever existed, despite the fact they flew a combined total of more than 30 million miles during the war, performing tasks that ranged from the simply necessary to the dangerous and even life threatening. More than three decades passed before the surviving WASP veterans were accorded military veteran status.

After the War

With the end of the war, women found themselves once again in an ambivalent position. No longer lionized as the symbol of patriotism, women workers were now seen as a stumbling block for war veterans to make a smooth transition from the military back into civilian life and jobs. A barrage of propaganda from both public and private sources was soon exhorting women to go back home, to revert to their traditional roles as homemaker and mother. Indeed, women themselves, when polled, expressed the opinion that returning veterans should have job priority. But their response was not as simple as it appeared on the surface, for too much water had passed under the bridge for women workers to return to a prewar world. As independent workers, women had come to enjoy managing their own funds, their own resources, their own lives.

Still, women left the work force in droves, persuaded that their first duty was to home and family. Many of the prejudices applied to women through the ages came back full force, including the notion that the career-oriented businesswoman was not natural and not really a woman. Although the new head of the Women's Bureau, Frieda Miller, endorsed working women, hers was a voice in the wilderness. The women's movement, or what was left of it, was in disarray, with very little sympathy for the issues traditionally supported by advocates of women's rights. The ERA, for example, was pretty much a dead issue by the early 1950s. And, despite the fact that women eventually began to go back into the work force, especially after it became clear that fears of a resumption of the depression once the war industry was disbanded were unfounded, they did not view themselves as either career women or permanent fixtures in the work force. Rather, they considered themselves temporary contributors to the family income, even when their "temporary" status stretched into years. The marriage rate rose sharply in 1946 and the birth rate rose as sharply beginning in 1947, with the first wave of "baby boomers" making their appearance. The cult of domesticity was in full force as never before, as families began settling into suburban life, with even fewer opportunities for women to interact with each other or with other people generally. Social gatherings tended to focus more on family events, such as church gatherings, PTA meetings, scouting events, little league, and picnics and barbecues. Women began to disappear from public life and even the movies reflected this trend. For several years after the war, the Katharine Hepburns and Bette Davises lost out in popularity to the June Allysons and Doris Days, stars with images that reflected domesticity and old-fashioned, traditional values. There were, of course, some women who retained a public identity, but they stood out all the more because there were so few of them.

Eleanor Roosevelt

When Franklin Delano Roosevelt died on April 12, 1945, Eleanor Roosevelt wasted little time in vacating the White House and returning to her Hyde Park cottage, Val-Kill. Reporters, soliciting her about future plans, were told that she was now retired from public life. "The story," she said, "is over." If anyone, including herself, actually believed that this dynamic women would remain out of the public eye, they were wrong. Roosevelt wrote long letters to

Truman, encouraging him to go forward with civil rights, to maintain the Fair Employment Practices Commission, and to work for a foreign policy where atomic weapons would not be negotiating chips in international relations. Late in 1945 Truman appointed Roosevelt to the United States delegation to the United Nations. On New Year's Eve, she flew to London for the initial meeting of the United Nations.

Because Roosevelt was the only woman delegate, many of the old hands in the State Department doubted Roosevelt's ability to rise to the occasion as a diplomat, despite her long experience in politics. They might have better expended energy on more productive concerns. For two years, in exhausting meetings in Geneva, Paris, New York, and San Francisco, Roosevelt chaired the Human Rights Commission. An endless series of quarrels developed between those who wanted human rights to revert to individual nations and those, like Roosevelt, who wanted a universal declaration of human rights. Indeed, Roosevelt was the main proponent of the universal declaration. Facing down Communists who consistently impugned the motives of the United States—although never Roosevelt's motives—the document that eventually was brought forth from the Human Rights Commission stood as a beacon for all the world to emulate and aspire to. The United Nations Declaration of Human Rights was a victory of human rights over states' rights. On December 10, 1948, the Universal Declaration of Human Rights, fundamentally the creation of Eleanor Roosevelt, was adopted. In honor of her monumental effort to secure the universal declaration, Roosevelt was accorded a standing ovation by the full United Nations body. Even those critics who had been most adamantly opposed to Roosevelt's appointment to the United Nations retracted their criticism. Notably, her old adversary from New Deal days, Senator Arthur Vandenberg of Michigan, declared, "I want to say that I take back everything I ever said about her, and believe me, it's been plenty." The woman who had often been a figure of scorn and ridicule by conservative opponents during the New Deal was quickly becoming a national heroine. Shortly after her death in 1962, Roosevelt became the posthumous recipient of the first United Nations Human Rights Prize. "What other human being," Adlai Stevenson asked at her memorial service, "has touched and transformed the existence of so many?"

There were, of course, other women, both those working in traditional areas as housewives and mothers, and those who remained in the public sphere, who were knowingly or unknowingly laying the groundwork for a revival of the women's movement and feminism. The path to that revival lay, in part, through the civil rights movement that was about to burst onto the American scene in full force.

• • • • •

Margaret Chase Smith, the Conscience of the Senate
1897–1995

Senator Margaret Chase Smith, a Republican from the state of Maine, was the first woman to be elected to both the House of Representatives and the United States Senate. A former schoolteacher from Skowhegan, Smith first went to Congress in 1940, winning the congressional seat previously held by her late husband. In 1948 Smith decided to make a run for the United States Senate, to replace the retiring incumbent. To do so, she had to oppose the Republican Party, for whom she was not even a second choice for the nomination; both a former governor and the current governor wanted the nomination. In all she faced three opponents in the primary, and in the end the voters of Maine endorsed Smith by choosing her with more votes than that of the other three candidates combined. As a senator, Smith joined other freshmen senators, including John F. Kennedy and Richard M. Nixon. For more than 30 years, she represented the people of Maine with unquestioned integrity and dedication. As a senator, Smith eventually served on the Rules Committee, the Appropriations Committee, and the Armed Services Committee, all three of which carried significant clout.

Smith generally did not seek the limelight, but she found herself in it on several occasions during her political career. Her 1960 campaign for re-election was widely covered because it was the first time that two women ran head-to-head for the same Senate seat. And in 1964, fearful that the right wing was overtaking the Republican Party, Smith announced her candidacy for president. In a year in which Republicans seemed to outdo each other in making excessive statements to prove their conservatism, Smith's was one of a handful of moderate Republican voices that tried to keep the party from moving to the extreme right. Her 27 first-ballot votes were insignificant compared to the ground swell for Barry Goldwater, the nominee, but Smith once again came away with integrity and principle reaffirmed.

Throughout her career, Smith never toed the party line. She voted for as many Democratic proposals as did some of her Democratic colleagues. A consistent supporter of the National Institute of Health, Smith was just as insistent in not supporting increases in Defense Department spending on experimental weapons systems. She was also one of the Republicans who sided with the Democrats in rejecting two of President Richard M. Nixon's controversial Supreme Court nominations.

But Smith's most courageous stand came during her first term as senator, shortly after Senator Joseph McCarthy of Wisconsin began making wild accusations about so-called communists in the State Department and in other government agencies. As McCarthy continued to make his charges and as the media began to churn the waters with daily headlines, the Senate Foreign Relations Committee appointed a subcommittee to investigate the charges. On June 1, 1950, Margaret Chase Smith rose in the Senate chamber to deliver a speech. It was, she said, her "declaration of conscience." Smith denounced the tactics used by McCarthy to smear his opponents and to gain fame for himself and publicity for his re-election campaign. She decried his willingness to place in jeopardy the smooth workings of the various government departments, especially the State Department, that McCarthy had attacked so indiscriminately. And she sympathized with those who had already been smeared by McCarthy's unfounded innuendoes and accusations.

That Smith's outspoken denunciation of McCarthy was an act of political courage there is no doubt. Others who had tried—and would try in the future—to defend those accused by McCarthy found themselves the targets of his invective. Part of McCarthy's success in keeping people persuaded that some of what he said must be true was his simple audaciousness in accusing even the most reputable people. One of his targets, for example, was George Marshall, the general-turned-statesman who had formulated the Marshall Plan to bring relief to people in Europe. The Foreign Relations subcommittee report, issued on June 20, 1950, declared that it found absolutely no proof to sustain any of McCarthy's accusations. Yet, by that time McCarthy and a willing public had already become determined to save the United States from the communists working within. When Smith ran for re-election in 1954, McCarthy endorsed her opponent in an effort to discredit his Senate adversary. But the Maine electorate stood behind Smith, and she won re-election by with 82 percent of the vote.

Smith remained in the Senate until 1972, when she was defeated in a close race. By then, she had become known as the Conscience of the Senate, the woman who could always be counted upon to do not the politically expedient thing, or even the politically correct thing, but the right thing. It is a measure of the respect that her colleagues held for her, even her adversaries like Everett Dirkson, who had opposed Smith when she fought to have the rose rather than the marigold declared the national flower. Smith won and was thereafter associated with the rose. When word was received of her death some years later, an anonymous member of the Senate placed upon the desk that had been occupied by Margaret Chase Smith a single red rose. It was a fitting tribute to a woman who had inspired so many others with her perseverance, her integrity, her simple presence, and always with her dignity for so long in the halls of Congress.

CHAPTER 12
. . . .

Civil Rights, Women's Rights

When Rosa Parks refused to give up her bus seat on December 1, 1955, claiming to be "just too tired" to move, many people interpreted her remarks to mean that her action had been a spur-of-the-moment decision made out of weariness after a long day's work. As a consequence, to many outside observers, Rosa Parks remained for a long time a peripheral, almost accidental, figure in the history-making bus boycott. Credit for initiating, sustaining, and successfully concluding the boycott went to civil rights leaders, including Martin Luther King, Jr., who not only emerged as the leader, but began his own journey that was destined to help change the face of America.

The truth was Rosa Parks had long been involved in efforts to change the Montgomery bus system. She, along with every other African American, hated having to enter the front door of the bus to pay a fare, and then get off and enter the bus again from the rear door; she hated the policy requiring African Americans to give up their seats if white people were standing; and she hated the disrespect with which African Americans were treated by drivers who felt no compunction about leaving people standing in the roadway after they had paid their fares or ejecting people who were not deferential enough. Parks had also just completed a summer seminar at the Highlander Folk School in Grundy County, Tennessee. Highlander sponsored seminars for both African Americans and whites seeking to bring equality and civil rights to fruition. So when the opportunity to act presented itself, Rosa Parks, a mild-mannered seamstress in her mid-forties, was equal to the challenge. Her insistent refusals to give up her seat prompted the bus driver to call authorities, who arrested Parks.

When Jo Ann Robinson, a professor at Alabama State College who had also been involved in efforts to change the public transportation policy, heard about Parks's arrest, she immediately swung into action. Without waiting for other civil rights activists to determine whether the Parks case was the proper vehicle to begin a boycott, Robinson ran off 50,000 flyers calling for a general boycott of all Montgomery buses the following Monday, December 5, 1955. And so began a year-long struggle between public officials and African Americans in Montgomery.

From the start the bus boycott was a monumental success. Boycott leaders, again motivated by Robinson and other women, organized the Montgomery Improvement Association (MIA) to direct boycott strategy and elected Martin Luther King, Jr., a young Baptist pastor, as president. While King, Ralph Abernathy, and Ed Nixon assumed the leadership roles in the MIA, they relied heavily upon the women in the organization to carry out the day-to-day activities necessary to sustain the boycott. The primary support for the boycott came from thousands of women who chose to walk as much as 12 miles a day or to car-pool. One typical elderly woman promised King that she would walk every day until the boycott ended. When King protested that her feet must be tired, she acknowledged that they were and added, "but my soul is rested." Such determination could scarcely fail to bring success. When the Supreme Court ruled, in *Browder v. Gayle* in November 1956, that Alabama's state and city bus segregation policies were unconstitutional, the MIA called off the boycott, almost one year from the day it began. The Court's decision also gave civil rights leaders the motivation to continue their activities in other areas.

The Montgomery bus boycott is generally credited with being the first step forward in the modern civil rights movement. Only a year before, in 1954, the United States Supreme Court had ruled, in *Brown v. Board of Education,* that separate schools were inherently unequal. The Court ordered segregated schools to begin integrating their student bodies with, as the order read, "all deliberate speed." Unfortunately, school integration dragged on for years, while white school districts—primarily in the South—resisted the Court's ruling with one delaying tactic after another. But the Brown decision helped to spark a grassroots movement that had been building up for years.

From the start African American women were crucially involved in the civil rights movement. Although most of the leadership was male and re-mained so, the women of the South made up the vast army of foot soldiers willing to put everything on the line to get out from under the yoke of oppression. When Tougaloo College student Anne Moody was asked to join a Woolworth lunch counter sit-in in Jackson, Mississippi, in 1963, she was one of a few students to respond positively. In her view she had nothing to lose. Already a three-year veteran of the civil rights struggle, Moody was committed to the cause, despite the threats of physical violence or worse that were made against her, her family, and anyone else who dared to join the National Association for the Advancement of Colored People (NAACP). Through occasional periods of doubt, Moody remained involved, as did many other women, both black and white. Gradually, under the sheer weight of numbers and the law, the South began to change its attitude and its practices towards African Americans. Whether the change came about because of sincerity on the part of enlightened white Southerners or because they were forced to change or face prosecution, jail, and the threat of withdrawal of federal funds, change happened.

FANNIE LOU HAMER

In August 1964 Fannie Lou Hamer, a Mississippi civil rights activist, led a contingent of dissenters to the Atlantic City Democratic National Convention. With little real hope of succeeding but intent nevertheless on pressing the issue, Hamer, the founder and vice-chairwoman of the Mississippi Freedom Democratic Party (MFDP), protested before the convention and a national television audience the seating of the all-white Mississippi delegation to the convention. Democrats Hubert Humphrey and Walter Mondale tried to organize a compromise that would have seated two members of the MFDP, but the Democratic party refused to entertain the compromise. Fearing that it would look too reactionary, the Democratic party made an unprecedented pledge guaranteeing to the MFPD that no delegations that excluded African Americans would be seated at the 1968 convention.

Hamer, who acted as spokesperson for the MFPD, had already been through more on behalf of civil rights than most Americans could comprehend at the time. One of 20 children of Mississippi sharecroppers, Hamer had experienced the myriad ways in which African Americans were discouraged from even thinking about getting ahead. When her father, after years of saving, had put together enough money to purchase two mules to help with the farming chores, whites poisoned the mules as an object lesson in maintaining one's place. In August 1962, inspired by civil rights activist Ella Baker, Hamer organized a voter registration drive at the Sunflower County Courthouse in Mississippi. Registration officials spent most of the day creating new reasons why they could not register. On the way home, their bus was stopped, and the driver arrested for violating a segregation law. Hamer was fired when her boss heard of her actions. She was evicted from her home. Her husband and daughter were falsely arrested. The Hamers were billed $9,000 by the water department for a home that had no running water. Hamer became a target for violent racists. She was threatened with bodily harm and death. She was put through all of this simply because she tried to register to vote. Instead of being discouraged, Hamer was motivated. As she told a congressional committee sometime later, she was "sick and tired of being sick and tired."

Hamer continued to work for civil rights in the South. The year after her attempt to register, Hamer and Annelle Ponder opened a citizenship school in their town, for teaching and training political activism and organizing voter registration drives and other movements. For this they received a severe beating at the hands of the local police. Although the Justice Department brought charges against the five men responsible, the presiding judge at their trial directed the jury to bring in a not-guilty verdict. Still, Hamer persisted. In an audacious move, she qualified to run for Congress from her home district. Although it is difficult to determine how many votes she won because all the ballots with her name on them were disqualified, it is safe to say by comparing the number of voters with the total number of votes that were counted that she picked up a significant percentage of the votes cast.

One of Hamer's most profound experiences was traveling to New Guinea, where she was greeted by government officials. It was the first time that Hamer had been anywhere where people of color were the government. "You don't know what that meant to me," she later said. In January 1965 Hamer challenged the legality of the Mississippi delegates to Congress on the grounds that African Americans had been denied the right to vote. After nine months the MFPD lost. Hamer continued to serve as vice-chairwoman of the MFPD, but over the next several years increasingly deteriorating health limited her activism. In 1977, at the age of 59, Hamer died of cancer.

PRESIDENT'S COMMISSION ON THE STATUS OF WOMEN

While the civil rights movement was building up steam in the South, other events that affected the lives of all women were taking place as well. In 1961 President John F. Kennedy established the President's Commission on the Status of Women. While Kennedy was very dependent on women's votes, he was not at all committed to promoting women's rights. It seems somewhat ironic, then, that he should be the one to establish the Commission, particularly because former presidents Dwight Eisenhower and Harry S. Truman had been similarly lobbied to create a commission, and both had refused. For Kennedy there were good political reasons for doing so.

Esther Peterson, the head of the Women's Bureau and the highest-level woman appointee in the Kennedy administration, first came forward with the suggestion. Peterson had two reasons for doing so: first, she wanted to deflect any potential pro-Equal Rights Amendment (ERA) activity, primarily because it was still opposed by organized labor; second, Peterson wanted to see legislation enacted that would guarantee to women equal pay for equal work, a measure for which the support of organized labor would be required.

Kennedy had already been criticized for not making any women Cabinet-level appointees. Indeed, his record of female appointees lagged behind those of his predecessors. When Peterson suggested the Commission, Kennedy viewed it as an opportunity to recoup some of his female support.

The Commission, composed of 13 women and 11 men, was chaired by Eleanor Roosevelt. It employed seven investigatory committees, on which many prominent women sat, as well as scores of consultants and Women's Bureau staff. In November 1962 Eleanor Roosevelt died. As a tribute to her memory, the Commission issued its report, entitled *American Women*, on October 11, 1963, Roosevelt's birthday.

As expected, the report declared that an equal rights amendment was not necessary at the present time because, in the opinion of respected constitutional scholars, the Fourteenth and Fifteenth Amendments guaranteed equal rights to women. Attorney Marguerite Rawalt, the only pro-ERA advocate on the Commission, insisted that the wording be such that it left open the question of whether an ERA might be appropriate in the future.

The 60-page report included a long list of conditions that required amelioration and made specific recommendations. Among other things the report advocated an end to the prohibition against women jurors and restrictions on married women's rights. It supported federally and privately funded child-care centers for working mothers, joint guardianship of children, continuing education programs for women, equal employment opportunities, paid maternity leaves, equal pay laws, increased vocational training, promotion of women to high-level government jobs, more appointments of women to policy-making jobs, and continued efforts on the part of the government to insure the rights of women.

Two special consultations arranged by the Commission provoked most of the controversy within it. Both were set up as afterthoughts, but they reflected to a great extent the concerns that emerged in the revived women's movement of the mid-1960s. The first was a consultation on "Images of Women in the Media." Sitting in on the symposium were writers Lorraine Hansberry, the author of *A Raisin in the Sun*, Marya Mannes, and Betty Friedan. Hansberry complained that women were constantly objectified in media images. Mannes noted that magazines tended to portray women as housewives and mothers, neglecting all of their other roles and categories. And Friedan criticized magazines for failing to convey the idea that women had goals and ideals outside of the narrowly defined stereotypes. A second commission, "The Problems of Negro Women," chaired by the president of the National Council of Negro Women, Dorothy Height, complained that too little attention was paid to the plight of African American families and their lack of opportunity.

Though the report of the Commission attracted little attention, it did result in passage of the first federal law prohibiting sex discrimination, the

Equal Pay Act, by the end of 1963. Moreover, Kennedy directed executive agencies to put a stop to sex discrimination in hiring and promoting practices, and a watchdog agency, the Citizen's Advisory Council on the Status of Women, was created. Finally, individual states began appointing their own commissions to make similar inquiries on statewide conditions. But perhaps the most lasting legacy of the Commission was that it served as a turning point, heralding a revitalization of the women's movement that would have far-reaching effects on American society.

Equal Pay Act

Throughout the history of industrialized America, women workers have been paid less than male workers for the same jobs. Until the Equal Pay Act of 1963, only Wyoming, of all the states, had enacted an equal pay. There were several reasons for this state of affairs, not the least of which was a culturally accepted tradition that men were entitled to earn more than women, even when they both did the same job, because men were the breadwinners and the heads of households. This idea was generally accepted even in the many cases where the head of the household was a woman. During World War II, when women went into the labor force in unprecedented numbers, they were still paid about half of what male workers received the same job.

The Equal Pay Act of 1963 was intended to remove that disparity. The act provided for equal pay for both men and women for jobs requiring equal skill, responsibility, and effort. It also prohibited employers from lowering the wages of one sex to avoid raising the wages of the other. Unions were forbidden from causing or trying to cause employers to violate the law. The circumstances under which exceptions could be made were wages based on seniority, merit, quantity or quality of production, or differentials based on any reason other than sex.

Since its inception the Equal Pay Act was difficult to enforce fairly because of the variances in interpreting what constituted equal effort, skill, and responsibility. Moreover, jobs were often categorized by personnel departments as either male or female, with job descriptions that could be altered just enough to make a provable case that the jobs were not comparable. Until the 1970s even help-wanted advertisements in the newspapers were segregated into "Help Wanted, Male," and "Help Wanted, Female," so determining equality in employment was, at best, vague and imprecise.

THE FEMININE MYSTIQUE

Betty Friedan, who had served on the President's Commission on the Status of Women, published her pathbreaking book, *The Feminine Mystique*, the same year that the Commission issued its report and Congress passed the Equal Pay Act. Friedan described the problem that afflicted many women in post–World War II America as a vague feeling of discontent and aimlessness that persisted despite the fact that both science and popular culture told them their most fulfilling roles in life were wives, mothers, and homemakers. It was, said Friedan, "the problem that has no name." Although the publisher of *The Feminine Mystique* expected reasonably good sales, W.W. Norton limited the first printing of the book to 2,000 copies. No one, including Friedan, anticipated the explosive response to the book. Within 10 years, *The Feminine Mystique* sold 3 million hardcover copies and many more in paperback.

Friedan's experience as a suburban housewife in the 1950s and memories of her mother's discontent at abandoning a career in favor of marriage led her to question the validity of the popular viewpoint. Although she had written for women's magazines, she accused them of helping to circumscribe the options open to women outside of the home by determining for all women where their self-worth ought to come from. A survey of Friedan's class of 1942 Smith College graduates also led her to believe that the problem was far more widespread than anyone might suspect. According to the popular viewpoint, scientifically corroborated by social scientists and reported in page after page of a variety of women's magazines, from *Redbook* to *Ladies' Home Journal* to *Cosmopolitan*, American women could find no greater fulfillment than in devoting their lives to their husbands and in raising their children in a nurturing environment. Most women who were unhappy with this predetermined life believed that they alone were out of step, somehow lacking in appreciation for all that they had. It was both a revelation and a release to discover that they were not alone. Friedan's book helped to break the long silence over issues such as equal pay for equal work, limited opportunities for women, and women's relative powerlessness in family and society. It was, therefore, an important step when Congress passed the Equal Pay Act and an equally important step when the Civil Rights Act of 1964 was passed.

CIVIL RIGHTS ACT OF 1964

Because the Civil Rights Act was such an ambitious piece of legislation, covering discrimination in public places, voting rights protection, and employment discrimination, among other things, the bill had to overcome a great deal of opposition. Octogenarian Representative Howard W. Smith of Virginia introduced an amendment to the Title VII of the Civil Rights Act that he was convinced would help to ensure the defeat of the entire piece of legislation. His amendment called for the prohibition of employment discrimination on the basis of not only race, but sex as well. Smith, who had appeared on the television program *Meet the Press* a short time before, had apparently taken a serious suggestion put to him by senior White House correspondent May Craig, and decided that including a provision outlawing sex discrimination would render the bill as ludicrous to everyone else as it was to him.

The Smith amendment elicited the kind of response he hoped for. Both liberals and women's groups, including the League of Women Voters, objected to endangering the cause of civil rights by tying it to the women's issue. One member of Congress voiced the fear that acceptance of such a provision might "endanger traditional family relationships." Congressmen also suggested that it might affect hard-won privileges such as alimony and child custody. President Lyndon Johnson was determined that the Civil Rights Act would be passed, however, and he began to put pressure on members of Congress to secure the necessary votes. He also enlisted the help of Michigan Representative Martha Griffiths and Maine Senator Margaret Chase Smith. On July 2, 1964, the Civil Rights Act of 1964 was passed into law, complete with Title VII and its sex discrimination clause. The new law provided for an Equal Employment Opportunity Commission (EEOC) to enforce the provisions of Title VII. The failure of the EEOC to enforce the sex discrimination clause as vigorously as it enforced civil rights violations became one of the catalysts for the founding of the National Organization of Women (NOW) two years later.

Additional legislation that helped both the civil rights movement and the women's movement included Executive Order 11246, a follow-up to the Civil Rights Act of 1964, and Title IX of the Education Act of 1972. In the spirit of the Civil Rights Act of 1964, President Johnson signed Executive Order 11246, which established a policy of affirmative action as a means to both eliminate discrimination in hiring and to persuade corporations to make a good faith effort to remedy past discrimination. The policy applied to specific categories, including race, color, religion, and national origin, and it forbade corporations who held government contracts to discriminate in their hiring practices against individuals solely because they possessed one of those characteristics. Although it was by no means a panacea against discriminatory hiring practices, it did give the government leverage over corporations because the government could withdraw federal contracts that it had awarded to them. In 1968, therefore, Johnson broadened affirmative action by including sex as one of the categories against which corporations were prohibited from discriminatory hiring practices.

The Office of Federal Contract Compliance (OFCC), which oversees corporate compliance with the regulations in cases where the federal contract is in excess of $1 million, can choose from several penalties, depending on the degree of noncompliance by the offending corporation. It can withhold funds until compliance has been achieved, it can prohibit the corporation from receiving future federal contracts, or it can refer the case to the Justice Department or to the EEOC. Corporations holding federal contracts are provided with strict guidelines and timetables under which they must reach compliance.

Theoretically, such a policy should effectively prohibit discriminatory practices. In fact, the policy has not worked as it was intended to for several reasons. First, understaffed agencies charged with carrying out the policy have made it difficult to monitor holders of government contracts. Second, an ongoing controversy over the issue of establishing numerical goals has divided those who oppose affirmative action and some government agencies including the Justice Department. And finally, during the 1980s, the administration of President Ronald Reagan attempted to weaken the regulations governing government contracts.

Hopes for a renewed effort to impose sanctions against violators and to require compliance came in 1988 when Congress overrode Reagan's veto of the Civil Rights Restoration Act. By overriding the veto, the intent of Congress was re-established and actually strengthened as a result.

TITLE IX

When the education amendments of 1972 were being debated in Congress, efforts were made to exclude intercollegiate athletics from the provisions. Advocates of the exclusion were unsuccessful, and virtually overnight, Title IX changed the face of college sports programs for women. Women had always been interested in competitive and recreational sports, but different constraints at different times discouraged the widespread participation that characterized men's sports. In the late 19th century, conventional wisdom determined that participating in physical activity would be detrimental to a woman's more fragile constitution. Because working-class girls and women did not have access to sports to the same degree that middle- and upper-class women did, the social rules that proscribed women's participation were directed more at middle-class sensibilities. While sports participation was encouraged and even expected as part of men's rites of passage, and though young girls might be encouraged to take up moderate forms of physical activity, by the time girls reached their teen years, they were made to understand that it was unladylike and unacceptable for women to engage in excessive physical activity. Even well into the 20th century, the constraints against women in sports were overwhelming, although more and more women were participating on both the amateur and professional levels. Notably for women, golf and tennis proved to be avenues to career sports and a respectable, even very lucrative, livelihood, although that aspect is a much more recent phenomenon.

One area where women remained fairly low-key in sports participation was at the college level. With the exception of the women's schools, like Wellesley, Smith, and Mount Holyoke, where physical activity was always encouraged and, consequently, athletic programs were funded, most women attending colleges and universities found only a rudimentary physical education program, if that. Virtually all monies spent for athletic programs went to men's sports. As a result, women who wanted to compete in sports had to make do with underfunded programs characterized by shoddy equipment, shabby uniforms, and a competitive schedule that was determined more by the ease with which teams could get together than any competitive equity. Nevertheless, dedicated women coaches and players kept the programs alive in the leanest of times.

When Title IX was included in the education amendments of 1972, it fairly revolutionized women's sports programs in colleges and universities. By 1975 the growing awareness of the impact of Title IX and the guidelines set forth by the Department of Health, Education, and Welfare, produced enormous changes for women's programs. In 1970 the number of women students participating in intercollegiate athletic programs was about 7.5 percent; by 1978 that number had increased to almost 32 percent. An astounding 570 percent increase in the number of women athletes during these years, compared to the 13 percent increase in the number of male athletes, was dramatic proof of the effectiveness of the federally mandated equal funding for women's sports programs.

Opponents of Title IX, including the Reagan Administration, seeking to find loopholes in the tough enforcement mechanism, finally succeeded when the United States Supreme Court virtually gutted Title IX with its decision in the case of *Grove City College v. Bell* in 1984. Until then, colleges were forced to abide by Title IX for fear that they would be stripped of federal funds, regardless of whether those funds were used for athletics, if it could be determined that the institutions were discriminating against athletic programs for women. In *Grove City College v. Bell*, the court ruled that federal funds could be stripped only from those programs found to be discriminatory. In other words, a college that received no federal funds earmarked for sports programs and that discriminated against women in funding such programs could not be stripped of federal funds or grants used to support, for example, scientific research. It was a huge blow to women's sports programs. But advocates in Congress, refusing to accept defeat, passed a Civil Rights Restoration Act in March 1988, reinstating the former institutionwide penalty for sex discrimination. Proponents were able to build a coalition strong enough to override a Reagan veto of the act, by allowing a provision that enabled colleges and universities to refuse to provide abortion-related services without threat of penalty.

Title IX continues to underpin the athletic programs for women in colleges and universities, encouraging women to participate in sports and to compete. One irony of its success, however, is that women coaches and athletic directors have become the expendable victims of revamped programs. In 1983 the Association for Intercollegiate Athletics for Women was dissolved when women's sports came under the aegis of the male-dominated National

Collegiate Athletic Association. As schools combined their athletic programs under one structure, it was more often than not the women coaches and staffs that were let go in favor of the male administration and coaching staffs. And, as salaries for coaches of women's teams increased, male coaches began to take more interest and eventually took over many of the coaching duties previously performed by women. So, while Title IX has certainly been a boon for women athletes and women's sports programs, the victory has been somewhat bittersweet.

NATIONAL ORGANIZATION OF WOMEN

At the Third Annual Conference of the President's Commission on the Status of Women held in Washington in 1966, those in attendance had no thought to found a new organization. Three days before the conference, Representative Martha Griffiths delivered a blistering speech to Congress accusing the EEOC of not taking sex discrimination seriously. She contended that the first director of the EEOC, aware that sex discrimination was thrown in only in an effort to defeat the Civil Rights Act and believing that race discrimination was really the mandate of the EEOC, simply ignored the complaints filed by women. Griffiths was furious. Moreover, she had the support of women employees of the EEOC, who were also distressed by the executive director's attitude towards complaints of women. The EEOC women believed that if women had an organization behind them to apply pressure in the way that the NAACP did for racial issues, then women's issues would not be ignored. Members of the Commission on the Status of Women wanted to submit a resolution urging the EEOC to consider seriously complaints filed by women, but commission leaders did not think that an appropriate issue to take up. As a result, 28 women met after the conference and took the first steps in establishing an organization to address the civil rights of women.

The first organizational meeting of the National Organization of Women was held in October 1966, with Betty Friedan chosen to serve as the first president. NOW's statement of purpose rejected tokenism and demanded "fully equal partnership of the sexes, as part of the worldwide revolution in human rights." NOW opposed any policy or practice that denied opportunities to women, as well as those that fostered in women "self-denigration, dependence, and evasion of responsibility . . . and fostered contempt for women." The members rejected the idea that men had to carry the entire burden of supporting their families, as well as the idea that women had to be entirely responsible for maintaining and nurturing home, marriage, and family. They also rejected the idea that a woman had to choose between marriage and career. Above all, the members of NOW declared that they rejected "the assumption that these problems are the unique responsibility of each individual woman, rather than a basic social dilemma which society must solve." With the organization of NOW, women finally had a political pressure group to lobby on their behalf. Again, it was a measure of the widespread discontent with the status quo that NOW expanded rapidly from 28 members to over 15,000 members.

In an informal way, the civil rights and the women's movement fueled and were fueled by each other. Particularly in the beginning, at least half the civil rights volunteers from the North who went south to provide assistance were women. And the gains made in civil rights helped women in general to realize once again that their own position in society had regressed since the early years of the century. Both movements moved on parallel, though not necessarily intersecting, paths for awhile. But as the women's movement became a more and more middle-class movement, black women were not at all certain that their needs would be addressed by the women's movement. Eventually, more black women came into the women's movement, but for awhile there was a good deal of suspicion regarding motives. But enough women recognized that women were treated as second-class citizens in both the civil rights movement and white-dominated movements, such as the antiwar movement. These women could identify with the frustration felt when Stokley Carmichael declared that the position of women in the civil rights movement was "prone." However women stood on the issues, the reality was that successes in either movement were beneficial to all women. Forums dedicated to women's issues spoke to all of the differences that divided people. The best known of these was Ms., the feminist magazine founded in the early 1970s.

MS. MAGAZINE

Ms. magazine, the first national publication created by women specifically for women readers, was perhaps the most creative innovation to come out of the women's movement of the 1960s and 1970s. Gloria Steinem, one of the acknowledged leaders of the women's movement, invited a group of feminist writers and journalists to her home early in 1971, for the purpose of discussing ways in which they might reach out to women who were not members of any of the organizations that had sprung up to discuss the status of women and to promote women's rights. Steinem, one of the founders of the successful New York magazine, wanted to create a magazine that would address crucial issues and that would be directed at a very specific female audience. Those present, including Betty Friedan and Pat Carbine, responded enthusiastically and began immediately to use their combined journalistic experience to find the necessary financial support.

The format of the new magazine was clearly defined. It would avoid the advice, cooking, and beauty columns traditionally found in women's magazines. At the same time, the founders did not want a magazine that relied on dogmatic partisanship or ideological debates that would almost surely prohibit broad readership. The goal was to provide a forum for feminist trends and ideas, presented in a low-key fashion that would not alienate women who did not consider themselves feminists. One of the most innovative editorial policies decided upon was that the magazine, under no circumstances, would accept advertising that portrayed women in a demeaning way.

Steinem approached her *New York* colleague, Clay Felker, and persuaded him to include a preview copy of *Ms.* as an insert in an issue of *New York*. The *New York/Ms.* issue was released at the end of 1971. The now-famous first cover of *Ms.* featured, appropriately enough, Wonder Woman. That particular issue of *New York* proved to be the magazine's all-time sales leader. Steinem and Felker had agreed on a 300,000-copy run, which they believed would last for eight weeks, right up to the projected spring debut of *Ms.* All 300,000 copies were sold in eight days. It was a stunning first outing.

Since its inception, *Ms.* editors (Steinem was the editor for the first 15 years) have published articles on issues concerning contemporary women both at home and in the workplace. A hallmark of its editorial style was a noncondescending and forthright discussion of issues that appealed greatly to its readers. In addition, *Ms.* featured articles on women's history, and poetry and fiction by some of the best contemporary writers.

The success of *Ms.* led to other ventures, including the Ms. Foundation for Women, Inc., organized in 1975 as a tax-exempt educational and charitable foundation that provided grants for research projects. A year later the Free To Be Foundation was established to fund nonsexist children's programming and to promote unbiased development. An outgrowth of Marlo Thomas's successful *Free to Be . . . You and Me* book and television show, the foundation used royalties to fund multimedia children's projects.

By 1982 *Ms.* boasted a solid subscription base of 200,000 readers. As the politically conservative 1980s wore on, however, the economic difficulties that beset the nation generally began to make themselves felt at the magazine. In the mid-1980s, with Steinem anxious to step down and pursue other ventures, the magazine underwent a reorganization that was intended to shore up its financial base. By 1988, however, the publishers had to sell *Ms.* to a more lucrative publishing company that could afford to continue its publication. Although *Ms.*, under its new ownership, was redirected slightly to a more mainstream product, it nevertheless continued to promote and support women writers and women's issues as the core of its monthly content.

ERA

For the women's movement, a major political goal was passage of an equal rights amendment. In 1923, under a mandate from the National Woman's Party (NWP), of which she was the founder, Alice Paul penned the simple lines of an equal rights amendment modeled on the recently passed Nineteenth Amendment: "Men and women shall have equal rights throughout the United States and every place subject to its jurisdiction. Congress shall have the power to enforce this article through appropriate legislation." The amendment, which in its final form changed only slightly, was immediately, on its introduction to Congress in December 1923, dubbed the Lucretia Mott Amendment. But if advocates hoped that naming the amendment after the renowned Quaker pacifist might help in eliminating some of the controversy surrounding it, it was purely wishful thinking.

From the start the women's movement was divided over the issue of the ERA. Radical feminists, like Paul, believed that until and unless the nation was willing to guarantee equal rights to women through a constitutional amendment, true equality would be nonexistent. Moderates, including virtually the entire women's movement, led by women such as Florence Kelley, Carrie Chapman Catt, Mary Elizabeth Dreier, Margaret Dreier Robbins, and Mary Anderson of the Woman's Bureau, feared that adoption of an ERA would nullify all of the protective legislation for women and children that had taken years of lobbying to put into place. It was a legitimately heartfelt difference of opinion that kept the women's movement divided for several decades and caused Paul and her supporters to redefine their strategy. Whereas Paul had initially planned to mount an ERA campaign much like the suffrage campaign, resistance from other women's groups made it clear that the NWP would first have to lobby among its own and gain the support of a majority of American women.

It was not until after World War II that women's groups, such as the General Federation of Women's Clubs and the League of Women Voters, were persuaded that an ERA was necessary, partially because the women's movement that had provided the impetus for the Nineteenth Amendment had dispersed after its passage. In the final years of the suffrage campaign, the National Woman Suffrage Association's strategy to mobilize women was to convince them that the vote was an end in itself. Once suffrage was secured, women would not have to campaign for reform because reforms would be secured at the polls. Ninety percent of the suffragists who had put in months and years of volunteer work for the cause wanted nothing more than to return to their private lives. They were not prepared to embark on another political campaign, nor did they want to.

In the 1960s, with a re-emergence of the women's movement, feminists began to focus again on an ERA. When the amendment was passed by Congress, women believed that the fight had finally been won because the majority of Americans supported the ERA. Within a year 28 states had ratified the ERA. After that opponents began to mount a counter-campaign. Led by Phyllis Schlafly, the editor of the *Phyllis Schlafly Report* and the *Eagle Forum Newsletter*, opponents rallied support from people across America by playing on their fears about what a world with an equal rights amendment would look like. According to Schlafly, women would be subject to the military draft and would have to leave their homes and children while they served in the armed forces. Equality like that, Schlafly argued, would destroy the family. Schlafly also used an existing element of resentment to drive a wedge between, in her view, two diametrically opposed camps: feminists and housewives. In part, the feminists had helped to create the mistrust by not validating those women who found satisfaction as housewives. But Schlafly was more than skilled at creating a chasm where none really existed. As she toured the country speaking against the ERA, resistance began building up. By 1977, 35 states had ratified the ERA, but with time running out, another three states were needed. Against the objections of Schlafly's STOP ERA organization, Congress granted a four-year extension for ratification.

In actuality, once Congress placed a limitation on the amount of time they would allow for ratification, they had really insured that with any kind of organized opposition, the ERA would have little chance of ratification. When the suffrage amendment was passed in 1919, opponents tried to impose a similar time limit for ratification. That effort was recognized for what it was, and Congress refused to attach limits to the ratification process. Opposition melted away almost overnight. Opponents were quite clear about why they gave up the fight. With a finite amount of time to ratify the suffrage amendment, the opposition could dig in their heels and put all their resources into those states where they had the best chance of defeating ratification. Without a time limit, the opposition believed that they could not sustain the support necessary to hold out indefinitely. With the ERA, the opposition got their time limit. They had only to organize their anti-ERA campaign in key areas to prevent ratification in the time allowed. When the time extension ran out in 1982, ratification was still three states shy of the necessary 38.

ABORTION

If the ERA left a bitter taste, the other major controversial issue that affected all women in the early 1970s and well before—abortion—was settled in favor of the woman's right to choose, which, for many, was a clear-cut victory. Abortion had been illegal since the mid-19th century when the government, aided and abetted by the American Medical Association, outlawed it. Women without the means to do otherwise had to obtain illegal and dangerous abortions or bring the pregnancy to full term. In Texas, where *Roe v. Wade* originated, a pregnant woman referred to as Roe brought suit against Henry Wade, the district attorney of Dallas County, challenging his right to prevent her from obtaining an abortion. Roe won in the lower court, and when Wade appealed to the Supreme Court, the lower court decision was upheld. In its ruling the Supreme Court refused to define the point at which life begins, preferring to take as a measure of when abortion could legally be prevented, the point at which a fetus becomes viable and able to survive outside of the mother's womb. The Court declared that because the state has a compelling interest in potential human life at the point of viability, the state's interests supersede those of the mother. Before that point the state has no right to interfere in a woman's right to privacy.

The most vociferous critic of the Court's decision was the Roman Catholic Church, which characterized the decision as horrifying. But many women viewed the decision as a great stride forward, because it overturned all of the assumptions previously held regarding the right of government to restrict women's free choice. Since *Roe v. Wade*, several attempts have been made to overturn the Court's decision. Thus far, the Court has made only minor adjustments, for example in allowing states to impose waiting periods before women could obtain abortions and in requiring that minors get permission from both parents before undergoing abortion. However, the fundamental right to a legal abortion has been preserved. But one of the consequences of *Roe v. Wade* has been the birth of a right-to-life movement that, in recent times, has become more assertive, and, at times, more violent as opponents of abortion seek ways to shut down clinics.

Advances made by women from World War II to the early 1980s have been significant. Many women would argue that the failure of the ERA did not really amount to anything because women had already achieved much of what an ERA would give them. It is certainly true that women are able to enter virtually any profession or occupation they want. The service academies of West Point, Annapolis, the Air Force Academy, and others are now all open to women, and quickly women proved themselves the equal to male cadets and midshipmen by grabbing the top graduating class honors on several occasions. Resistence to full participation by women in some areas of military service and institutions proved to be more stubborn. Only recently women have been authorized for fighter pilot training—considered one of the last impediments to full participation in military careers and advancement. And one of the last bastions of all-male military education was forced to modify its attitude towards women when the courts upheld the right of a woman to enter The Citadel after she had been unwittingly admitted in the normal application process. The Ivy League also opened its doors to women, and there, too, women have graduated at the top of the class at Princeton, Yale, Harvard, and other previously all-male institutions. Women have been appointed to the Supreme Court and to more and more cabinet and other high-ranking political posts. The age-old double standard that has often made many women victims of sexual harassment with no recourse became a public issue when Anita Hill testified on prime-time television against her former boss, Supreme Court nominee Clarence Thomas. Issues of personal safety, including date rape and spousal abuse, have become more prominent as societal concerns that can no longer be ignored. More and more women have been elected to both the House and the Senate, as well as heads of state governments and other high ranking posts.

• • • • •

Lorraine Hansberry, Playwright
1930–1965

Lorraine Hansberry, born in Chicago in 1930, grew up in a world peopled by the activists, politicians, professionals, and artists with whom her parents associated. Her love of the theater and particularly of playwrighting matured when she was a student at the University of Wisconsin in the late 1940s. She left there before earning her degree and settled in New York to begin serious writing. When Hansberry's brilliant play, *A Raisin In the Sun*, opened on Broadway in 1959, critic Walter Kerr wrote that Hansberry had "taken the precise temperature of a race at that time in its history when it cannot retreat and cannot quite find the way to move forward." Her starkly drawn characters represented "three generations . . . poised and crowded on a detonating cap." Hansberry's play altered the American theater, forever changing what producers of Broadway productions considered acceptable subject matter. Ironically, the play almost did not make it to Broadway because the so-called "smart money people" did not believe that the American public was ready to support a play about an African American family. Hansberry, however, had faith, both in her creation and the theater-going public. When producers wanted to change the play in ways that they thought would make it more acceptable but that significantly altered the content, Hansberry refused, preferring instead to raise money in other ways to stage the play. With no guarantee of a Broadway house, Hansberry and her colleagues raised enough cash to take the play on the road. Its success in other cities, including Chicago, New Haven, and Philadelphia, finally convinced doubters that America was ready for such a play. *A Raisin in the Sun* won the New York Drama Critics' Circle Award in 1959, the first time that an African American, male or female, had been so honored. Hansberry was also the youngest playwright to ever win the award, and only the fifth woman.

Hansberry was only 28 when *A Raisin in the Sun* opened on Broadway. The theme of the play was inspired by poet Langston Hughes's poem, *Harlem*, in which he asked: "What happens to a dream deferred? . . . Does it dry up like a raisin in the sun? . . . Or does it explode?" Lorraine Hansberry did not allow her dreams to be deferred. A civil rights activist as well as an author and a playwright, it was she who coined the term "young, gifted, and black" for a speech honoring winners of the United Negro College Fund's writing contest in 1964. By then, Hansberry already knew she was dying of cancer. Yet she refused to allow that to stop her from achieving her goals. She managed to complete her next play, *The Sign in Sidney Brustein's Window*, and saw it open to mixed reviews in October 1964 at the Ethel Barrymore Theater. Its theme was a call for intellectuals to become involved with social problems, and it surprised critics to see that an African American woman would write a play about whites, perhaps because Hansberry had by then become so identified with the civil rights movement. But Hansberry had learned long before that profound human suffering transcends race and class, an understanding that made her work so universally accepted and at the same time so powerful.

Hansberry's plays also reflected her own feminist sensibilities. Most of her works feature female characters who, through sheer willpower, hope, and aspiration, provide the cultural and emotional links that unite her protagonists with the human family. The character of Mama in *Raisin* and the Parodus sisters in *Sidney Brustein* both reflect Hansberry's concern with acknowledging women's contributions to life and culture.

Hansberry died in January 1965 at the age of 34. Her star had shone over American theater for a brief six years. The work she did as a playwright, an author, a civil rights activist, a feminist, a political commentator, and a humanist, despite the discrimination she faced as an African American woman and her painful illness, is permanent testimony to the innate courage of the human spirit.

Dolores Huerta, Labor Organizer and Negotiator
1930–

In the late 1950s, in Stockton, California, labor organizer Fred Ross recruited young Dolores Huerta, persuading her to work with him in a grassroots group called the Community Service Organization (CSO). Huerta worked through the CSO in voter registration drives to get more Chicanos into the electorate. She also helped to bring public attention to the ongoing police brutality against Chicanos. It was as a CSO volunteer that Huerta met Cesar Chavez. Working together, they helped to establish more than 20 CSO locals throughout the state and in Arizona. Huerta also worked as a lobbyist on behalf of Chicanos and first-generation Mexicans living in California. Her skills were amply demonstrated when she was able to persuade legislators in Sacramento to include first-generation Mexicans, regardless of citizenship, in an old-age pension program. During that period, Huerta also succeeded in getting farm workers included in disability coverage, a remarkable feat because the Chicano population was not yet organized enough to wield political power at the polls. When the CSO objected to plans made by Huerta and Chavez to set up a rural program, they left the organization.

Chavez went first to Delano, California, and began organizing agricultural workers. In California most agricultural workers were Hispanic in origin and represented the last large unorganized workers' group, characterized by extremely low wages, long seasonal hours, and extremely poor working conditions.

Huerta soon joined Chavez in Delano, and together they organized the United Farm Workers (UFW) union. Huerta served as vice-president and chief negotiator for the UFW. In September 1965 the Delano grape strike began in California—an action that lasted almost five years before it was settled. In the course of the strike, a number of influential unions and civil rights organizations supported the grape pickers. They also secured the support of Robert F. Kennedy, which brought a great deal of national media attention to the strike. Their red flag bearing a black Aztec eagle and the word "Huelga," Spanish for "strike," became a commonly recognized symbol, as did the long marches that characterized the strike. Huerta and Chavez mounted a campaign to pressure growers into negotiating with them by organizing, as part of the strike, a nationwide consumer boycott of grapes.

Although the *machismo* culture of Hispanics militated against accepting women into their union, people like Huerta set an example of accomplishment that was hard to deny. Women ultimately became very important in the strike, establishing themselves as the chief proponents of the union's nonviolent philosophy. When the very first contract was drawn up with the grape growers, Dolores Huerta was the chief negotiator. She continued to negotiate the contracts herself for another five years.

Wilma Mankiller, Chief of the Cherokee Nation
1954–

When Wilma Mankiller accepted the position of deputy chief of the Cherokee Nation, she vowed to "make things happen." Two years later, only midway through her first term as deputy chief, Mankiller was chosen as principal chief, the first time in tribal history that a woman led the Cherokee Nation.

Mankiller, who announced in April 1994 that this would be her last term as principal chief, was not yet 32 when she was elected the Cherokee leader in 1985. As a young child in 1957, she had left Oklahoma for San Francisco as part of the Bureau of Indian Affairs' relocation program. Two decades later she returned to Oklahoma with two daughters, an undergraduate degree in social sciences from the University of Arkansas, and the beginnings of a graduate degree in community planning. Despite her young age—or perhaps because of it— Mankiller made things happen. Convinced of the value of self-help, particularly because the Bureau of Indian Affairs had traditionally not acted in the best interest of the Indians, Mankiller pushed through new training, education, and health-service programs; water line installations; and new housing and upgrading of old housing. Before her election she established, then managed, a multimillion-dollar community development department that has improved the quality of life for hundreds of Native Americans in rural northeastern Oklahoma. She was also a founding member of Rainbow Television Workshop, Inc., which produced programs about minorities, and she is a task force member for Save the Children, Inc.

Mankiller has had a profound influence on the lives of hundreds of Cherokee Nation members because of the work she has done on behalf of her constituents. But more than that, she is also an important role model, and not only for women. At a time when unemployment and alcoholism, the by-products of 200 years of systematic mistreatment and cultural misunderstanding, seem to be the only lasting characteristics of Indian life, Wilma Mankiller's fight to restore self-esteem and dignity to the Cherokee Nation is nothing less than heroic.

EPILOGUE

•••••••••

W hile it is incontrovertibly true that women have made substantial gains in status, there are enough disquieting aspects in present-day society to suggest that women's rights are an ongoing struggle. Increased public awareness of the prevalence of sexual harassment, demonstrated during the Anita Hill–Clarence Thomas controversy, did not prevent the Tailhook scandal or the U.S. Navy's efforts to whitewash the affair. Several female appointees in the administration of President Bill Clinton were held to a higher standard when it was revealed that they neglected to pay social security taxes for their hired help—nannies and housekeepers. This issue was only marginally raised for male nominees and was quickly forgiven and forgotten, presumably because women and not men are still considered primarily responsible for raising children and maintaining the home. When Geraldine Ferraro became the first female nominated for the vice-presidency by a major party, she spent her campaign defending herself against charges made regarding her husband's activities. Women are still paid much less than are men for virtually the same work, and there are still far fewer women in the top echelons of corporate America. Contemporary American women continue to face limitations, most of them long-standing, which affect their daily lives.

Abortion is a divisive subject and remains an important campaign issue for any candidate. In its over-20-year opposition to abortion, the well-organized and well-funded right-to-life movement has exacted a toll on the availability of the procedure around the country. The vast majority of people who oppose abortion do not support violence; however, according to recent surveys, one-third of the physicians who were performing abortions in 1993 have stopped because of threats made to them and their families (*ABC News*, October 1994). Since abortion's legalization in 1973, violent demonstrations have taken place at some clinics. Two physicians have been killed, and there have been numerous bombings and arson attacks on facilities where abortions are performed. As recently as January 1995, a misguided anti-abortion zealot killed three clinic staffers and wounded several others in attacks on three separate clinics in Massachusetts and Virginia. Pro-choice advocates have criticized the federal, state, and local authorities for failing to provide adequate protection to clinics and clinic personnel in the face of escalating acts of violence. Some 84 percent of the counties throughout the United States have no abortion facilities at all.

The singular difficulty in the widening chasm between pro-choice and anti-abortion forces is that much of the issue is bound up in religious beliefs. American citizens have always held in high regard the concept of separation of state and church, but the abortion issue is testing the strength of that concept as perhaps no other issue in our nation's history. Anti-abortionists, most of whom are not violent in their opposition, believe profoundly that life begins at conception, a belief grounded in religious ideology. Indeed, for some that belief extends to their opposition to any form of birth control because, in their view, that is interrupting God's plan. Because of that, it is difficult, if not impossible, for the anti-abortionists to tolerate another viewpoint or to accept any compromise, such as waiting periods or parental notification. Most pro-choice advocates, on the other hand, believe that it is each individual woman's right to make a decision about terminating a pregnancy and that the choice is constitutionally protected by a right to privacy.

ROE V. WADE

Roe v. Wade continues to be challenged in the United States Supreme Court. In an effort to tighten the restrictions on abortion in his state, the governor of Pennsylvania, William Casey, initiated legislation requiring a waiting period and the consent of both parents when the individual seeking the abortion was a minor. Surprisingly, when *Pennsylvania v. Casey* went to the Supreme Court in April 1992, the Court did not overturn *Roe v. Wade*, but in some ways strengthened the landmark decision. A majority of the Court determined that *Pennsylvania v. Casey* did not warrant a reconsideration of *Roe*. To overturn *Roe* under the circumstances, the majority contended, would have been a political decision and would have damaged the Court as a consequence. On the other hand, the majority opinion did allow that states had the right to impose certain restrictions on abortion, including those initiated by Casey. Several states have adopted similar constraints. Whatever the courts may decide in the future, it is almost certain that, in the short run at least, the abortion issue will continue to spark more debate and perhaps more violence.

WORK-RELATED ISSUES

Women in the 1990s still face a variety of work-related issues, from child care to unequal pay scales to limited potential for advancement. Most women work, and they do so regardless of race, ethnicity, marital status, maternal status, religious orientation, or economic standing. The middle-class concept of young women working until they have a family no longer holds. In the current environment, based on trends of the last two decades, most women will continue to work, full time, part time, or sporadically depending on the circumstances of their lives. Although most occupations are now open to women and some women earn salaries that are commensurate with those of their male colleagues, on average women still earn 66 cents for every dollar earned by men when education and experience levels are equal. More often than not the ratio is even more unbalanced. Many more women than men are likely to hold minimum wage jobs. Women have fewer opportunities to advance in corporate jobs, especially if they are married and have children. And few women have managed to break through the so-called glass ceiling, the invisible barrier that keeps them from upper-level management. Women are perceived as being unable to make a 100 percent commitment to the corporation. Because the pool from which chief executive offices, chief financial officers, and board chairmen are most often selected is that consisting of top-level managers, few women are even in a position to be considered for these key positions.

For married women and especially female heads of households, child care continues to be crucial. Working mothers are faced with a lack of affordable day care for their preschool children or adequate after-school supervision for school-age children. Options in the private sector are frequently too expensive for many working women. To avail themselves of private day care would place many women in the ludicrous position of working to keep their children in day care. The alternatives for these women are arranging for relatives to care for the children, leaving younger children

Sally K. Ride, the first American woman in space.

in the care of older siblings who may themselves need supervision, or arranging for often inexperienced, untrained babysitters willing to work for minimal compensation. Those women lucky enough to have family members who can provide care for the children are indeed fortunate. For too many women and their children, the choice must be made from the latter three options, none of which is either ideal or desirable. Though some corporations are beginning to recognize the problem and are either setting up in-house day care or subsidizing day care for their employees, these programs are few and far between. More often than not, employers fail to make any accommodations, including refusing to institute measures such as flexible hours.

The other major problem for women regarding the day-care industry is quality. In too many instances, even high-priced day-care facilities are not bound by—or ignore—any restrictions regarding personnel and/or curriculum. The result is that the quality of the day-care programs can be wildly uneven. Ironically, although the various levels of government, from federal down to local, have maintained a hands-off attitude to this important issue, the children of elected officials, for example the members of Congress, often have access to the finest-quality child care available at a minimal cost. The congressional day-care facility is not only well funded and well staffed, it also offers an enriching program to the children who attend.

Career women and professionals of child-rearing age also are faced with the prevalent perception that they will be committed to their jobs only until they decide to start a family. Furthermore, mothers who work often experience prejudices from their coworkers that they can give only so much to their careers and will always put their families first. It is also a widely held misperception that these women are working out of choice, not economic necessity. Equally mistaken is the perception that the enormous guilt women experience over leaving their children every day will cause them to quit precipitously. It is undeniable that many employers view women with children as less serious candidates for promotion and less reliable employees. Mothers reentering the work force after staying home with young children for a few years frequently face the kind of resistance expressed recently by a Maryland career woman: "The mere suggestion that professional women who took time off to raise children should just jump back into the work force at the level and salary they would have had had they stayed, belittles the hard work of those of us who did stay" (New York Times, October 1994).

Still, the picture for career-track women with children is not all bleak. Sheila Wellington, the president of Catalyst, an agency that works with businesses and the professions to bring about change for women in the workplace, notes that corporations are beginning to recognize the value of those women generally relegated to the nonserious "mommy track." Indeed, with women making up about half the work force, earning more than half the undergraduate degrees, almost half of the law degrees, and a third of the MBAs, companies who choose to ignore this pool of workers or ask of them less than they are capable of producing, run the danger of losing their competitive edge.

Sexual Harassment

Another job-related issue that remains problematic for women is sexual harassment. In the year following law professor Anita Hill's testimony against Supreme Court nominee Clarence Thomas, the reported cases of sexual harassment almost doubled, from 6,883 in 1991 to more than 12,000 in 1993. Harassment was not even recognized by the Supreme Court as a form of sex discrimination until 1986, when it stated that employees have the right to work in an environment free from discriminatory conduct and insults. The Court followed up in 1993 when it said that harassment victims did not have to prove severe psychological damage to bring suit against an abusive employer. The result is that sexual harassment in the workplace has become more and more a serious concern for companies. Individual suits, such as the 1994 case where a legal secretary was awarded $7.1 million in punitive damages against her former employer of three months who was found guilty of harassment, have made companies pay closer attention to their own potential exposure. Indeed, many firms now have guidelines for their employees. Nevertheless, because of the potential fallout, it still takes a great deal of resolve and courage for a woman to bring a sexual harassment suit. For career women especially, the risk of being branded a troublemaker can derail a career not only in the firm in which she had the difficulty but in other firms that might be dissuaded from hiring her.

PUBLIC ASSISTANCE

A separate though related issue that women in the 1990s still grapple with is that of public assistance. Women heads of household are especially vulnerable to the problems associated with public assistance or welfare. The fastest-growing poverty groups in the United States today are women heads of households, their children, and elderly single women. In addition, the almost epidemic occurrence of teen pregnancy pushes more and more single mothers onto public assistance. For recipients of public assistance, the issue is multi-faceted. Women on public assistance tend to have less education and fewer job skills and therefore cannot easily locate employment that will pay enough to support themselves and their families. Yet, the prevailing attitude towards the so-called welfare mothers is that they are willfully cheating the system by remaining unemployed. Because of the way the welfare system is structured, with crucial items like health care dependant on remaining on the welfare rolls and a limitation on how much an individual can earn before they are cut from the rolls, it remains a difficult proposition for even the most ambitious person to withdraw from welfare assistance without sinking hopelessly into even greater poverty. In addition, with the growing numbers of teen pregnancies, more and more single mothers have need of public assistance. Exacerbating the problem are the unmarried or divorced fathers who do not contribute to the support of their children. Increasingly, an already tax-burdened middle class grows more resentful of anyone on welfare.

There is no easy solution to this problem. The overwhelming Republican poliltical victory at the polls in November 1994 promises—or threatens, depending on one's political point of view—to address the problem of welfare and make sweeping changes in the system. And clearly the system does need fundamental changes to break the cycle of poverty. But just as clearly, the problems that contribute to the staggering number of welfare recipients are complex and will not be corrected by simple solutions, such as transferring responsibility from the federal to state level on limiting the amount of time an individual may remain on the welfare rolls.

The pattern of women's rights in the United States is one of waxing and waning—periods of incremental or even great strides forward, interspersed with periods of movement backward. As each new generation grapples with home versus career, equal pay issues, sexism, and lack of opportunity, it is almost as though a national amnesia wipes away the memory that all of these issues have been raised before, argued before, and fought for before. Author Susan Faludi, in her book *Backlash* (1991), argues forcefully that the regressions are more than coincidental. She believes that whenever women make significant advances that threaten to change their role in fundamental ways, deliberate pressure is brought to bear by a conglomerate male power structure to preserve the status quo. The modern women's rights movement, begun in the 1960s, has already gone through periods of ebb and flow, and has struggled to maintain the gains made in the 1970s against the conservatism of the 1980s and 1990s. Indeed, even to describe someone or something as "feminist" is enough to draw fire from many younger women who are the beneficiaries of the struggle for women's rights. It seems likely that, without a real equal rights amendment to the Constitution, the same issues will continue to be reargued and discussed with each new generation.

CHRONOLOGY

•••••••••

1607   First European women arrive at Jamestown Colony.

1638   Anne Hutchinson is expelled from Massachusetts Bay Colony.
        Hutchinson was tried and convicted of religious heresy, the
        punishment for which was banishment.

1692   Salem Witch Trials occur. In a town gripped by witch hysteria,
        scores of women were accused of practicing witchcraft. A series of
        trials resulted in the execution of 20 of the accused.

1769   Daughters of Liberty support Non-Importation Agreement.

1773   A volume of Phillis Wheatley's poetry becomes first published book
        by an African American.

1776   Abigail Adams admonishes John to "remember the ladies."

1792   Mary Wollstonecraft publishes *Vindication of the Rights of Women*.

1818   Emma Willard asks for taxpayer support to educate females.

1826   American Society for the Promotion of Temperance is established.

1830   *Moral Physiology* is published, the first tract in favor of birth
        control.

1833   Oberlin College is founded, America's first coeducational college.

1833   Prudence Crandall opens Canterbury School, one of the first to
        accept black females as students.

1833   Female Anti-Slavery Society of Philadelphia is founded.

1833   National temperance movement begins.

1833   Lydia Maria Child publishes first anti-slavery book in the United States.

1834   Lowell mill girls strike to restore wages.

1834   American Female Moral Reform Society is founded, its goal to eliminate prostitution and other immoral activities.

1837   Mount Holyoke Seminary, the first women's college, is founded by Mary Lyon.

1839   Margaret Fuller initiates "conversations" with prominent Boston women.

1840   Abolition movement divides over women's rights issue.

1840   Lucretia Mott is denied seat at World Anti-Slavery Conference.

1843   Dorothea Dix exposes harsh treatment accorded the mentally ill.

1844   Lowell Female Labor Reform Association is organized.

1848   Maria Mitchell is elected to the American Academy of Arts and Sciences.

1848   Seneca Falls Convention is the first women's rights convention.

1849   Elizabeth Blackwell is the first woman to graduate from medical school.

1850   Harriet Tubman first leads slaves to freedom.

1851   Sojourner Truth addresses women's rights convention.

1852   Harriet Beecher Stowe writes *Uncle Tom's Cabin*.

1852   Emily Dickinson begins writing poetry.

1853   Antoinette Blackwell becomes first woman ordained as a minister.

1859   American Medical Association announces its opposition to abortion.

1869   Suffragists organize.

1872   Victoria Woodhull runs for president of the United States.

1873   Women's uprisings and temperance actions occur.

1873   Congress passes Comstock Law, which prohibits the mailing of obscene material and defines birth-control information as "obscene material."

1874   Frances Willard joins the Women's Christian Temperance Union.

1874   Supreme Court decides *Minor v. Happersett*, the suit brought against the registrar of voters in St. Louis, Missouri, because he refused to place Virginia Minor's name on the eligible voters list.

1878   Woman Suffrage Amendment is first submitted to Congress.

1879   First woman attorney appears before the United States Supreme Court.

1881   Clara Barton founds the American Red Cross.

1888   Illinois Women's Alliance organizes coalition of women's groups.

1889   Jane Addams founds Hull House in Chicago.

1889   Nellie Bly goes around the world in 72 hours using a combination of transportation methods.

1890   General Federation of Women's Clubs is founded.

1890   National American Woman Suffrage Association is founded.

1892   Illinois becomes first state to limit work hours for women. Women are prohibited from working more than 10 hours a day.

1893   Mary Elizabeth Lease runs for United States Senate.

1895   Henry Street Settlement is founded by Lillian Wald.

1898   Charlotte Perkins Gilman publishes *Women and Economics*.

1899   Florence Kelley accepts position with National Consumer's League.

1900   *Sister Carrie* reveals harsher side of urban living. The novel, written by Theodore Dreiser, reveals the conditions that most working women have to endure.

1903   National Women's Trade Union League is founded.

1904   Ida Tarbell publishes *History of the Standard Oil Company*. Tarbell's exposé of John D. Rockefeller's conglomerate oil company helped to initiate reforms in business practices.

1906   Congress passes a Pure Food Act. The act establishes federal guidelines for the preparation and inspection of food products and is the result of widespread efforts by women reformers and Upton Sinclair's *The Jungle*.

1908   Supreme Court upholds protective legislation in *Muller v. Oregon*. The decision upholds the rights of states to enact laws intended to safeguard female employees.

1909   International Ladies' Garment Workers' Union is established and the "Uprising of the 30,000" takes place.

1911   Dr. Alice Hamilton publishes the first study of occupational diseases.

1911   The Triangle Shirtwaist Company Factory fire kills scores of young women workers.

1911   Kansas City, Missouri, passes the nation's first mothers' pension law.

1912   Alice Paul leads protest at Woodrow Wilson's inauguration. Suffragists march to promote voting rights for women.

1912   United States Children's Bureau is established.

1915   Woman's Peace Party is founded.

1916   Jeannette Rankin is the first woman elected to the United States Congress.

1916   Margaret Sanger opens the first birth-control clinic.

1917   American Women's Hospitals Service helps female physicians serve in World War I.

1919   League of Women Voters is founded.

1919   Women secure congressional passage of the Nineteenth Amendment, which gives women the right to vote; ratified the following year.

1920   Edith Wharton wins a Pulitzer Prize for *The Age of Innocence*.

1921   Congress passes the Sheppard-Towner Act, which is intended to improve health care for infants and children, as well as mothers and pregnant women.

1921   The Miss America Pageant attracts tourists to Atlantic City, New Jersey.

1921   M. Carey Thomas opens Bryn Mawr Summer School for Women in Industry.

1923   The Supreme Court strikes down minimum wage laws.

1925   Florence Sabin is elected to the National Academy of Sciences and to membership in the Rockefeller Institute.

1928   Margaret Mead publishes *Coming of Age in Samoa*. The anthropological study of adolescence in primitive society has enormous implications in America.

1929   Women pilots organize the Ninety-Nines, Inc.

1930   Association of Southern Women for the Prevention of Lynching is founded.

1931   Jane Addams is awarded the Nobel Peace Prize.

1931   Journalist Dorothy Thompson interviews Adolf Hitler.

1932   Amelia Earhart flies the Atlantic Ocean solo.

1932   Frances Perkins becomes the first woman Cabinet Officer.

1935   Mary McLeod Bethune accepts government position as Minority Affairs Adviser.

1935   Congress enacts the Social Security Act.

1935   National Council of Negro Women is organized.

1936   Eleanor Roosevelt transforms role of first lady.

1936   Federal court rules that the Comstock Law's definition of obscenity cannot include birth control.

1938   Pearl Buck wins the Nobel Prize for Literature.

1938   Fair Labor Standards Act establishes minimum wages.

1939   Marian Anderson sings at the Lincoln Memorial. After the Daughters of the American Revolution refused Anderson permission to appear at Constitution Hall, Eleanor Roosevelt arranged for open-air concert at the Lincoln Memorial.

1939   Grandma Moses exhibits her paintings at the Museum of Modern Art.

1940   Dorothea Lange and Margaret Bourke-White win honors for their photographic essays.

1941   Women are accepted into the armed forces in roles other than nursing.

1941   World War II increases demand for women workers.

1942   WASPs are created by Jackie Cochran and General Hap Arnold.

1945   Eleanor Roosevelt is appointed to the United States Delegation to the United Nations.

1946   Emily Greene Balch is awarded the Nobel Peace Prize.

1949   Babe Didrikson Zaharias is named Woman Athlete of the 20th Century.

1950   Margaret Chase Smith delivers "A Declaration of Conscience" speech. Chase was one of the first public officials to denounce Joseph McCarthy.

1950   Althea Gibson breaks color barrier in professional tennis.

1950   Gwendolyn Brooks wins Pulitzer Prize for *Annie Allen*.

1952   Playwright Lillian Hellman testifies before House Un-American Activities Committee.

1955   Rosa Parks refuses to give up her seat to a white passenger on a Montgomery, Alabama, bus.

1960   Food and Drug Administration approves "The Pill," an oral contraceptive.

1962   Dolores Huerta helps found United Farm Workers.

1962   *Silent Spring* alerts public to dangers of pesticides. Author Rachel Carson becomes the first to study the effects of pesticides on the environment and to attempt to warn the government and the public that irreparable harm was being done.

1963   President's Commission on the Status of Women is created.

1963   Congress passes Equal Pay Act of 1963.

1963   *The Feminine Mystique* by Betty Friedan is published.

1964   Civil Rights Act includes prohibition against sex discrimination in employment.

1964   Fannie Lou Hamer organizes Mississippi Freedom Democratic Party.

1966   National Organization of Women is founded.

1967   Executive Order 11375 broadens affirmative action to include gender.

1968   Shirley Chisholm is the first African American congresswoman elected to the House.

1971   *Ms.* magazine is founded.

1971   National Women's Political Caucus is founded.

1972   Title IX prohibits discrimination on the basis of sex in federally funded education programs.

1972   Congress passes Equal Rights Amendment.

1973   *Roe v. Wade* strikes down anti-abortion laws.

1976   Military service academies begin admitting women.

1978   Nancy Landon Kassenbaum is the first woman elected to the United States Senate in her own right.

1981   Sandra Day O'Connor is the first woman appointed to the United States Supreme Court.

1983   Astronaut Sally K. Ride is the first American woman to travel in space.

1984   Geraldine Ferraro accepts the nomination as the Democratic Party's vice-presidential candidate.

1985   Wilma Mankiller becomes principal chief of the Cherokee Nation.

1991   Anita Hill testifies at Clarence Thomas's Supreme Court confirmation hearings.

1992   The American Association of University Women reports on sex bias in schools, revealing that female students receive less attention, encouragement, and praise for their academic achievements. The study provides explanation for the heretofore unaccountable decline in female academic achievement, which begins to show up at around the age of 10 or 11.

1993   African American writer Toni Morrison wins the Nobel Prize for Literature.

1993   African American poet Maya Angelou composes and reads poem at President Clinton's inauguration.

GLOSSARY

· · · · · · · · ·

Abolitionism: Abolitionism included measures that supported or encouraged the dismantling of the slave system and the abolishment of slavery and the slave trade. The abolitionist movement gained significant strength in the non-Southern states in the early 19th century and continued to exert a growing influence until the Civil War and the dissolution of slavery.

Cable Citizenship Act: Prior to 1922, women who married noncitizens or men who gave up their citizenship lost their own citizenship rights as a consequence. The Cable Act granted to a married woman independent citizenship rights regardless of her husband's status.

Civil Rights Act of 1964: The Civil Rights Act of 1964, the fifth in a series of civil rights acts enacted since 1863, was particularly significant for women because it prohibited, for the first time, discrimination in employment based on race, color, religion, national origin, or gender.

Civil Rights Restoration Act: After the Supreme Court gutted Title IX of the Education Act of 1972 (see Title IX, below), Congress acted to reestablish the original intent of the act by passing the Civil Rights Restoration Act in 1988. The Restoration Act once again prohibited colleges and universities from discriminating on the grounds of sex, race, age, or disability if they received federal funds, and provided for the loss of all federal funds if the college or university did so.

Comstock Law: Self-styled moral arbiter Anthony Comstock, the head of the New York Society for the Suppression of Vice, lobbied successfully for a law that would make illegal the publication of materials that were deemed obscene and/or illicit. The law was passed by Congress in 1873. In addition to defining obscene material, the law prohibited the transportation of such material through the United States Postal Service. Included in the list of obscene materials, according to Comstock, was anything related to birth control, contraception, or abortion. Not until 1971 were these materials excluded from the definition of obscene and illicit.

Declaration of Sentiments: The first women's rights convention was held in Seneca Falls, New York, in 1848. The organizers were Elizabeth Cady Stanton and Lucretia Mott. The seminal document arising out of the convention was Stanton's Declaration of Sentiments. The Declaration, purposefully crafted to resemble the Declaration of Independence penned nearly a century earlier by Thomas Jefferson, contained a list of grievances against women, including denial of property rights and guardianship of their children. This list of grievances became the basis for reforms sought by the women's movement for a century thereafter and included the demand for voting rights.

Equal Pay Act: The Equal Pay Act of 1963 provided for equal pay for men and women performing jobs requiring equal skill, responsibility, and effort. It also prohibited employers from lowering the wages of one gender to avoid raising the wages of the other gender. Unions were forbidden from causing or attempting to cause employers to violate the law. The circumstances under which exceptions to the provisions of the law could be allowed included wages based on seniority, merit, quantity or quality of production, or differentials based on any other reason than gender.

Equal Rights Amendment: After intense lobbying by feminists and other proponents of equality, Congress passed an Equal Rights Amendment by overwhelming majorities in both houses of Congress in 1972. The amendment's major clause stated simply, "Men and women shall have equal rights through-out the United States and any place subject to its protection." The amendment was three states short of ratification when time ran out in 1982.

Fair Labor Standards Act (FLSA): The FLSA, passed in 1938, established minimum wages and maximum hours in businesses engaged in interstate commerce. It also prohibited child labor in the same industries. After decades of effort by women to prohibit child labor, defined as work by anyone under the age of 16, the reformers achieved their goal through the FLSA.

Feminism/Radical Feminism: Belief in the political, social, and economic equality of women and men, as well as organized activity in pursuit of women's rights and interests. Feminism has been defined by feminists as the "radical" notion that women and men are equal.

Feme Covert: A legal designation applied to married women in which all of their rights and possessions reverted to their husbands upon marriage. By the mid-19th century, many states were beginning to abolish, modify, or at least question this legal designation.

Fugitive Slave Act of 1850: This act amended the Fugitive Slave Law of 1793 by placing fugitive slave cases under the direct jurisdiction of the federal government. Fugitive slaves could be returned from free states to slave states and handed over to their so-called owners, under warrants issued by special United States commissioners. Penalties for aiding and abetting runaway slaves substantially increased, with fines and prison sentences imposed on those found guilty. Thus, the stakes were much higher for people like Harriet Tubman, a mainstay of the Underground Railroad.

Grange Movement: The Order of the Patrons of Husbandry, commonly referred to as the Grange, was organized in Washington, D.C., in 1867, as a secret organization. The Grange was particularly concerned with promoting agricultural interests, including controlling freight prices and monopolistic practices, both of which placed the farmer at a disadvantage. Significantly, from its inception the Grange accepted women as fully participating members and lessened the sense of isolation that many women in the vast rural stretches of the Midwest experienced so profoundly. Education and social functions sponsored by the Grange became an avenue for women to regularly interact with other women in similar circumstances.

Indentured Servants: Beginning with the earliest immigrants, many contracted with an individual who would pay the cost of their transportation from Europe to the Colonies. In exchange, the immigrant would agree to work as a servant for a period a years. The law upheld the practice of indenture, and any efforts to shirk servant duties could result in a penalty of an extended period of servitude.

Keating-Owen Child Labor Act: In 1916 Congress passed the Keating-Owen Child Labor Act, capping several decades of lobbying by progressive reformers. The act prohibited interstate shipping of any goods or articles produced using child labor. The Supreme Court struck down the law in 1918, and a subsequent effort to enact a similar law was also struck down by the Court in 1922. An acceptable child labor law would not be put into place until passage of the Fair Labor Standards Act in 1938 (see above).

Lanham Act: Congress passed the Lanham Act in an effort to provide women workers with the necessary child-care solutions during World War II. In 1943 funds were allocated to establish child-care centers. Ten different agencies were involved in administering the funds and setting up the centers. But government, including the agencies entrusted to establish the child-care centers, were reluctant to appear to favor any shift in family values. With no real government commitment to succeeding, only 10 percent of women with child-care needs had access to such care. Once the war ended, funds were cut off, and by 1946 the program was completely phased out.

Manumission: Freeing slaves.

Married Women's Property Acts (MWPAs): By 1839 a number of states were beginning to acquiesce to pressure to eliminate the laws of coverture that said that women could not retain control over possessions or property that they brought with them to marriage, nor could they be legally responsible for themselves and/or their children. Mississippi passed the first Married Women's Property Act in 1839, with a few other states following suit. Most of the MWPAs provided only partial relief, allowing women to retain rights to their possessions and property. For most women, relief would not come until well into the 20th century.

Mothers' Pensions: One of the many issues raised by progressive reformers in the early 20th century dealt with the often instantaneous state of poverty in which women found themselves under certain circumstances, including death of a spouse, desertion, and loss of a job. A 1909 White House conference on the care of dependent children resulted in passage of the first mothers' pension law in Kansas City in 1911. By 1919, 39 states had enacted some type of "mothers' pension" law. It was the first time that government acknowledged that it had some responsibility to assist poor women and their children. In 1935 the Social Security Act incorporated the mothers' pensions into a program called Aid to Dependent Children.

Muckraking: A style of journalistic exposé that focuses on revealing corporate and/or personal graft and corruption. Muckraking gained legitimacy during the late 19th century with exposés such as Ida Tarbell's study of Standard Oil, Lincoln Steffens's exposé of corruption in city government, Ray Stannard Baker's reports on Jim Crow laws in the South, and Upton Sinclair's description of the meat-packing industry.

National Industrial Recovery Act (NIRA): A centerpiece of New Deal legislation, the NIRA, passed in 1933, authorized the creation of the National Recovery Administration (NRA). In an effort to promote economic recovery, the NRA established a series of fair competition codes, which industry was obligated by law to observe. By far the most significant part of the NIRA was Section 7a, which guaranteed labor's "right to organize and bargain collectively through representatives of their own choosing." Although the NIRA was ultimately declared unconstitutional, labor unions grew in strength. Thereafter, labor could negotiate with management on a much more equal footing than that of before.

Nativism: Favoring native inhabitants over immigrants. From time to time throughout American history, immigrant groups have had to endure prejudicial behavior from nativist groups, in a variety of areas including work, wages, and housing. Generally, nativism became rampant during times of domestic economic downturn.

Nineteenth Amendment: The 19th amendment, ratified in 1920, enabled women to exercise the right to vote in elections. In effect, it legitimized women's status as citizens with all the rights and privileges of citizens as defined by the Constitution.

Pure Food and Drug Act: The lack of sanitary regulations concerning the meat-packing industry had long been a serious concern for reformers. Legislation making its way through Congress in 1905 suddenly became bogged down and failed to be enacted. In 1905 novelist Upton Sinclair published a book, entitled *The Jungle*, that exposed the horrendous conditions in Chicago's meat-packing plants. When President Theodore Roosevelt read the book, he insisted that the appropriate persons in his administration take immediate action to rectify the situation. As a result, the Pure Food and Drug Act was passed on June 29, 1906. The act authorized organization of the Food and Drug Administration to oversee the production and safety of products intended for consumption by consumers.

Sheppard-Towner Act: In the first two decades of the 20th century, nearly 250,000 infants died yearly in the United States, primarily because of the unavailability of prenatal care to a significant part of the population, particularly the poor and those who lived in isolated rural areas. In 1921, partially because of the fear that newly enfranchised women would retaliate at the polls, Congress passed the Sheppard-Towner Act. The law provided for initial funding of $1.25 million to establish a series of public health centers and prenatal clinics. Although the clinics made significant headway in lessening the rate of infant mortality, by 1929 conservative forces succeeded in repealing the Sheppard-Towner Act, arguing that the program smacked of "Bolshevism." At a time when every other industrialized nation was establishing permanent preventive health-care facilities, the United States dismantled its own already successful program.

Social Feminism: Social feminists were concerned primarily with winning the franchise to promote other reform issues, including temperance, settlement work, protective legislation, and unionization of working women. The social feminists, the vast majority of women in the late 19th and early 20th centuries, were committed to social reform and public service. Unlike the so-called radical feminists, they were not interested in achieving political, social, or economic equality with men.

Social Security Act: The Social Security Act, passed in 1935 and another cornerstone of the New Deal, for the first time provided the elderly with federal unemployment insurance and retirement funds. In addition, it provided insurance for widows with young children that was unprecedented in its scope. Much of the impetus for shaping the act rested with influential women within the Roosevelt Administration who were committed to social reform. Their concerns for the welfare of the aged, the infirm, and the very young helped to produce legislation wherein, for the first time, those most vulnerable to economic chaos would not be left without some resource.

Suffrage Movement: The suffrage movement began in 1848 with the first women's rights convention at Seneca Falls, New York (see Declaration of Sentiments). The women's rights movement focused on suffrage—securing the vote for women—as a first step in redefining their status in society. It took more than 70 years for women to succeed in their goal of securing a federal suffrage amendment (see Nineteenth Amendment).

Temperance Movement: Sobriety as a desirable characteristic of society concerned large numbers of people from the earliest years of nationhood on. As the caretakers of values, women especially became interested in establishing a temperate society. Indeed, the temperance movement was the first such activity in which women participated on a large scale. In the late 19th century, under the direction of Emma Willard, the Women's Christian Temperance Union became the premier organization pursuing temperance. The Eighteenth Amendment, ratified in 1919, outlawed alcohol consumption. The temperance victory was only short-lived, as organized crime soon controlled a vast illegal empire of alcohol sales to an all-too-willing public. Because adequate controls could not be imposed in the face of overwhelming public opposition to temperance, the amendment was repealed in 1933.

Thirteenth, Fourteenth, Fifteenth Amendments: The Civil War amendments that, respectively, abolished slavery, insured citizenship for former slaves, and guaranteed voting rights for former male slaves. The Fifteenth Amendment specifically limited the vote to males, the first time that such a limitation had been consciously inserted into the Constitution. Although custom and tradition had successfully excluded women from the full protection of the Constitution, the Fifteenth Amendment legitimized this exclusion.

Title IX: In 1972 Congress passed an education act that provided, under Title IX of the act, that institutions of higher education that received federal funds had to provide equal programs—including sports programs—for men and women. The immediate consequence of Title IX was that participation by women in interscholastic sports programs jumped from 7.4 percent in 1970–1971, to over 30 percent by 1978. It was a clear indication that the threat of tough enforcement caused institutions to distribute funding for programs more equitably. In 1984, however, the Supreme Court reopened the door for discriminatory practices by ruling in *Grove City College v. Bell* that federal funds would be withheld only from programs found to be discriminatory. The result was that institutions could once again fund programs as they wished as long as they could present proof that the disparity in funding was not discriminatory, and moreover, the institution would not lose funding applied to other programs in any case.

SELECTED
BIBLIOGRAPHY

• • • • • • • • •

Addams, Jane. *The Second Twenty Years at Hull House*. New York: Macmillan, 1930.

————. *Twenty Years at Hull House*. New York: Macmillan, 1910.

Bailyn, Bernard. *The Great Republic, A History of the American People*. Lexington, Mass.: D.C. Heath Co., 1985.

Banner, Lois W. *American Beauty*. New York: Knopf, 1983.

————. *Women in Modern America: A Brief History*. New York: Harcourt, Brace, Jovanovich, 1984.

Barker-Benfield, G.J., and Catherine Clinton, eds. *Portraits of American Women from Settlement to the Present*. New York: St. Martin's Press, 1991.

Barton, Clara. *The Red Cross: A History*. Washington, D.C.: American Red Cross, 1898.

Bateson, Mary Catherine. *With a Daughter's Eyes*. New York: Washington Square Press, 1984.

Bell, Winifred. *Aid to Dependent Children*. New York: Columbia University Press, 1965.

Bird, Caroline. *Enterprising Women*. New York: W.W. Norton Books, 1976.

Brooks, Paul. *The House of Life: Rachel Carson at Work*. Boston: Houghton Mifflin, 1972.

Brownlie, W. Elliot, and Brownlie, Mary M. *Women in the American Economy: A Documentary History*. New Haven: Yale University Press, 1976.

Brownmiller, Susan. *Shirley Chisholm, A Biography*. Garden City, N.Y.: Doubleday, 1971.

Campbell, D'Ann. *Women at War with America*. Cambridge, Mass.: Harvard University Press, 1984.

Carson, Rachel. *The Sea Around Us*. Boston: Houghton Mifflin, 1951.

————. *Silent Spring*. Boston: Houghton Mifflin, 1962.

Catt, Carrie Chapman, and Nettie Rogers Shuler. *Woman Suffrage and Politics*. New York: Scribner, 1923.

Chafe, William. *The American Woman: Her Changing Social, Economic, and Political Roles*. New York: Oxford University Press, 1972.

Cheney, Anne. *Lorraine Hansberry*. Boston: G.K. Hall, 1984.

"Cherokee Nation Principal Chief Wilma Mankiller." *Cherokee Nation*, 1994.

Chicago, Judy. *The Dinner Party: A Symbol of Our Heritage*. Garden City, N.Y.: Anchor Books, 1979.

Clinton, Catherine. *The Other Civil War: American Women in the Nineteenth Century*. New York: Hill and Wang, 1984.

Cochran, Jacqueline. *The Stars at Noon*. Boston: Little, Brown, 1954.

Cott, Nancy, and Elizabeth Pleck. *A Heritage of Her Own*. Ithaca, N.Y.: Cornell University Press, 1978.

Current, Richard N., et al. *American History: A Survey*. New York: Knopf, 1983.

Davis, Allen F. *American Heroine*. New York: Oxford University Press, 1973.

————. *Spearheads for Reform: The Social Settlements and the Progressive Movement 1890–1914*. New York: Oxford University Press, 1967.

David, Kenneth C. *Don't Know Much About History*. New York: Avon Press, 1990.

Degler, Carl N. *At Odds: Women and the Family in America from the Revolution to the Present*. New York: Oxford University Press, 1980.

Douglas, Ann. *The Feminization of American Culture*. New York: Alfred A. Knopf, 1977.

Douglas, Emily Taft. *Remember the Ladies*. New York: G.P. Putnam, 1966.

Dublin, Thomas. *Women at Work: The Transformation of Work and Community in Lowell, Massachusetts 1826–1860*. New York: Columbia University Press, 1979.

DuBois, Ellen. *Feminism and Suffrage: The Emergence of an Independent Woman's Movement in America, 1848–1869*. Ithaca, N.Y.: Cornell University Press, 1978.

Dulles, Rhea Foster. *The American Red Cross: A History*. Westport, Conn.: Greenwood Press, 1971.

Dye, Nancy Schrom. *As Equals and as Sisters: Feminism, Unionism, and the Women's Trade Union League of New York*. Columbia, Mo.: University of Missouri Press, 1980.

Ehrenreich, Barbara, and Deirdre English. *For Her Own Good: 150 Years of Experts' Advice to Women*. New York: Anchor Press, 1978.

Evans, Sara. *Born for Liberty: A History of Women in America*. New York: The Free Press, 1989.

Faludi, Susan. *Backlash: The Undeclared War against American Women*. New York: Crown Publishers, 1991.

Ferraro, Geraldine. *Ferraro: My Story*. New York: Bantam Books, 1985.

Flexner, Eleanor. *Century of Struggle: The Women's Rights Movement in the United States*. New York: Atheneum Press, 1974.

Flynn, Elizabeth Gurley. *Rebel Girl, An Autobiography*. New York: International Publishers, 1973.

Foner, Philip S. *Women and the American Labor Movement*. New York: Free Press, 1979.

Fowler, Robert B. *Carrie Catt, Feminist Politician*. Boston: Northeastern University Press, 1986.

Friedan, Betty. *The Feminine Mystique*. New York: W.W. Norton: 1963.

————. *It Changed My Life*. New York: Random House, 1976.

Garrow, David. *Bearing the Cross: Martin Luther King Jr. and the Southern Leadership Conference*. New York: Morrow, 1986.

Gibson, Althea. *I Always Wanted to Be Somebody*. New York: Harper & Row, 1958.

Gilman, Charlotte Perkins. *The Living of Charlotte Perkins Gilman*. New York: Appleton-Century, 1935.

Goldmark, Josephine. *Impatient Crusader: Florence Kelley's Life Story*. Urbana, Ill.: University of Illinois Press, 1953.

Goldstein, Leslie Friedman. *The Constitutional Rights of Women*. New York: Longman, 1987.

Gordon, Linda. *Women's Bodies, Women's Right: A Social History of Birth Control in America*. New York: Penguin Books, 1976.

Green, Elizabeth Alden. *Mary Lyon and Mount Holyoke: Opening the Gates*. Hanover, N.H.: University Press of New England, 1979.

Hall, Helen. *Unfinished Business*. New York: Macmillan, 1971.

Hall, Jacquelyn Dowd. "Disorderly Women: Gender and Labor Militancy in the Appalachian South." *Journal of American History*. September 1986: 354–382.

————. *Revolt Against Chivalry: Jessie Daniel Ames and the Women's Campaign against Lynching*. New York: Columbia University Press, 1979.

Harrison, Cynthia. *On Account of Sex: The Politics of Women's Issues 1945–1968*. Berkeley, Calif.: University of California Press, 1988.

Haskell, Molly. *From Reverance to Rape: The Treatment of Women in the Movies*. 2nd ed. Chicago: University of Chicago Press, 1987.

Hellman, Lillian. *Pentimento*. Boston: Little Brown & Co., 1973.

————. *Scoundrel Time*. Boston: Little, Brown & Co., 1972.

Hine, Darlene Clark, et al., eds. *Black Women in America: An Historical Encyclopedia*. Brooklyn, N.Y.: Carlson Publishing Co., 1993.

Hoff-Wilson, Joan, and Margaret Lightman. *Without Precedent: The Life and Career of Eleanor Roosevelt*. Bloomington: Indiana University Press, 1984.

Ingrehma, Claire, and Leonard Ingrehma. *An Album of Women in American History*. New York: Franklin Watts, 1972.

Irwin, Inez Haynes. *The Story of the Woman's Party*. New York: Harcourt Brace, 1921.

James, Edward T., et al. *Notable American Women: A Biographical Dictionary*. Cambridge, Mass.: The Belknap Press of Harvard University Press, 1971.

Jones, Jacqueline. *Labor of Love, Labor of Sorrow*. New York: Basic Books, 1985.

Josephson, Hannah. *Jeannette Rankin: First Lady in Congress*. Indianapolis: Bobbs-Merrill, 1974.

Kennedy, David. *Birth Control in American: The Career of Margaret Sanger*. New Haven, Conn.: Yale University Press, 1970.

Kennedy, Susan E. *If All We Did Was to Weep at Home*. Bloomington, Ind: Indiana University Press, 1979.

Kessler-Harris, Alice. *Out to Work: A History of Wage-Earning Women in the United States*. New York: Oxford University Press, 1982.

King, Billie Jean. *Billie Jean*. New York: Viking Press, 1982.

Kirber, Linda, and Jane DeHart Mathews. *Women's America: Refocusing the Past*. New York: Oxford University Press, 1982.

Kraditor, Aileen. *The Ideas of the Woman Suffrage Movement, 1890–1920*. NewYork: Columbia University Press, 1965.

———. *Means and Ends in American Abolitionism*. New York: Pantheon Books, 1969.

Lanker, Brian. *I Dream a World: Portraits of Black Women Who Changed America*. New York: Stewart, Tabori & Chang, 1989.

Lash, Joseph. *Eleanor and Franklin*. New York: W.W. Norton Books, 1971.

———. *Eleanor: The Years Alone*. New York: W.W. Norton Books, 1972.

Lemons, J. Stanley. *The Woman Citizen: Social Feminism in the 1920s*. Urbana, Ill.: University of Illinois Press, 1973.

Lerner, Gerda. *The Grimké Sisters of South Carolina: Pioneers for Women's Rights and Abolition*. New York: Schocken Books, 1967.

Levenson, Dorothy. *Women of the West*. New York: Franklin Watts, 1972.

Lisle, Laurie. *Portrait of an Artist: A Biography of Georgia O'Keefe*. Albuquerque, N.M.: University of New Mexico Press, 1986.

Lunardini, Christine A. *From Equal Suffrage to Equal Rights, Alice Paul and the National Woman's Party 1910–1928*. New York: New York University Press, 1986.

Martin, George. *Madam Secretary*. Boston: Houghton Mifflin, 1976.

Martin, Wendy. *An American Triptych: Anne Bradstreet, Emily Dickinson and Adrienne Rich*. Chapel Hill, N.C.: University of North Carolina Press, 1984.

Marshall, Helen. *Dorothea Dix: Forgotten Samaritan*. Chapel Hill, N.C.: University of North Carolina Press, 1937.

Melder, Keith E. *Beginnings of Sisterhood: The American Woman's Rights Movement*. New York: Schocken Books, 1977.

Norton, Mary Beth. *Liberty's Daughters: The Revolutionary Experience of American Women, 1750–1800*. Boston: Little Brown & Co., 1980.

O'Neil, William. *Divorce in the Progressive Era*. New Haven, Conn.: Yale University Press, 1967.

————. *Everyone Was Brave: The Rise and Fall of Feminism in America*. Chicago: Quadrangle Books, 1969.

Rothman, Sheila M. *Woman's Proper Place: A History of Changing Ideals and Practices 1870 to the Present*. New York: Basic Books, 1978.

Roudebush, Jay. *Mary Cassatt*. New York: Crown Publishers, 1972.

Rupp, Leila. *Mobilizing Women for War*. Princeton, N.J.: Princeton University Press, 1978.

Ryan, Mary P. *Womanhood in America: From Colonial Times to the Present*. New York: New Viewpoints/Franklin Watts, 1984.

Sanger, Margaret. *My Fight for Birth Control*. Orig. pub. 1931; rpt. Elmsford, N.Y.: Maxwell Reprint Company, 1969.

Schlafly, Phyllis. *A Choice, Not an Echo*. Alton, Ill.: Pere Marquette Press, 1964.

Sicherman, Barbara, and Carol Hurd Green, eds. *Notable American Women, The Modern Period*. Cambridge, Mass.: The Belknap Press of Harvard University Press, 1980.

Solomon, Barbara Miller. *In the Company of Educated Women*. New Haven, Conn.: Yale University Press, 1985.

Stanton, Elizabeth Cady, et al., eds. *The History of Woman Suffrage*. 6 vols. New York: NAWSA, 1888–1922.

Starkey, Marion L. *The Devil in Massachusetts*. New York: Knopf, 1949.

Sterling, Dorothy. *Black Foremothers: Three Lives*. Old Westbury, N.Y.: Feminist Press, 1979.

————. *Lucretia Mott: Gentle Warrior*. Garden City, N.Y.: Doubleday, 1964.

Van Voris, Jacqueline. *Carrie Chapman Catt: A Public Life*. New York: Feminist Press, 1987.

Vorse, Mary Heaton. *Labor's New Millions*. New York: Modern Age, 1938.

Wald, Lillian. *The House on Henry Street*. New York: Holt, 1915.

Ware, Susan. *Beyond Suffrage: Women in the New Deal*. Cambridge, Mass.: Harvard University Press, 1981.

Weatherford, Doris. *American Women's History*. New York: Prentice Hall, 1994.

Wertheimer, Barbara Mayer. *We Were There: The Story of Working Women in America*. New York: Pantheon Books, 1977.

Withey, Lynn. *Dearest Friend: A Life of Abigail Adams*. New York: Free Press, 1981.

Wolf, Naomi. *Fire with Fire: The New Female Power and How It Will Change the 21st Century*. New York: Random House, 1993.

Woloch, Nancy. *Women and the American Experience*. New York: Alfred A. Knopf, 1984.

Wood, Mary Louise, and Martha McWilliams. *The National Museum of Women in the Arts*. New York: Abrams, 1987.

Zophy, Angela Howard, ed. *Handbook of American Women's History*. New York: Garland Press, 1990.

INDEX

• • • • • • • • •

by
James Minkin